I0759721

WELSH WOMEN ON THIS DAY

WELSH WOMEN ON THIS DAY

366 Amazing Facts and Daily Stories

Huw Rees and Sian Kilcoyne

2025

www.uwp.co.uk

British Library Cataloguing-in-Publication Data
A catalogue record for this book is available from the British Library.
ISBN: 978-1-83760-027-4

Cover artwork and illustrations by David Wardle
Typeset by Agnes Graves
Printed and bound by CPI Group (UK) Ltd,
Croydon, CR0 4YY
The publisher acknowledges the financial support of the Books Council of Wales

For all General Product Safety Regulation (GPSR) enquiries, please contact: Logos Europe, 9 rue Nicolas Poussin, 17000, La Rochelle, France. contact@logoseurope.eu

Our history, heritage and culture has always been important to us. Some years ago Huw started a daily blog under the title *The History of Wales.* The aim was to publish, every day of the year, one nugget of Welsh history relevant to that day. The collection of articles grew as the years went by and we were able to share more moments in Welsh history. Today we have over 200,000 followers engaging regularly with our posts.

In 2022, Calon published *Wales on This Day: 366 Facts You Probably Didn't Know*, a compilation of entries from the blog. With an entry for each day of the year, readers can work through chronologically, or to dip in randomly as time and inclination dictate. We had far more material than one volume could contain when it came to compiling that collection. We had material that covered Welsh history from ancient times. Our collection covered writers, artists, actors, politicians, social reformers, philanthropists, scientists, engineers and entrepreneurs. Our collection covered Welsh legend and tradition. And we also celebrated the eccentric individuals who provide humour and quirkiness to the Welsh story. And so we faced some difficult decisions as to what to include, but our choices resulted in a publication of which we are proud.

Our theme for a second miscellany of Welsh history came quite quickly. From the time of tenth-century king, Hywel Dda, who recognised the right of women to possess land and to wield power, women have been central to Welsh society and have played a crucial role in its history. In *Welsh Women on This Day* we pay tribute to some of those women.

Within these pages you will learn about the women from the Age of Saints who inspired the spirituality of our nation; women in Welsh mythology whose representations appear in our works of art, literature and music; historical figures who not only gave birth to kings and princes but who ruled themselves and often led rebellions.

We look to modern times to acknowledge the huge, and often unsung, contributions made by women to the broad social spectrum that exists in Wales today. We celebrate those who have stood against injustice; who have excelled in the fields of education, medicine and social reform; and those who have sought equality of gender and race in sport, enterprise, engineering and medical research. Many are now honoured in Wales with Purple Plaques as part of a national campaign to celebrate remarkable women.

We are a nation of pioneers and innovators, and this book will introduce readers to remarkable women who were born here, were inspired by Wales, have influenced Wales and who form part of its wide diaspora.

For breaking the mould, and for stepping beyond the artificial boundaries of social expectation, we thank and salute these women.

Huw Rees and Sian Kilcoyne

NOTE TO READERS

Unavoidably, there are distressing elements involved in the histories of some Welsh women. To help you decide which entries to read or not, some entries are marked with a ⚠ as a warning of disturbing content such as suicide, domestic abuse or sexual violence.

For Leo Kilcoyne
24 December 2023–17 April 2024

1 JANUARY

Released on 1 January 2024, the television drama *Mr Bates vs The Post Office* proved to be one of the most-watched programmes of the last decade. It captured the attention of the whole of the UK and sparked outrage among its millions of viewers when it related the story of Post Office sub-postmasters who were wrongly accused of theft and false accounting as a result of a software fault.

One of the more than 900 people who faced prosecution when the faulty software made it look like money was missing from their branches, was Margery Lorraine Williams. Margery was a sub-postmistress in Llanddaniel Fab near Llangefni, on Anglesey. The Post Office insisted that Margery had stolen £14,000 and she faced fraud charges. Facing the possibility of a prison sentence, she felt forced to accept a plea bargain in 2012. In return for pleading guilty, she was given a fifty-two-week prison term, suspended for eighteen months with two hundred hours of unpaid work, and told to pay the Post Office back the money. Margery lost her home and she found further work opportunities were restricted. She was ostracised by friends and her daughter was bullied in school. She also developed type 2 diabetes and scarring alopecia.

Margery's wrongful conviction was eventually overturned in 2021. Margery was one of the many people who gave evidence at the inquiry in 2022. The scandal has been described as one of the greatest miscarriages of justice in UK history. New legislation to clear victims' names and pay them compensation came into effect in May 2024.

2 JANUARY

On 2 January 1909, a luxury car was found hanging over the edge of a fifty-metre-high cliff in Penmaenmawr. Strewn on the ground beside it was a ladies' flat bonnet hat and a diary belonging to Violet Gordon Charlesworth. It was assumed that Violet had been thrown through the windscreen and into the sea. However, no body was found and it soon emerged that Violet had tried to fake her own death to escape major financial debts and was now on the run.

Violet and her mother, Miriam Davies, had invented the story that Violet was the goddaughter of the famous British major general Charles Gordon, and that she was therefore a lucrative prospect for a wife as she was set to inherit a significant sum of money. Using this falsehood, they defrauded potential suitors of over £2 million in today's money and were enjoying a lavish and luxurious lifestyle.

A major police search was launched to find Violet, and the story – dubbed the 'Welsh Cliff Mystery' – made headlines all over the world. Eventually, Violet was found in Scotland and admitted that, in fear of being exposed as a fraudster, she had staged the crash at Penmaenmawr. Violet and her mother were convicted and sentenced to two years of hard labour.

3 JANUARY

Catherine of Valois (born 27 October 1401), wife of Henry V and queen of England from 1420 until 1422, died on this day in 1437.

Catherine was the daughter of King Charles VI of France and Isabella of Bavaria. She married Henry as part of a peace treaty between France and England in 1420. When Henry died in 1422, Owen Tudor, a descendant of a prominent family from Anglesey, was appointed as the keeper of Catherine's household. They became lovers, subsequently married and had at least six children. Their eldest son, Edmund, would go on to become father to Henry VII of England, who was born at Pembroke Castle in 1457.

As Henry VII's grandparents, Catherine and Owen are often regarded as the founders of England's Tudor Dynasty.

4 JANUARY

National Trivia Day takes place each year on 4 January. Here are some of the more unusual and interesting facts and records involving Welsh girls and women – and one very special sheepdog.

On 28 December 2022, Seren Isla Price, a five-year-old girl from Llangennech, accompanied by her dad Glyn, became the youngest person to climb the highest mountains of Wales (Yr Wyddfa), England (Scafell Pike) and Scotland (Ben Nevis) within forty-eight hours.

On 3 February 2021, at an auction organised by Farmers Marts in Dolgellau, a twelve-month-old, female, red-and-white border collie called Kim became the world's most expensive sheepdog when she sold for £28,455.

In August 1934, Henrietta (Hettie) Langdale Bussell from Newport became Britain's first female railway engineer. She secured a job with Great Western Railway after finishing second in a national exam. She later served as president of the Women's Engineering Society.

On 10 July 2022, eight-year-old Anne Winston of Pontprennau Primary School in Cardiff became the youngest person to correctly recite every single capital city and currency for all 195 countries of the world, achieving the world record in seven minutes and fifteen seconds.

Ida Gaskin from Pontardawe became the first woman to win the New Zealand version of *Mastermind* in 1983. Her specialist subject was Shakespeare, but she also fielded questions on opera, gastronomy, *Winnie the Pooh*, tantric yoga and the production of sulphuric acid.

DID YOU KNOW?

The six-foot-high words on the front of Cardiff's Wales Millennium Centre, *CREU GWIR FEL GWYDR O FFWRNAIS AWEN* – IN THESE STONES HORIZONS SING, are thought to be the largest representation of a poem in the world. They were written by Gwyneth Lewis, National Poet of Wales from 2005 to 2006.

CREU GWIR IN THESE STONES
FEL GWYDR HORIZONS
O FFWRNAIS AWEN SING

5 JANUARY

Johanna Frances (née Dooyeweerd), or 'Hanny', was born on 5 January 1936 into a wealthy and intellectual Dutch family. Her father was an internationally renowned professor of philosophy. By 1940 Germany had invaded Holland, and the attic of their house became a hiding place for Jews and others being sought by the Gestapo.

After the war, Hanny visited her sister who had married a policeman and settled in Pontnewydd. There she met and instantly fell in love with Robert 'Bob' Frances, a penniless, dishevelled but handsome farmer of forty acres in Mamhilad, near Pontypool.

Despite her father's misgivings, they were married in a lavish wedding in Amsterdam. On their first night together at the farm in Wales, Hanny cut up her wedding dress to make curtains on a freezing night. There followed years of hardship, laborious toil, failure and poverty. The couple kept hens, then pigs, processed food waste and ran a minibus service. Hanny's new life was so very different from the high society she had been born into. Despite this and their financial difficulties, the love between Hanny and Bob endured for forty-five years until his death in 2000.

Hanny died in 2021 and the couple's beautiful love story is told in the book *Fields of Orange: A True Welsh Love Story*, written by Johanna's daughter, Jantien Powell and son, Alan Francis and published in 2022.

6 JANUARY ⚠

Dorothy Edwards, born on 18 August 1902 in Ogmore Vale, Glamorgan, was a critically acclaimed author who died tragically on 6 January 1934 before fulfilling her enormous potential.

After the death of her father when she was fourteen, Dorothy moved to Rhiwbina where her mother had taken up a teaching post. She graduated with a degree in Greek and philosophy from Cardiff University, but did not, as expected, become a teacher like her mother. Instead she decided to become a writer. In 1926, Dorothy and her mother travelled to Austria, where Dorothy began writing, completing a ten-story collection entitled *Rhapsody* and her only novel, *Winter Sonata,* which was published in 1928. It was considered by leading critics of the time to be a work of genius.

When Dorothy returned to Wales, her writing came to the attention of David Garnett, the London author and member of the Bloomsbury Group, who invited her into his social circles. Living in London gave Dorothy a deep understanding of national and class divisions and she frequently felt she was regarded as inferior by her London friends. She became increasingly drawn to socialism and the Welsh nationalist movement. She returned to Cardiff to live with her mother following the end of her affair with the married Welsh cellist Ronald Harding.

Reeling from the break-up and frustrated by her circumstances, Dorothy wrote a note that read: 'I am killing myself because I have never sincerely loved any human being. All my life I have accepted kindness and friendship, and even love, without gratitude and given nothing in return.' She died by suicide later that day.

7 JANUARY

On 7 January 1971, Nerys Hughes (born in 1941 in Rhyl) made her first appearance on the successful BBC television series *The Liver Birds*. The series followed the lives and loves of Sandra Hutchinson (played by Nerys) and Beryl Hennessey (Polly James), two young, single women sharing a flat in Liverpool. This turned out to be a breakthrough role for Nerys, who subsequently became a household name throughout the UK.

Between 1984 and 1987, Nerys starred in *The District Nurse*, a series which was devised especially for her and for which she won the Variety Club Television Actress of the Year Award. Nerys was educated at Howell's School in Denbigh and Rose Bruford College, a drama school in London.

8 JANUARY

Dame Shirley Bassey was born on 8 January 1937 in Tiger Bay, Cardiff, and raised in the working-class neighbourhood of Splott. Shirley found fame in the mid-1950s and is perhaps best known for recording the theme songs to the James Bond films *Goldfinger*, *Diamonds Are Forever* and *Moonraker*. She is an internationally recognised and much-loved figure in the music industry and one of the world's most popular female vocalists.

Her mother was from Yorkshire and her father was a Nigerian seaman. Shirley worked in an enamelware factory before making her professional debut at sixteen with her first major hit, 'The Banana Boat Song'. In January 1959, Shirley became the first Welsh singer to hit number one in the UK singles chart, with 'As I Love You', and has since become the first female artist to claim a Top 40 album in seven consecutive decades.

In 2019, Shirley was awarded the freedom of her hometown, Cardiff.

DID YOU KNOW?

In 2018, Rheilffordd yr Wyddfa (Snowdon Mountain Railway) named one of their train carriages *Dame Shirley Bassey* in the singer's honour.

9 JANUARY

Sarah Jane Rees, better known by her bardic name Cranogwen, was born in Llangrannog on 9 January 1839. Over the course of her lifetime, she was a ship's captain, a navigational and nautical trainer, a campaigner for the temperance movement, a supporter of women's rights, a poet and a magazine editor.

Sarah Jane was the daughter of a sea captain and after leaving school decided to follow him and work at sea. She attended local navigational colleges and finished her nautical education by gaining a master's certificate in London, which qualified her to take command of sea-going vessels. Sarah Jane then returned to Wales to establish a renowned school of navigation in Llangrannog.

Sarah Jane won the crown for her poetry at the Aberystwyth National Eisteddfod in 1865, competing under the bardic name of Cranogwen. Her victory brought her national fame and encouraged her to publish a book of poems, *Caniadau Cranogwen,* and to edit the women's journal, *Y Frythones.*

In later life, Sarah Jane became a popular lay preacher and established the South Wales Women's Temperance Union in 1901 as well as founding a home for destitute girls in Tonypandy. She also remained actively involved in education as a pioneer of the 'tonic sol-fa' method of music teaching.

A statue to honour Sarah Jane was unveiled in Llangrannog in June 2023.

10 JANUARY

Eluned Phillips, born in Cenarth on the banks of the River Teifi on 27 October 1914, died on 10 January 2009. She was the only female poet to have won the bardic crown twice at the National Eisteddfod of Wales, in 1967 and 1983.

Eluned achieved this despite a backdrop of misogyny and poetic prejudice. The complex craft of *cynghanedd* (Welsh-language verse) was considered an exclusively male preserve. She was consistently doubted, ridiculed and accused of plagiarism, despite having been a published poet from the age of seven and studying literary structure through her teens, inspired by her admiration for the medieval Welsh poet Dafydd ap Gwilym.

Eluned was raised by a family of formidable women, including her beloved Aunty Hannah, a renowned fisherwoman of the Teifi, and her inspirational *mam-gu,* whose advice to her granddaughter was, 'Go for it, girl! Give it your best shot!'

EISTEDDFOD
CENEDLAETHOL FRENHINOL CYMRU

Eluned certainly heeded this advice. She embraced a bohemian lifestyle, mixing with the likes of Augustus John, Edith Sitwell and Dylan Thomas. She spent time in Paris where she became friends with Édith Piaf, Jean Cocteau, Maurice Chevalier and Pablo Picasso, who showed Eluned his iconic masterpiece *Guernica* when the paint was still wet on the canvas.

Her European travels were halted by the Second World War and she began writing for women's magazines and published Mills and Boon-type romances. Back in Wales after the war, she continued writing poetry and the boom in radio gave her opportunities to write radio scripts for BBC Wales and to work as a roving reporter, travelling extensively to Ireland, Eastern Europe, Australia and America.

For her ninetieth birthday she bought her first computer (nicknamed Siencyn) to write her autobiography, *The Reluctant Redhead*. It was published in 2007, and in it she describes herself as 'a country girl with itchy feet'.

Poignantly, she also wrote of herself, 'Perhaps after I've gone, someone will tell the truth about me.'

11 JANUARY

On 11 January 1997 the first women priests were ordained into the Church in Wales in the cathedrals of St Asaph, Bangor, St Davids, Monmouth and Llandaff, with more ordinations taking place in Brecon the following day. In total, sixty-four women were ordained as priests over the two days.

Among the first women ordained was the Right Reverend Joanna Penberthy, who, on 21 January 2017, became the first woman to become a bishop in the Church in Wales when she was consecrated as the Bishop of St Davids.

Born in Swansea in 1960 and educated at Cardiff High School, Joanna graduated from Newnham College, Cambridge and trained for the ministry at both St John's College, Nottingham and Cranmer Hall, Durham. Prior to her appointment as a bishop, she served as Rector of Glan Ithon, in the Diocese of Swansea and Brecon, based in Llandrindod Wells, and as a deaconess and priest in the Dioceses of Llandaff, St Asaph and St Davids.

She was also awarded a PhD in Philosophy in July 2019 by the University of Nottingham for her studies in theology and science.

12 JANUARY

On 12 January 2000, the British Government announced that gay and lesbian citizens could serve openly in Her Majesty's Armed Forces.

Hannah Graf (née Winterbourne) from Cardiff was selected for military training at fifteen and, after obtaining a degree in electronic engineering at Newcastle University, completed officer training at Sandhurst in 2010. There, she identified as an openly gay man but increasingly realised that it was only a way to express herself 'to a certain degree'. She had 'very early memories of wanting to express [herself] female' and, in 2013, she began her transition while serving as a captain in the Royal Electrical and Mechanical Engineers in Afghanistan. Hannah became the highest-ranking transgender officer in the British Army and took on the role of advising the army on transgender issues. In 2015, Hannah was named as 'Ultimate Trailblazer' in the Cosmopolitan Women of the Year Awards, and in 2016 she received an honorary fellowship from Cardiff University.

Following her retirement from the British Army in 2019, Hannah has since become a patron of Mermaids, a charity that helps young people who feel 'at odds' with their birth gender, and also served as an ambassador for Sport Cymru, which promotes the inclusion of the LGBTQ+ community all over the country. In 2019, she was made an MBE for 'services to the LGBTQ+ community in the military' and Stonewall named her their 'Trans Role Model of the Year'.

Hannah married the actor and film-maker Jake Graf, who is a trans man, in 2015. In 2020, the couple welcomed their daughter Millie. Their experience as transgender parents was broadcast later that year in the Channel 4 documentary *Our Baby: A Modern Miracle*, which followed the couple's journey to parenthood at the height of the Covid-19 pandemic. The couple announced the birth of their second child in 2022.

13 JANUARY

On 13 January 1840, Joan Williams witnessed the end of the trial of her husband, Zephaniah Williams, one of the leaders of the Newport Rising of 1839. Along with his co-accused, John Frost, a draper and tailor from Newport, and William Jones, a watchmaker from Pontypool, he was found guilty of high treason and sentenced to death by hanging, drawing and quartering. This sentence was later reduced to transportation to Tasmania for life.

Zephaniah was a coal miner and the innkeeper of the Royal Oak at Nantyglo, which was home to the thriving Blaina Female Chartist Lodge run by Joan. Following her husband's transportation, she continued running the Royal Oak, held the family together and vigorously campaigned for Zephaniah's pardon which was eventually granted in 1854. Joan then joined him in Tasmania. They were subsequently instrumental in establishing the Tasmanian coal industry, which made them extremely wealthy.

Chartism was a working-class movement that emerged in the early 1800s to campaign for a more democratic political system in the UK through the six demands of a People's Charter. It was particularly popular among working people in the industrial towns of south Wales and the wool-producing areas of mid-Wales. It declined in the second half of the nineteenth century due, in large part, to the political establishment's repressive measures and the discouragement of the church. However, all but one of the six demands (for annual parliaments) have long since been made a part of our parliamentary system.

14 JANUARY

The film *Save the Cinema* was released in the United Kingdom on 14 January 2022.

It is based on the true story of Liz Evans, a hairdresser and manager of the Lyric Theatre in Carmarthen, who began the campaign in 1993 to save the Lyric cinema from demolition.

The Lyric relied on high-profile blockbuster films to survive and had been let down by a London distribution company that had failed to send the cinema a copy of the film *Jurassic Park*. A message was sent to the film's director, Steven Spielberg, explaining how important the film was to the town and how angry and disappointed the local people were to not be able to see it. Six days later, they received a reply from the managing director of United International Pictures, who not only agreed to send a copy of the film but announced that the Lyric Theatre had been chosen to host a premiere of the film on the same evening as its star-studded London premiere on 15 July 1993. Today the theatre is still operational and shows occasional films.

15 JANUARY

The story of Pembrokeshire-based Patricia Mawuli Nyekodzi is one of a life-changing chance meeting, followed by years of dedicated hard work and a remarkable career in aviation.

On 15 January 2016, Patricia became a director and co-founder, alongside her husband Jonathan, of Metal Seagulls Ltd, one of the UK's leading and most innovative aviation engineering businesses. Since 2021, the company has been based at Haverfordwest Airport.

Patricia was brought up in a small Ghanaian village. There in 2007, at the age of nineteen, while collecting firewood near Kpong Airfield in southwest Ghana, she decided to follow a plane coming in to land at the airport. There, she met Jonathan Porter, who was in charge of aerial training, and persuaded him to let her volunteer at the airport clearing runways. As she worked, she also studied the aircraft on the site and soon she was able to help Jonathan assemble aeroplanes. He taught her how to fly and, in 2009, she became the first civilian woman to obtain a pilot's licence in Ghana. In 2010, Patricia and Jonathan married and set up an aviation school, training girls from rural backgrounds to fly, build and maintain aircraft. The following year, she was appointed managing director of operations at Kpong Airfield, and was also a volunteer pilot with Medicine on the Move, providing medical supplies and services to Ghana's remote communities. She was the first woman and first Black African to be certified to build Rotax aircraft engines.

In 2015, Patricia and Jonathan moved to the UK to set up their new aviation engineering company, ending up at their current location in Haverfordwest Airport. In 2019 Patricia was selected as an Aviation Ambassador for the UK Department of Transport, and in 2022 she was awarded an OBE for services to aviation.

16 JANUARY

Charlotte Maria Shaw Mason died on this day in 1923. Born 1 January 1842 in the hamlet of Garth, near Bangor, she became a much-respected and pioneering educator whose revolutionary teaching methods and educational philosophy helped to change the way in which children were taught across the country.

As an only child, Charlotte was mostly educated at home by her parents. When they died when she was sixteen, Charlotte embarked on a teaching career, first at Davison Girls' School in Worthing and then Bishop Otter Teacher Training College in Chichester.

By her forties, she had developed her ideas for educating the whole person, not just their mind, and disregarding their social class. Her approach included the discipline of good habits, nutritional choices and physical education as well as encouraging children to think and formulate ideas rather than just giving them dry facts.

By the late nineteenth century, even though state

schooling had been fully established, there was still a significant number of parents who were educating their children at home and Charlotte became aware of a generally poor standard of the education provided by governesses in private households.

Between 1880 and 1892, she began publishing her ideas for providing a broad curriculum and wrote a series of books outlining her approach. In 1887, she established the Parents' National Educational Union to provide support and guidance for home-schooling. Then, in 1891, she founded an educational training school for governesses at Ambleside in Cumbria.

17 JANUARY

Isabel Marshal died on 17 January 1240. Isabel was born at Pembroke Castle in October 1200, the daughter of one of England's greatest knights, William the Marshal, and his wealthy heiress wife, Isabel de Clare the Countess of Pembroke. Isabel de Clare was the daughter of Richard de Clare, 2nd Earl of Pembroke, commonly known as Strongbow and famous for his leading role in the Anglo-Norman invasion of Ireland. He owned extensive estates in Wales, England and Ireland.

In 1217, the younger Isabel married Gilbert de Clare, Lord of Glamorgan. She managed the family lands when Gilbert was on campaign defending Glamorgan from the native Welsh lords under the leadership of Llywelyn ap Iorwerth (Llywelyn the Great). Despite the twenty-year age gap between them, the marriage seemed a happy one and the couple had six children. Robert the Bruce, King of Scots, was among their descendants.

Gilbert died in 1230 and the following year, Isabel married the brother of King Henry III, Richard, Earl of Cornwall. During their marriage, it was widely expected that Isabel would become Queen of England as Henry was unmarried and had no legitimate heir. This all changed when Henry married Eleanor of Provence in 1236 and had five children with her, including the future Edward I, who was born in 1239.

Isabel died of liver failure, contracted while in childbirth, on 17 January 1240. Upon her deathbed, she asked to be buried next to her first husband, Gilbert de Clare, at Tewkesbury Abbey. Although Richard had her interred at Beaulieu Abbey, he did send her heart to Tewkesbury in a silver casket.

18 JANUARY

On 18 January 2019, the result of the BBC's 'Hidden Heroines' vote was announced.

There are many statues of male industrialists, soldiers, statesmen, musicians and sporting icons throughout Wales but, at the time, there were only two of women: Queen Victoria and Boudica. The 'Hidden Heroines' campaign aimed to bring Welsh women who had been largely forgotten to history, and yet whose incredible achievements have helped to shape modern Wales, to public attention.

Monumental Welsh Women, a not-for-profit organisation, worked with the Women's Equality Network (WEN) Wales to produce a list of a hundred Welsh women who had made a notable contribution to the history and life of Wales. From this list, a panel of experts drew up a shortlist of five women so that the public could vote on who they would like to be immortalised with a public statue.

The five shortlisted were Elizabeth Andrews (see 30 October), Betty Campbell (see 6 November), Cranogwen (see 9 January), Elaine Morgan (see 18 March) and Lady Rhondda (see 12 June). Following the public vote, Betty Campbell was announced as the first 'Hidden Heroine'.

19 JANUARY

The funeral of Winifred Cochrane (née Bamford Hesketh, born 1859), Countess of Dundonald took place on 19 January 1924 at St Cynbryd's Church, Llanddulas. She had died in London but her coffin was brought back by train.

Winifred was the wealthy heiress of the Gwrych Castle Estate and, like her parents, was a Welsh speaker and an enthusiastic supporter of Welsh art, music and literature.

In 1878, Winifred married Lieutenant General Douglas Cochrane, 12th Earl of Dundonald. He spent most of his time in Scotland on military campaigns, while Winifred remained in north Wales raising their five children and managing her large estates.

She became a highly respected figure for her involvement in many national and local organisations and campaigns. She was a patron of The United Gentlewomen's Handicrafts Society, Gwynedd Ladies' Art Society, the Women's Institute, and the Society for the Abolition of Vivisection. She was president of the Denbighshire division of the Welsh Industrial Association and of the Vale of Clwyd Toys company, which employed and trained disabled soldiers. Winifred was also an active supporter of the NSPCC and a leading member of the Children's Happy Evenings Association, which raised money to fund the purchase of sports equipment. She founded a north

Wales harp competition and was heavily involved in the organisation of the Colwyn Bay National Eisteddfod in 1910, at which she was inducted into the Gorsedd, taking the bardic name Rhiannon.

During the First World War, she converted two of her London homes into military hospitals. She donated land to build Colwyn Bay Community Hospital and had a church hall built for Llanddulas. She donated firewood from her estates to keep vulnerable people warm and ensured that her elderly tenants were protected from eviction.

When she died in 1924, Winifred bequeathed £5,000 and land for building almshouses in Abergele. She bequeathed Gwrych Castle to Prince George, later King George V, in the hope that it would become the official Welsh residence of the Prince of Wales. However, the gift was refused. It passed instead to the Venerable Order of St John and is now owned by Gwrych Castle Preservation Trust.

DID YOU KNOW?

Gwrych Castle shot to fame during the Covid-19 pandemic as the alternative venue for the reality television show *I'm a Celebrity… Get Me Out of Here!*

20 JANUARY

Dame Margaret Lloyd George (née Owen), who was one of seven women appointed as magistrates in 1919, died on this day in 1941.

Born 4 November 1864, Margaret was the only child of Richard and Mary Owen of Mynydd Ednyfed Fawr, a sizeable farmstead just to the north of Criccieth. She was educated at Dr Williams' School for Girls in Dolgellau. Margaret first met her future husband and future Prime Minister, David Lloyd George, in 1885 when they were both members of the Criccieth Debating Society. They were engaged in 1886 and married in 1888.

When Lloyd George became a member of parliament, Margaret moved with him to London. As well as being appointed one of the first female magistrates, Margaret was made a dame after raising the equivalent of £15 million for her First World War Troops Fund.

Margaret found life in London very difficult and her heart was in Criccieth. The couple's five children were all born in north Wales. In 1919, she was elected to the Criccieth Urban District Council and she later became the first female Justice of the Peace in Caernarfonshire and was president of the Women's Liberal Federation of North and South Wales.

Her relationship with her husband became distant. Nevertheless, following the end of the war, Margaret conducted an unprecedented programme of campaigning on behalf of her husband's Liberal Party throughout England and Wales. She later also helped both her son Gwilym and her daughter Megan (see 22 April) to become members of parliament.

21 JANUARY

On 21 January 1549, Blanche Parry was temporarily promoted from the position of second in the household of Princess Elizabeth (later Elizabeth I) to chief gentlewoman. Her promotion followed the arrest and imprisonment of Kat Ashley for her unsubstantiated involvement in the flirtatious behaviour of Thomas Seymour towards the fourteen-year-old Elizabeth. After Kat Ashley died in 1565, Blanche was appointed permanently as the chief gentlewoman of the privy chamber, controlling access to Elizabeth, who was by then queen. She was in charge of the queen's jewels, personal papers, clothes, furs and books.

Blanche was born in 1507 or 1508 in St Faith's, Bacton, in the Welsh Marches and was involved in Elizabeth's life from the princess's birth, serving as nursemaid, personal attendant and confidante before her promotion to chief gentlewoman. It is widely believed that Blanche, who was Welsh speaking, sang Welsh lullabies to baby Elizabeth and later taught her to speak Welsh. It is suggested that the two would talk in Welsh to disguise their discussions about attendants and suspected conspirators at court.

22 JANUARY

On 22 January 2018, Yasmin Khan became the Welsh Government's National Adviser for Violence Against Women. Her role involves working with victims and survivors to shape and inform improvements in the way services are planned, commissioned and delivered.

Yasmin founded the Halo Project, an award-winning national charity that supports Black and minoritised victims and survivors of domestic abuse, sexual violence and hidden harms including forced marriage, female genital mutilation, and honour-based abuse. As part of the Tees Valley Inclusion Project, Halo has helped over 2,500 women to date, including many with children. The goal of the project is to help survivors move on from situations of violence and lead independent lives safe and free from harm.

23 JANUARY

The Llandudno branch of the National Union of Women's Suffrage Societies (NUWSS) was formed on 23 January 1907 at the Cocoa and Coffee House on Mostyn Street. It is regarded as the first society in Wales to campaign for women to be allowed to vote in parliamentary elections. The Llandudno branch's first secretary was Susan Edith Champneys, who joined the Women's Police Service in 1916 and worked her way up to the position of chief inspector.

The Cardiff and District branch was formed the following year. Beginning with a membership of seventy, it rapidly grew and, in 1914, it was the largest branch outside London. Each branch carried a banner with regional or national emblems: Llandudno's banner featured a leek and Cardiff's featured a dragon.

The NUWSS differed from the more militant Women's Social and Political Union (WSPU), known as the suffragettes, in that they sought parliamentary and public support through political and peaceful means. The two groups were identifiable by the predominant colours they wore: red, white and green by the NUWSS and purple, white and green by the WSPU.

24 JANUARY

Marged ferch Ifan, famous wrestler and harpist, was buried in Llanddeiniolen on 24 January 1793.

Marged was born in 1696 in the area around Mynydd Drws-y-Coed on the Nantlle ridge in Eryri (Snowdonia). Later, with her husband Richard Morris, she ran a pub frequented by copper miners. Marged could shoe horses and she made harps which she played to entertain her customers. She was an imposing woman – over six feet tall – and apparently had hands like shovels. It was said that she could wrestle any man and she took on challenges well into her seventies, beating men much younger than herself. She was also said to have been violent to Richard.

Marged and Richard later moved to Nant Peris, where she built a boat to ferry miners to their work across Llyn Peris and Llyn Padarn, earning her the name 'Queen of the Lakes'. On one occasion she threw a passenger into the lake over a disagreement over the fare and only hauled him back in when he agreed to pay her a guinea.

25 JANUARY

St Dwynwen, the patron saint of friendship and love, is celebrated in Wales on 25 January.

According to legend, the fifth-century king of Brycheiniog, Brychan Brycheiniog, was thought to have had twenty-four children and Dwynwen was one of his prettiest daughters. Her story varies but the generally accepted version is that Dwynwen was already betrothed to another when she fell in love with a local man called Maelon Dafodrill. Distraught, Dwynwen fled into the woods and prayed that God would help her forget him.

There, she fell asleep and received a visit from an angel, who gave her a potion to make her forget him but which also turned Maelon into ice.

God then granted Dwynwen three wishes. She asked for Maelon to be thawed, for God to grant true lovers all their hopes and dreams and also that she would never marry. The three wishes were granted and Dwynwen dedicated the rest of her life to God. The remains of Dwynwen's church are still visible today on Ynys Llanddwyn, an island off Anglesey. Here there is also a well, which legend says is home to a sacred fish, whose movements forecast the romantic future of visiting couples.

Traditionally on St Dwynwen's Day, decoratively carved love spoons were presented to young women by their loved ones as a token of affection. Love spoons were usually made from a single piece of sycamore or poplar. A small pocket knife was often used to carve symbols into the spoon: hearts representing passion; balls within cages representing the number of children desired by the couple; chain links representing faithfulness; keys representing security; and wheels representing the carver's intention to work hard and provide for his loved one.

26 JANUARY

Edith Elizabeth Downing, renowned artist and sculptor, is thought to have been born in Cardiff on 26 January 1857.

Edith sold much of her work to support the suffragette movement. She was arrested during an extensive window-smashing campaign in London in March 1912 and sent to Holloway Prison where she joined fellow suffragettes on hunger strike. She was one of the victims

of the extremely controversial policy of force-feeding of suffragette prisoners. This involved the prisoner being restrained while a rubber tube was forced into their mouth or nose. Mixtures of liquid foods were then poured into the stomach. The victims often suffered broken teeth, bleeding, vomiting and choking as a result of the practice.

In recognition of her bravery and her suffering, Edith was awarded a Hunger Strike Medal by the Women's Social and Political Union (WSPU). Between 1909 and 1914, a hundred Hunger Strike Medals were awarded to other Welsh women including Edith's sister, Caroline Lowder Downing. Other recipients included Frances Olive Outerbridge, a nurse from Swansea, and Kate Williams Evans from Llanymynech in Montgomeryshire. Like Edith, Kate was also arrested in 1912 and imprisoned in Holloway Prison. Her medal, along with her arrest warrant and her autograph book, containing the signatures of suffragettes such as Emily Davison, Emmeline Pankhurst and Sarah Benett, were purchased in 2018 by Amgueddfa Cymru (Museum Wales).

27 JANUARY

International Holocaust Remembrance Day is 27 January – the day that, in 1945, Auschwitz concentration camp was liberated – and commemorates the genocide of approximately six million Jewish people, along with countless members of other minority groups, by Nazi Germany between 1933 and 1945.

Holocaust survivor Eva Clarke was born on 29 April 1945 at Mauthausen in Austria, one of the most brutal and severe of the Nazi concentration camps. Eva's mother,

Anka, was a Czech Jew who had arrived at Mauthausen the day after the gas chambers had ceased to function; within three days it was liberated by the United States Army.

Returning to Prague with Eva, Anka discovered that her husband (and Eva's father) Bernd Nathan, a German-Jewish architect, was dead. Her son, Dan (Eva's brother), had already died of pneumonia in the Theresienstadt ghetto in 1944, aged two months. Anka remarried: her new husband was Karel Bergman, a Czech Jew who had escaped to the United Kingdom in 1939 and returned to Czechoslovakia (as it was then) as a translator in the Royal Air Force. In 1948, they relocated to Cardiff with Eva. Karel found work at a factory on the Treforest Trading Estate near Pontypridd and Eva was educated at Rhydypenau Primary School and Lady Mary Secondary High School in Cyncoed. She later married Malcolm Clarke, a lawyer from Abergavenny, and they had two sons.

Eva is now a speaker for the Holocaust Educational Trust, aiming to combat modern-day instances of racism and prejudice by sharing her family's experiences of the Holocaust. She was awarded the British Empire Medal in 2019 for her efforts in sharing testimonials for future generations.

28 JANUARY

On 28 January 1457, Margaret Beaufort gave birth to Henry Tudor (later King Henry VII) at Pembroke Castle. Margaret was the great-great-granddaughter of Edward III, which gave Henry his claim to the English crown.

In 1455, Margaret married Edmund Tudor, the son of Owen Tudor and Catherine of Valois, the widow of Henry V of England, which made him a half-brother of King

Henry VI. Margaret was twelve years old and Edmund was twenty-four. This was at the time of the dynastic civil wars known as the Wars of the Roses (1455–85) between the supporters of Henry VI (House of Lancaster) and those of Richard, 3rd Duke of York (House of York). A year after their wedding, Edmund died of the plague after being captured while defending Carmarthen Castle for the Lancastrians. Seven months pregnant, Margaret was taken by Edmund's brother Jasper to Pembroke Castle, where she gave birth to a son. It is thought that the birth was extremely difficult because she was so young and it may have done her permanent physical injury. Despite two later marriages, she never had another child and, later in life, she produced a set of proper protocols regarding the birth and upbringing of royal heirs.

The Yorkists took Pembroke in 1461. Henry was a leading Lancastrian claimant to the crown, so Jasper took him into hiding and they eventually fled to Brittany. During this time, Margaret saw her son only occasionally, although they corresponded. When Edward IV died unexpectedly in 1483, Margaret and Edward's widow, Elizabeth Woodville, plotted to bring Henry back from exile to take the crown. They also committed for Henry to marry Elizabeth's daughter, also Elizabeth (Elizabeth of York), thereby uniting the Houses of Lancaster and York and ending the Wars of the Roses.

Margaret remarried twice, first to Sir Henry Stafford and then, in 1472, to Thomas Stanley, 1st Earl of Derby. Stanley had initially been a Yorkist supporter of Edward IV's brother Richard III, but it was his decision to change his allegiance and fight for Henry Tudor at the Battle of Bosworth in 1485 that proved crucial in Henry's victory and his coronation as Henry VII. Margaret subsequently exerted considerable political influence within the Tudor court in her role as 'My Lady the King's Mother'. When Henry died in 1509, Margaret was the chief executor of his will and arranged both the funeral of her son and the coronation of her grandson Henry VIII.

Margaret died on 29 June 1509 and, although she specified in her will that she wanted to be buried alongside Edmund Tudor, she was buried at Westminster Abbey, probably on the orders of Henry VIII.

DID YOU KNOW?

Margaret Beaufort was also a benefactor of academic and religious establishments. Christ's College and St John's College at Cambridge were founded by her and she organised the building of the chapel overlooking St Winefride's Well in Holywell.

29 JANUARY

It was on 29 January 2021 that reports first emerged that four-year-old Lily Wilder had discovered a well-preserved dinosaur footprint while walking with her father at Bendricks Bay, Barry, in the Vale of Glamorgan.

The footprint was found to be 220 million years old and had been preserved in mud. While it is impossible to tell what type of dinosaur left it, the print is ten centimetres long and would have belonged to a creature likely to have been about seventy-five centimetres tall. It would have been a slender animal which would have walked on its hind legs and actively hunted other small animals and insects.

Scientists acknowledged that Lily's discovery could help establish how dinosaurs walked. Museum Wales palaeontology curator Cindy Howells described it as 'the best specimen ever found on this beach. Its spectacular preservation may help scientists establish more about the actual structure of their [dinosaur] feet as the preservation is clear enough to show individual pads and even claw impressions.'

The footprint is now on display at the National Museum Cardiff, with Lily Wilder credited as the finder.

30 JANUARY ⚠

Dorothy 'Dot' Miles, poet and activist in the deaf community, died on this day in 1993. Born 19 August 1931, she is regarded as the pioneer of British Sign Language (BSL) and her work laid the foundations for modern sign language poetry in the US and UK. She also compiled the first teaching manual for BSL tutors and helped establish the first university course for deaf people to become BSL tutors.

Dot was born in Cadole, Flintshire and moved with her family to Rhyl by the time she was eight years old. In 1939, she contracted cerebrospinal meningitis, which left her deaf and initially unable to walk. She attended the Royal School for the Deaf, Manchester, and the Mary Hare School in Berkshire (the first grammar school for the deaf) before attending university in Washington DC, where she began composing sign language poetry. After returning to Britain in 1977, Dot worked with the BBC to develop its provision for deaf people and helped initiate the *See Hear* BBC television series.

By the early 1990s, Dot began suffering from severe depression. In 1993, she fell from the window of her second-floor flat in London. An inquest concluded that she had died by suicide.

31 JANUARY

On 31 January 2021, Barbara McGregor from Bryn, near Maesteg, retired with the longest career of any woman ever to serve in the Royal Navy: forty-three years and 189 days.

Barbara joined the Women's Royal Naval Service as a radio operator in 1977. Following service as a trainer of new recruits she was appointed as the most senior warrant officer of the Royal Naval Careers Service. She was also involved with the NATO Summit when it was held in Cardiff in 2014.

The Women's Royal Naval Service (WRNS; popularly known as the Wrens) was first formed in 1917 as a branch of the Royal Navy for the First World War. It was disbanded in 1919 and then reformed in 1939 at the beginning of the Second World War. The WRNS was finally integrated into the Royal Navy in 1993 when women were allowed to serve on board navy vessels as full members of the crew.

1 FEBRUARY

Merthyr-born academic, journalist, lecturer and writer Ursula Masson (1945–2008) was an influential figure in the establishment of Honno Press, a Welsh publisher specialising in women's writing. Honno Press published their first books on 1 February 1987.

As a history lecturer, Ursula was a leading figure in the field of women's history, especially Welsh women's social and political history.

In 1998 she co-founded Archif Menywod Cymru (Women's Archive Wales), and initiated a series of Wales Women's History Roadshows, where people were encouraged to contribute and discuss material relating to the social history of women in Wales. The results subsequently became part of The People's Collection Wales.

She also established, along with Professor Jane Aaron, the Centre for Gender Studies in Wales, where the annual Ursula Masson Memorial Lecture is still given.

2 FEBRUARY

The Christian festival of Candlemas takes place each year on the 2 February. It is thought to originate from the Celtic festival of Imbolc, the celebration of the arrival of spring, which honours the pagan Irish goddess Brigid. Over time, the goddess was adopted into Christianity as St Brigid or Sant Ffraed in Welsh.

According to Welsh legend, Brigid visited Wales, crossing the Irish Sea on a floating turf of grass and landing at Trearddur Bay on Holy Island, Anglesey. An eight-foot-high cross commemorating her still stands here. She is also remembered in the names of seventeen churches and chapels in Wales associated with her.

This day is also known in Wales as *Gŵyl Fair y Canhwyllau* (Mary's Festival of the Candles). This festival marked the end of *amser gwylad* (time of vigil) the darkest time of the year where candles would be put aside with the increase in daylight and the approach of spring.

3 FEBRUARY

Born on 3 February 1932 in Pontycymer in the Garw Valley near Bridgend, Molly Parkin went on to have a long and illustrious career as an artist, journalist, novelist, fashion guru and colourful media personality.

After attending Goldsmiths College and Brighton College of Art, she exhibited widely from the late 1950s to the mid-1960s.

In 1964 she started making hats and bags for the trendsetting shop Biba and founded *Nova* fashion magazine before becoming fashion editor of *The Sunday Times*. She helped to establish designers such as Paco

Rabanne and Manolo Blahnik, and was awarded Fashion Editor of the Year in 1971.

Her flamboyant personality and style made her a popular guest on television and radio shows, although she was once banned by the BBC for swearing. She gave up fashion and began writing erotic novels. She later started painting again when she gave up alcohol and cigarettes at the age of fifty-five and has been painting ever since.

4 FEBRUARY

Deirdre Beddoe, born in Barry on 4 February 1942, is an Emeritus Professor of Women's History at the University of Glamorgan and a highly respected expert on the history of women in Wales. She co-founded and became the first chair of Archif Menywod Cymru (Women's Archive Wales) in 1998 and is a broadcaster and the author of several books on women's history.

After graduating from Aberystwyth University, Deirdre committed herself to rescuing the lost history of women in Wales and to making their stories accessible to a wide audience. She has researched and written extensively about women's suffrage and their lives during the First and Second World Wars. As a member of Cardiff Women's Action Group, Deirdre was also heavily engaged in the Women's Liberation Movement of the 1970s and 1980s and organised the first conference on women's history in Wales in 1983.

Her books include *Back to Home and Duty: Women Between the Wars, 1919–39*, regarded as a pioneering work on the subject, and *Out of the Shadows: A History of Women in Twentieth-Century Wales*, which was published in 2001 and is her most popular work, detailing the education, health, home life, leisure, politics and waged work of Welsh women during the twentieth century.

5 FEBRUARY ⚠

Born in Port Talbot on 5 February 1908, Millicent Lilian Entwistle, known as Peg, was a stage and screen actress who gained notoriety when she died by suicide after jumping from the 'H' of the Hollywood sign at the age of just twenty-four.

Although her life was brief, her Hollywood career influenced the now-legendary Hollywood star Bette Davis to go into acting. It was after seeing Peg in a Broadway production of Ibsen's *The Wild Duck* that Bette decided to embark on an acting career. She told her mother, 'I want to be exactly like Peg Entwistle.'

DID YOU KNOW?

Bette Davis herself had Welsh roots through her father, Harlow Davis.

6 FEBRUARY

On 6 February, New Zealanders celebrate their national day, known as Waitangi Day, which marks the date in 1840 that the Indigenous Māori people and the settlers signed a treaty regarded as the founding document of the country.

There are many notable Welsh women associated with New Zealand.

In 1850, Charlotte Godley (née Griffith Wynne), born in Voelas House, near Betws-y-coed, accompanied her husband John Robert Godley to New Zealand. He was the leader of an expedition to establish a British colony in Canterbury and a capital at Christchurch. Charlotte was an active community leader and her letters home to her mother are regarded as an important historical account of life in this period. Published as *Letters from Early New Zealand,* they describe Māori customs and give an insight into the lives of the settlers.

Eveline Willet Cunnington (1849–1916) was born in Briton Ferry and emigrated to New Zealand in 1875. Eveline was a strong advocate for ending the exploitation of children and young women and for prison reform. She was also a founding member of the National Council of Women of New Zealand.

Brewery owner Mary Innes (née Lewis, 1852–1941), born in Llanvaches, Monmouthshire is credited with bringing the soft drink industry to New Zealand. Her once family-owned company is today owned by the Oasis Group. In 2013, Mary was recognised and inducted into the New Zealand Business Hall of Fame.

Dame Sian Elias has a Welsh mother, and became the first woman to serve as chief justice of New Zealand between 1999 and 2019. She was the presiding judge of the Supreme Court of New Zealand and acted as administrator to the government on several occasions.

7 FEBRUARY

British-Nigerian solicitor Professor Uzo Iwobi was born on 7 February 1969 and is the first Black woman to be appointed as Specialist Policy Adviser on Equalities to the Welsh Government.

Uzo is the founder and chief executive of Race Council Cymru, which has the mission of bringing together key organisations to cooperate on promoting integration and championing justice and race equality in institutions and society in Wales. She has served as a commissioner for Racial Equality UK and has worked with the police authority as a strategic adviser.

Among her many appointments, Uzo became the first international chair of diversity at the Royal Welsh College of Music and Drama and a representative for Wales as a board member of the Universities Association for Lifelong Learning.

8 FEBRUARY

Today is, by some accounts, the feast day of St Ciwa – also known as St Kew or the 'Wolf Girl' – who, according to legend, was raised by wolves in Gwent in the sixth century. She is said to have built a church in the village of Llangiwa (Llangua) near Abergavenny. Ciwa then travelled to Cornwall, where she tamed a fierce bear that had been terrorising the area and set up a hermitage and church at current-day St Kew, which is named in her honour.

This period is often referred to as 'The Golden Age of Saints' as it was when the foundations for the Christian Church were laid in ancient Wales following the Roman period. While the pagan Anglo-Saxons gained influence over much of England, Christianity flourished along the seaways between Wales, Cornwall, Brittany and Ireland during this time.

Other notable Welsh female saints with a connection to Cornwall are:

- **Materiana** is the eldest daughter of King Vortimer. She went on to rule over Gwent with her husband Prince Ynyr. She is patron of the churches of Minster and Tintagel.
- **Morwenna, Menefrida and Endelienta** (see 29 April) were the daughters of Brychan, the legendary fifth-century founder and ruler of the kingdom of Brycheiniog (now modern-day Breconshire). Morwenna made her home near Morwenstow, from where she could see her homeland of Wales. It is said that on her deathbed, she asked to be raised up so that she could see Wales for the last time. Menefrida is associated with the area of St Minver, near the Camel estuary.

9 FEBRUARY

Grace Williams from Barry (1906–77) is regarded by many as one of Wales's finest composers. The last page of the score for her most popular work, the symphony *Fantasia on Welsh Nursery Tunes,* was annotated on 9 February 1940 and this is regarded as its completion date. It's the work that brought her to prominence: a composition for a symphonic orchestra based on traditional Welsh nursery tunes and lullabies.

Grace was a pupil at the Royal College of Music, London and later studied under the composer Egon Wellesz in Vienna. She wrote mainly orchestral and choral music and, early in her career, was influenced by Vaughan Williams and Elgar. She is also well known for her suite of five movements for string orchestra *Sea Sketches* (1944), which she dedicated to her parents.

Grace was proudly Welsh and embraced her Welsh national identity within her work. In 1966, she turned down the offer of an OBE for her services to music.

DID YOU KNOW?

Grace Williams was the first British woman to compose the score for a feature film: 1949's *Blue Scar.*

10 FEBRUARY

Rachel Thomas, much-loved radio, film and television actress, was born on 10 February 1905 in Alltwen near Pontardawe.

Frequently cast in the role of the archetypal Welsh 'mam', she starred alongside Paul Robeson in the 1940 classic *The Proud Valley* and in the 1968 television version of *How Green Was My Valley*. In 1954 she was a member of the original cast of Dylan Thomas's radio play *Under Milk Wood,* and played Mary Ann Sailors in the 1972 film version.

She was, for many years, a mainstay of the BBC Wales

Welsh-language soap opera *Pobol y Cwm* (*People of the Valley*). In 1991 she received a special BAFTA Cymru award for her lifetime's work and achievements. Rachel died on 8 February 1995.

11 FEBRUARY

The iconic fashion designer Mary Quant was born on 11 February 1930. She is credited as being the creator of the miniskirt and the first designer to use PVC in her pieces. Her designs played a prominent role in the period of social and cultural change referred to as the Swinging Sixties.

Mary's Welsh parents were both schoolteachers who had moved to London, but she spent nearly all of her summer holidays with her aunt in Pembrokeshire, and spent time there as a child evacuee during the Second World War.

Her affordable clothing collection, Ginger Group, launched in 1963, and the clothing was manufactured by Steinbergs in its Pontypridd factory.

In 1990, Mary was awarded the prestigious Hall of Fame award by the British Fashion Council, recognising her contribution to the industry.

12 FEBRUARY

Megan Watts Hughes, singer, scientist and philanthropist, was born on 12 February 1842 in Dowlais.

Young Megan performed at local concerts in the Merthyr and Aberdare area. In 1864, she was enrolled at the Royal Academy of Music, London. She later toured north Wales with the renowned composer Joseph Parry, who described her as being one of 'our greatest vocalists'.

In 1885, she was experimenting with ways to measure the power of her voice. She crafted a device which featured a mouthpiece feeding into a receiving chamber, over which was stretched a rubber membrane sprinkled with sand. When she sang into the mouthpiece, she discovered that geometric patterns were formed from the resonance of her voice. She called these patterns 'voice-figures' and later substituted the sand and powder with a thin layer of liquid. She called the device an 'eidophone'. Megan was one of the first people to observe the phenomenon of visualising sound.

When Megan later demonstrated the eidophone at a meeting of the Royal Society, she became one of the very first women to make such a presentation. In 1904, she published a book on the subject: *The Eidophone Voice Figures: Geometrical and Natural Forms Produced by Vibrations of the Human Voice.*

Megan founded a home for homeless boys at Mountford House in Islington around 1871. She died on 29 October 1907 and was buried in Abney Park cemetery in London.

13 FEBRUARY

Kate Roberts was born on this day in 1891 in Rhosgadfan in Eryri (Snowdonia) and was one of the most prominent Welsh-language authors of the twentieth century.

Her childhood was firmly rooted in the slate quarrying and subsistence smallholding communities of Welsh-speaking northwest Wales.

The crushing poverty and harsh living of her early years are continually evoked in her writing, especially in her 1936 novel *Traed Mewn Cyffion* (*Feet in Chains*). Here she explores the devastating effects of the First World War, the changing role of women during the war years, the undermining influence of Anglocentric education systems on monoglot Welsh communities, and industrial unrest.

Her writing was initially a therapeutic coping mechanism for her, following the death of her brother Dei in Malta during the war and the devastating injuries sustained by her brother Evan in the Battle of the Somme, but her work rapidly won her national acclaim.

Known as '*Brenhines ein Llên*' ('The Queen of our Literature'), Roberts remains one of the most prolific and highly regarded writers of twentieth-century Wales.

14 FEBRUARY

Sources record that it was 14 February 1904 when, at a Sunday church service in New Quay, Cardiganshire, a local sixteen-year-old girl spontaneously got to her feet and publicly confessed, 'I love the Lord Jesus with all my heart.' Florrie Evans's testament had an unusually powerful effect and is generally considered to be the beginning of the 1904–5 Welsh Revival of Christianity.

The revival became national news and 'set the country on fire', according to one journalist, before spreading to the rest of Britain then sparking similar revivals in Scandinavia, North America, Latin America, India and Africa. It was characterised by services that included spontaneous tears of joy, fainting, hymn-singing, public confessions and mass conversions. The revival attracted young people, and young women in particular.

Florrie became a prominent leader of the revival and toured all over Wales and London with fellow New Quay native, singer Maud Davies. It is estimated that, over the course of the revival, around 100,000 people were converted to Nonconformist religion by the 'Baptism of the Holy Spirit' in Wales, and that up to a million people were converted across Britain.

15 FEBRUARY

The American novelist, travel writer and journalist Martha Ellis Gellhorn (born 8 November 1908), died on this day in 1998. She is considered one of the great war correspondents of the twentieth century.

Gellhorn covered the Spanish Civil War, the Second World War and conflicts in Vietnam and the Middle East during her career. She was the only female reporter at the Normandy landings in 1944 and one of very few who reported from the liberated Nazi concentration camps. The Martha Gellhorn Prize for Journalism is named after her.

In 1980, she moved to Kilgwrrwg, near Chepstow, after being charmed by Wales and its people. She came out of retirement to report on the 1984–5 miners' strike for *The Guardian*. She was driven around the south Wales valleys to talk to miners and their wives. She described the miners' strike as being 'exactly like a war; they were fighting for their territory, their community. They said "If the mine closes, the community dies."' In 2021 a Purple Plaque, designed to mark the achievements of women from all walks of life across Wales, was unveiled at her former home in Kilgwrrwg, where she lived for fourteen years.

16 FEBRUARY

On 16 February 1901, Constance Edwina Cornwallis-West married Hugh Grosvenor, 2nd Duke of Westminster, then one of the wealthiest men in the world.

Constance was born at Ruthin Castle in 1877. He father was William Cornwallis-West, the High Sheriff and Lord Lieutenant of Denbighshire, who later went on to be elected MP for Denbigh West. Her mother was Mary 'Patsy' Fitzpatrick, a leading socialite and mistress of the future King Edward VII.

Constance was one of only two women to compete at the 1908 Summer Olympics as the yacht owner and extra crew member of the team that won bronze medals in sailing. In 1919, her divorce settlement from Grosvenor of £13,000 a year was, at the time, the largest in British legal history.

During the First World War, she sponsored a military hospital in Le Touquet for which she was created a Commander of the Order of the British Empire (CBE). It was at this hospital that she met her second husband, Captain John Fitzpatrick Lewis.

17 FEBRUARY

On 17 February 1976, a police investigation which came to be named Operation Julie (after Police Sergeant Julie Taylor) was begun at a meeting in Brecon. The police operation involved chief constables and senior drug-squad officers and it eventually resulted in the break-up of one of the largest LSD manufacturing operations in the world.

Julie Taylor was one of a team of undercover surveillance officers based in a farmhouse in Tregaron, Dyfed, overlooking the cottage of chemist Richard Kemp, who was a key suspect in the drugs network.

The subsequent raid in 1977, after thirteen months of surveillance, on the LSD factory in Kemp's home in mid-Wales discovered six million tabs, which was one of the largest stashes of illegal drugs ever found and resulted in dozens of people being arrested.

18 FEBRUARY

On 18 February 1915, the German high command first implemented 'unrestricted submarine warfare' in the seas around Britain. Under this instruction, U-boat captains could sink merchant ships. Controversially, hospital ships were also viewed as legitimate targets.

Hospital ships were unarmed and easily identified. Among the thirteen British hospital ships sunk during the conflict were HMHS *Britannic* (sister ship to the *Titanic*) on 21 November 1916 and HMHS *Salta* on 10 April 1917.

Britannic hit a naval mine of the Imperial German Navy near the Greek island of Kea and sank, killing thirty of the more than a thousand passengers on board. There were three Welsh nurses on board, Annie Handley from Llandovery, M. A. Harries from Abergwili and another nurse known only by her surname, Edwards, from Cynwyd. All three survived and Annie and nurse Edwards reportedly spent the remainder of the war nursing soldiers in France. *Salta* hit a German mine while returning to pick up wounded soldiers at the port of

Le Havre, France. Of the 205 passengers and crew members on board, 130 were lost at sea, including Jane (Jennie) Roberts from Bryncrug, near Aberdyfi.

Thousands of young women volunteered to serve as nurses during the First World War. The number of registered nurses with the Queen Alexandra's Imperial Military Nursing Service increased from less than 300 to over 10,000, during the war. The courage and dedication of these nurses did much to change perceptions of the role of women in British society.

19 FEBRUARY

Lucy Thomas (1781–1847) from Llansamlet took over the running of her husband Robert's coal mining business when he died on 19 February 1833. Although she could neither read nor write, under her guidance their coal mine in Merthyr became one of the most successful mines in Wales. Described as a witty and clever businesswoman, and 'the mother of the Welsh steam coal trade', Lucy was one of the first to commission scientific reports on the efficiency of Welsh steam coal, which resulted in lucrative deals with London merchants.

Caroline Williams, from Bridgend, was another notable female colliery owner. In 1867, she inherited most of the Dinas Estate in Rhondda from her uncle, Walter Coffin III, who is regarded as the first person to mine the Rhondda Valley on an industrial scale.

Caroline contributed financially to the community at Dinas, and spent large sums of money on laying and improving local roads. She was also an active promoter of women's education. At Cardiff University, she donated

towards the establishment of Aberdare Hall as a residence for female students, provided the first scholarship for women at a Welsh university college and established a school of mining. The nearby village of Williamstown is named after her.

20 FEBRUARY ⚠

On 20 February 1336, Alice de Lacy (1281–1348) was arrested on the orders of Edward III of England. It was just one of the many dramatic events in her eventful life.

Alice was born at Denbigh Castle and was one of medieval Britain's richest heiresses. Alice's first marriage in 1294 was an arranged union with King Edward I's nephew Thomas, Earl of Lancaster. She was twelve and Thomas around sixteen. It appears that the two disliked each other intensely, which resulted in Thomas taking many mistresses and Alice living mostly alone. Alice was also, according to sources, unable to have children following a miscarriage in either 1307 or 1308.

In 1317, Alice was abducted by John de Warenne, Earl of Surrey. It is suggested that Alice may have been having an affair with him and was complicit in her own abduction. Although Thomas waged a private war on de Warenne for the humiliation, he made little effort to rescue his wife and little is heard of Alice for the next five years.

When Thomas was executed in 1322 for leading a revolt against Edward II, Alice reappeared in the history books. As Thomas's widow, she was imprisoned and had to forfeit all her land. It was only upon payment of an indemnity that she was released but only a small portion of her inheritance was restored.

In 1324, she married Baron Eubulus le Strange of Shropshire. When Eubulus died in 1335, Alice took a vow of chastity. But his death left her, as a wealthy, widowed landowner, vulnerable and in February 1336 she was abducted for a second time. Sir Hugh de Freyne, royal keeper of the town and castle of Cardigan forcibly removed her from her home at Bolingbroke Castle and raped her. The king arrested them both but they were later released and Alice became his wife. Hugh died on campaign in Scotland the following year and Alice returned to her vow of chastity.

Alice lived out the remainder of her life relatively peacefully having earned the respect and protection of Edward III. She died in 1348 and requested to be buried alongside Eubulus in Barlings Abbey in Lincolnshire.

21 FEBRUARY

Charlotte Church (born Charlotte Maria Reed) was born on 21 February 1986. She came to public notice when she made an appearance on *The Big Big Talent Show* in 1996 and was asked to sing. She stole the show and became an overnight sensation. More television and concert appearances followed, including at the Cardiff Arms Park, the London Palladium, the Royal Albert Hall, and as an opening act for Shirley Bassey in Antwerp. Charlotte, aged twelve, became the youngest person to top the UK's classical charts with the release of her album, *Voice of an Angel*.

Charlotte has since made the transition to pop music and in total has released six studio albums, selling more than ten million records worldwide. Alongside her continuing success as a singer, Charlotte presented her own entertainment television show, *The Charlotte Church Show* which launched in 2006, and has made several appearances on television and in films. She has also been outspoken on a number of political issues and, in 2016, declared her support for the Plaid Cymru and Welsh independence.

DID YOU KNOW?

At thirteen, Charlotte won the Best Female Artist at the 2000 Classical BRIT Awards, making her the youngest artist ever to receive the award.

22 FEBRUARY ⚠

On 22 February 1921, Kitty Armstrong returned to her home in Hay-on-Wye after a spell in the Barnwood mental hospital near Gloucester. Her physical and mental health had been bad upon admission but she had made a good improvement. Within a month, however, she was dead at forty-eight.

Kitty had been publicly distrustful of her husband, Major Herbert Rowse-Armstrong, who was a seemingly upstanding and respected solicitor. In her will dated 1917, she left the bulk of her substantial estate to her children. After her death Armstrong produced a different will, giving him sole control of her fortune.

A few months after her death, one of Armstrong's business rivals became violently sick after eating scones at his invitation, and his sister-in-law was also taken ill after eating a chocolate from an anonymously delivered box. There was also talk of another rival who had died unexpectedly after being in a dispute with Armstrong. Suspicions were aroused.

Kitty's body was exhumed and found to contain significant quantities of arsenic. Witnesses also recalled that Armstrong had been in the habit of purchasing unusually large quantities of arsenic for the purpose of 'controlling the dandelions' in his garden. He was put on trial, convicted and was subsequently hanged at Gloucester jail. Known as 'The Hay Poisoner', Armstrong remains the only solicitor ever to be hanged in Britain.

23 FEBRUARY

Elisabeth 'Betty' Evans (born c.1828) died on 23 February 1919.

Betty was the wife of Joseph Jenkins, reputedly 'the jolly swagman' of the popular song 'Waltzing Matilda', who spent twenty-seven years in Australia as a transient labourer and poet.

The story is that Joseph Jenkins left his family and home in Cardiganshire in 1868 to escape his wife, who was unfaithful to him and who beat him. However, the real story is much more intriguing than the legendary tale.

Betty was born in Ciliau Aeron, near Aberaeron, the daughter of a farmer. She married Joseph in 1846 and, within two years the couple moved to a farm near Tregaron. They had nine children and they won best farm in the county in 1851. However, Joseph became unpopular due to his support for the oppressive attitude of landowners towards their tenant farmers.

Betty and Joseph's relationship broke down following the death of their eldest son from tuberculosis in 1863. Their situation was made worse by Joseph's excessive drinking and neglect of the farm. His biographer, Bethan Phillips, notes that Joseph's diaries reveal him to be a tormented, melancholy and introspective man, who was seeking 'to exorcise his own demons by attempting to escape from them'. He decided to leave for Australia in 1869 to make his fortune in the gold mines.

Betty and her remaining children continued to run the farm successfully. When he returned in 1895 she allowed Joseph back into the house but they remained estranged. He died in 1898. Betty retired to Joseph's birthplace at Blaenplwyf and died aged ninety-one in 1919.

24 FEBRUARY

On 24 February 1797, Jemima Fawr (Jemima Nicholas) a cobbler from Fishguard, led a group of women to confront a force of French invaders who had landed in the bay of Carreg Wastad three miles west of the town, armed with only a pitchfork. She and her comrades rounded up twelve French soldiers, who were reputedly the worse for drink, and held them captive in a nearby church. The French commander surrendered shortly afterwards at the Royal Oak public house. The Battle of Fishguard is regarded as the last invasion of Britain and Jemima is known as 'The Heroine of Fishguard'.

Jemima's exploits are commemorated in the *Last Invasion Tapestry,* a hundred-foot-long work created by local women, commissioned by the Fishguard Arts Society to celebrate the 200th anniversary of the invasion. The tapestry is displayed in Fishguard Town Hall.

25 FEBRUARY

On 25 February 2003, the National Library of Wales announced the purchase of an important early album of photographs by Mary Dillwyn, thought to be the earliest Welsh female photographer. Her work provides an insight into the domestic lives of women and children of nineteenth-century Britain. The album includes a picture of a young boy – her nephew, Willy – smiling which is thought to be the first picture of a smile in Britain and probably the world.

Mary Dillwyn (1816–1906) was the daughter of Lewis Weston Dillwyn of Penllergaer, a prominent Swansea industrialist, and Mary Adams. When it came to photography, Mary preferred a smaller camera with a shorter exposure time as it provided her with the opportunity to take more spontaneous photographs.

DID YOU KNOW?

Mary Dillwyn is credited with taking the world's first photograph of a snowman in 1853.

26 FEBRUARY

On 26 February 1916, Joan Curran (née Strothers) was born in Swansea. Joan would go on to play a crucial part in the success of the 1944 Allied invasion of Europe that we know as D-Day.

Joan was a well-respected physicist who developed a way of disrupting enemy radar with strips of tinfoil which would be scattered in the path of enemy planes. The technique was code-named 'Window' and the strips became known as 'chaff'. Window was used along with hundreds of dummy parachutists as part of an elaborate diversion prior to D-Day to convince the German forces that the Allied assault would begin in the Pas-de-Calais area instead of Normandy.

Later in the war, Joan and her husband, Sir Samuel Curran, were invited to the US as part of a group of British scientists to take part in the Manhattan Project, to develop an atomic bomb.

DID YOU KNOW?

In 1935, when Joan was at university in Cambridge, she competed in the first women's rowing race against a team from the University of Oxford, which is recognised as being the world's first competitive women's rowing event.

27 FEBRUARY

On 27 February 2020, Nicky Walters from Llanybydder achieved a Guinness world record when she took 1 minute and 35.53 seconds to complete a fifty-metre pull of a nineteen-tonne narrowboat – the fastest time for a woman. In 2022, she achieved two further world records when she pulled a 7.5-tonne double-decker bus twenty metres

in 41.624 seconds and completed a pull of the heaviest vehicle (a cement truck weighing 8,260 kilograms) for a female using the upper body.

Nicky's achievements are all the more remarkable as she not only suffers from Crohn's disease but has been diagnosed with polycythaemia vera, a rare form of blood cancer.

Other notable Welsh strongwomen include:

- **Rebecca Roberts** from Bangor won the 2021 and 2023 World's Strongest Woman competition, becoming one of only four women in history to win multiple championships.
- **Jemma 'Stubbs' Stubbington** from Llangollen was the first Welsh woman to win the title of Britain's Strongest Woman in 2021. She has also held Guinness world records for car deadlifting and Atlas Stone lifts.

28 FEBRUARY

Born on 28 February 1962, Professor Karen Holford is a Welsh engineer, Professor of Mechanical Engineering and Vice Chancellor of Cranfield University.

Despite being actively discouraged at school from pursuing a career in engineering, which was then considered to be an exclusively male domain, Karen acquired an apprenticeship with Rolls-Royce who sponsored her to read mechanical engineering at Cardiff University. Her career has seen her repairing Harrier jump jet engines during the

Falklands War and working on automotive engineering projects with Jaguar, Rover and BMW.

An avid motorsport enthusiast and an accomplished racing driver, Karen sees Formula One engineering as an opportunity to be innovative and creative and is keen to encourage young women to seek experience and industrial placements in the automotive sector. In 2018, she received a CBE for services to engineering and the advancement of women in the field, and in 2019 received the Suffrage Science Award in Physical Sciences and Engineering.

29 FEBRUARY

There is a tradition of women proposing marriage on 29 February, which may go back to the time when the extra day of a leap year was not recognised by law and had no legal status. It was, therefore, acceptable to break with the courting tradition of men proposing marriage.

There are a number of other Welsh customs around marriage. In Pembrokeshire, a girl was said to dream about a future lover if a shoulder of mutton pierced by nine holes was placed under her pillow, her shoes were arranged in a T pattern and a rhyme spoken above her as she lay down.

Traditionally, a Welsh bride carried a bouquet containing myrtle leaves and gave cuttings from it to her bridesmaids. If the cuttings blossomed, then the girls would also soon marry.

Welsh brides believed that it was lucky to be woken by birdsong on the morning of their wedding. Also, if their wedding dress was torn on the wedding day, that piece of seemingly bad luck actually foretold a happy marriage.

1 MARCH

On St David's Day, it is customary for schoolchildren to wear traditional Welsh costume. Augusta Hall, the heiress to the Llanover estate near Abergavenny, is widely considered to have been instrumental in the adoption of the national costume.

During the 1830s, many people saw the increasing industrialisation of Wales as a threat to the country's traditional identity. Augusta was particularly active in trying to promote the use of the costume in order to protect that identity. She did extensive research and commissioned illustrations to win first prize at the 1834 National Eisteddfod for her essay on the costume. She learned to speak Welsh, issued her staff with national dress uniforms and organised balls at which her guests were encouraged to wear the national costume.

From the 1840s, Welsh costume dolls were being manufactured, and the dress appeared on prints, postcards and photographs as a means of promoting Wales as a tourist destination.

The Welsh traditional costume for women originates from the clothing worn by working rural women during the late eighteenth and early nineteenth centuries. It consists of a woollen *betgwn* (a bodiced, open-fronted gown) worn over a *pais* (a skirt or petticoat) with an apron, a shawl and kerchief. The traditional headgear was a black stovepipe hat or a black cockleshell bonnet. The costume was significantly different from those worn by the rural women of England.

DID YOU KNOW?

Author and journalist Margaret Williams claimed to be the most-photographed woman in Wales. She inherited the Smallest House in Great Britain, located in Conwy, and was photographed by countless tourists as she stood outside the building always dressed in her Welsh costume.

2 MARCH ⚠

The second day of March is largely recognised as the anniversary of the death of St Non, the mother of St David (Dewi Sant).

It is recorded that Non was born during the fifth century, and was the daughter of the nobleman Cynyr Ceinfarfog of Caer Goch in the Cantref of Pebidiog (in the northwest of current-day Pembrokeshire) and St Anna, daughter of

Vortimer Fendigaid, King of Gwerthefyriwg (Gwent). According to legend, Non's mother and father were also foster parents of King Arthur.

At a young age, Non joined a monastic community at Tŷ Gwyn above Whitesands Bay. She was a very beautiful woman and it is claimed that Prince Sandde of Ceredigion forced himself upon her and she became pregnant with David. Even from the womb David apparently performed miracles. During her pregnancy, Non entered a church and the priest was immediately struck dumb by the unborn David's presence. Non went into hiding to give birth, and David was born on the coast just south of Mynyw (St Davids) in the middle of a violent storm. This spot is marked by the now-ruined Capel Non (the Chapel of St Non) and a nearby holy well which, in medieval times, were among Wales's most-visited sites for Christian pilgrims.

Non named her son Dewidd, but he was commonly called Dewi (David is an English version taken from the Latin *Davidus*). Many of his fine qualities of character are attributed to his mother's early influence. Non subsequently travelled to Cornwall, where she is commemorated at the villages and holy wells at Pelynt and Altarnun. She ended her days in Dirinon in Brittany, where the chapel is now home to her tomb.

3 MARCH

On 3 March 1922, the Football Association of Wales (FAW) banned all its clubs, officials and players from participating in women's football. The contentious decision followed that of the English Football Association which had outlawed the playing of the game on Association members' pitches the previous year, stating that 'the game of football is quite unsuitable for females and ought not to be encouraged.'

A women's team in Norwood (Swansea) was recorded in March 1894. It was, however, during the First World War that its popularity soared. This was due mainly to the creation of teams such as Newport Ladies, the National Shell Factory Swansea and Powell's (Girls) Athletic in Wrexham. The teams sometimes grew up around munitions factories where women were required to work. Following the war, the women's game continued to grow with teams such as Llanelli Ladies' Football Club, Hengoed Girls, and Pengam Garden Village Girls attracting large crowds – sometimes in their thousands.

The ban remained for forty-eight years before finally being rescinded by FAW on 29 May 1970. The Wales Women played their first international match against the Republic of Ireland on 13 May 1973 and first entered the FIFA Women's World Cup and UEFA Women's Championship in 1995. On 3 December 2024, Wales Women defeated the Republic of Ireland in a qualifying tie for the Women's Euros in 2025. In 2023, FAW agreed on an equal-pay deal which resulted in women and men being paid the same for representing their country in the sport.

DID YOU KNOW?

The Welsh Women's football team's biggest victory (to date) was a 15–0 thrashing of Azerbaijan at Newtown in August 2010.

4 MARCH

On 4 March 1881, in a druidic ceremony at Y Maen Chwyf on Coedpenmaen Common, Pontypridd, twenty-one-year-old Gwenllian Llewelyn married Dr William Price on his eighty-first birthday.

Gwenllian, an orphan from Ynyscaedudwg Farm in Cilfynydd, came to Price's Llantrisant home to work as a maid in early 1881. It is said that, when he saw her for the first time, Dr Price clutched his hand to his head and exclaimed, 'Isis has come! The Mother of Gods has visited my habitation! Her forehead is high like that of the Goddess Juno, and her brow is like that of the Goddess Minerva!'

Price was a radical who held anti-establishment views and, until their union, rejected the notion of marriage. In Gwenllian, he found someone who understood his druidic beliefs and was prepared to accept his outlandish behaviour. He had held dreams of a god-like son and on 8 August 1883 when Gwenllian gave birth they named the baby Iesu Grist (Jesus Christ) Price. When the child died suddenly five months later, his mother brought the body of the child to Price, who performed a (then illegal) cremation ceremony. Gwenllian was made to face the judge and jury at Price's famous trial in Cardiff. He was acquitted.

Gwenllian remained faithful to William Price and bore him two further children: Iesu Grist II and Penelopen Elizabeth. After Price's death in 1893, Gwenllian fought to fulfil his wish to be publicly cremated in Llantrisant.

She later married publican John de Winter Parry. When the marriage failed, she continued to run the family farm in East Caerlan until her own death in December 1948.

5 MARCH

'Save Your Kisses for Me', one of the bestselling Eurovision Song Contest winners ever, was released by Brotherhood of Man on 5 March 1976. The song won that year's competition hosted by the Netherlands. Nicky Stevens was a member of the triumphant pop group but she was born Helen Thomas in Carmarthen. She is, to date, the only Welsh person to have won the Eurovision Song Contest.

Other Welsh women who have competed in the song contest include:

- **Mary Hopkin** came second with 'Knock, Knock Who's There' for the United Kingdom in 1970.
- **Emma (Emma Louise Booth)**, from Bridgend,came sixth with 'Give a Little Love Back to the World' in 1990. At fifteen, she became the youngest singer to have represented the UK in the contest.
- **Elaine Morgan**, from Cardiff, came nineteenth while representing France in the band Dan Ar Braz & L'Héritage des Celtes, with the Breton-language song '*Diwanit Bugale*' in 1996.
- **Jessica Garlick,** originally from Kidwelly came third with 'Come Back' in 2002.

- **Bonnie Tyler**,from Skewen, came nineteenth with 'Believe in Me' in 2013 for the United Kingdom.

- **Lucie Jones**, from Pentyrch was recruited for the United Kingdom entry in 2017 and came fifteenth with 'Never Give Up on You'.

6 MARCH

On 6 March 1984, the National Coal Board announced that it intended to cut four million tonnes of production and 20,000 jobs within a year. Miners across the UK went on strike in an attempt to save the coal industry and its communities.

Among those campaigning and organising support for the strikers was Siân James from the Swansea valley. A housewife married to a miner, she started volunteering to help other mining families. Eventually she helped to feed a thousand families across three Welsh valleys.

After the strike ended, Siân didn't want to stop campaigning. She took A levels and then a degree at Swansea University where she worked for the Students' Union. She became a fundraiser for Save the Children, a director of Welsh Women's Aid and, in 2005, was elected Labour MP for Swansea East, becoming the first woman to represent the constituency.

In 2014, Siân's story was a central plotline of the film *Pride* which tells the real-life inspiring tale of how Lesbians and Gays Support the Miners (LGSM), a group of activists from London, decided to fundraise in support of a mining community in south Wales during the 1984–5 strike. Siân, played by actress Jessica Gunning, is depicted as being one of the most passionate supporters of LGSM's efforts.

The National Union of Mineworkers (NUM) refused to acknowledge the support of LGSM at the time but eventually recognised LGSM's contribution to their cause. At the 1985 Labour Party Conference, a resolution committing the party to support gay rights passed, largely due to support from the NUM.

7 MARCH

The Bevan Foundation was formed on 7 March 2001. It was established to supply independent and apolitical ideas which would help to shape the public policy of the newly devolved government of Wales.

The foundation's director since 2002 has been Victoria Winckler, who is responsible for the foundation's strategic and policy development as well as funding and research. Her areas of expertise include tackling poverty and inequality, and economic development. Victoria developed and led the initiative that secured 'Objective 1' status (designating areas in need of special support as they were falling behind European standards of growth and GDP) for west Wales and the Heads of the Valleys area. She also proposed new devolved taxes that were implemented by the Welsh Government. Today she regularly gives expert evidence to the Senedd's committees.

Under Victoria's leadership, the Bevan Foundation is now internationally regarded as Wales's most innovative and influential think tank. In 2021 it was awarded *Prospect Magazine*'s prestigious Think Tank of the Year 'One to

Watch' Award. Victoria has been included in the Women's Equality Network (WEN) Wales list of a hundred Welsh women past and present who have made significant contributions to life in Wales.

8 MARCH

Today is International Women's Day: a day when we celebrate women's achievements, raise awareness about discrimination and support action to achieve gender equality.

The present struggle for equality for men and women has its roots in the mid-nineteenth century. What is less well known is that early Welsh history shows that women once had rights and opportunities that were lost and have only recently begun to re-emerge. Celtic women could choose their husbands, abortion was a right and they could own and inherit property. Women in ancient Wales fought for their tribes and could rise to become leaders of armies. In the tenth century, under the Laws of Hywel Dda, women could own property and not be forced to remain in a marriage they wished to leave. Significant change came after the Norman invasion of Britain in the eleventh century. The Normans imposed a feudal system which meant women had few legal rights and their property passed to male relatives.

The cause of women's suffrage was accelerated during the First World War when an estimated two million women replaced men in the home workforce. Women were eventually given equal voting rights with men in 1928 and although further legislation has improved women's equality, ongoing political activism, government intervention and community involvement are still needed to continue the journey towards a truly gender-equal society.

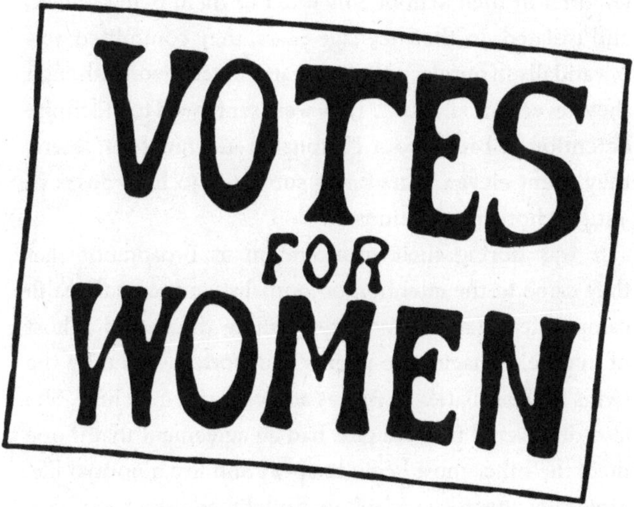

VOTES

FOR

WOMEN

9 MARCH

Jennifer Gibbons died on 9 March 1993. She and her sister June were known as the Silent Twins. They grew up in Haverfordwest after moving with their family from Barbados in 1974. The girls only communicated with each other using a secret language and were selectively mute to everyone else around them.

The twins and their only other sister were the only Black children in their school which led to them being bullied and isolated. In their teenage years, they committed acts of vandalism, burglary, theft and attempted arson although they never hurt anybody. They were sentenced to indefinite detention in Broadmoor Hospital at just nineteen. Here, they spent eleven years being subjected to high doses of antipsychotic medications.

It was during their incarceration at Broadmoor that they came to the attention of journalist and mental health campaigner Marjorie Wallace. Wallace discovered a host of intensely imaginative poems and stories written by the twins in their diaries as well as a novel written by June. She also discovered that the girls had an agreement that if one died, the other must begin to speak and live a normal life. Tragically, after the girls' release from Broadmoor to an open prison at Carswell, Jennifer died of a sudden inflammation of the heart. June lives near her parents in west Wales where she continues to write. She recently told her story in her own words on the BBC podcast *Voice of a Silent Twin*.

DID YOU KNOW?

The story of the Silent Twins inspired the 1998 Manic Street Preachers song 'Tsunami'.

10 MARCH

Princess Lilian of Sweden, Duchess of Halland and native of Swansea (born 30 August 1915) died on 10 March 2013.

Lillian May Davies was a fashion model when she met Prince Bertil, the third son of King Gustaf VI Adolf of Sweden, at a cocktail party in London for her twenty-eighth birthday. Soon after, they became lovers even though, at that time, she was still married to her first husband, the Scottish actor Ivan Craig, whom she divorced two years later in 1945.

A marriage between Lilian and Bertil was deemed inappropriate for an heir to the Swedish throne as Lilian was both a commoner and a divorcee. So, the couple lived together discreetly for over thirty years until Bertil's nephew, Carl XVI Gustaf, ascended the throne in 1973 and approved their marriage. The wedding ceremony took place on 7 December 1976 at the church of Drottningholm Palace. Lilian died in Stockholm, aged ninety-seven, sixteen years after the death of her husband.

11 MARCH

'Hen Wlad Fy Nhadau', the Welsh national anthem, was first recorded on 11 March 1899 by the Gramophone Company on Maiden Lane in London. It is also one of the first known recordings of a song in the Welsh language. The recording captured a performance by Madge Breese from Porthmadog, the niece of the Gramophone Company's chairman, Trevor Williams, from Meirionnydd. Very little is known about Madge, other than she was probably a music student in London at the time and that she is buried in Penrhyndeudraeth.

'Hen Wlad Fy Nhadau' was originally known as 'Glan Rhondda' ('Banks of the Rhondda') and was written by Evan James from Pontypridd, with the music composed by his son, James (who went under the bardic name of Iago ap Ieuan). It was first performed early in 1856 at Capel Tabor, Maesteg, by sixteen-year-old Elizabeth John, also from Pontypridd.

12 MARCH

Cardiff's Mary Sophia Allen, a policewoman, a political activist, a suffragette and later a prominent British fascist, was born on 12 March 1878.

Mary was an organiser for Emmeline Pankhurst's Women's Social and Political Union (WSPU) in the southwest and was imprisoned three times during WSPU campaigns in 1909 for smashing windows. At the outbreak of the First World War, when militant suffragist activities ceased, Mary joined the newly-formed Women Police Volunteers (later renamed the Women Police Service (WPS)) and rose to become its Sub-Commandant. She was awarded an OBE for her efforts in combating prostitution and the trafficking of vulnerable women.

After the war, the Metropolitan Police set up its own women's division with the expectation that the WPS would disband. They did not and, instead, changed their name to the Women's Auxiliary Service (WAS). Despite no longer being part of an organisation recognised by the authorities, Mary was invited to advise on policing in the Netherlands, Hungary, Czechoslovakia (as it was then), Turkey and Brazil. She also met with a number of fascist leaders such as Eoin O'Duffy in Ireland, Francisco

Franco in Spain, Benito Mussolini in Italy, and Adolf Hitler in Germany – for whom she publicly expressed her admiration.

Mary joined Oswald Mosley's British Union of Fascists in 1939 and was suspected of acting as a spy for the Nazis during the Second World War. Her home was searched, and internment was considered but not implemented as she was considered to be a 'crank … trailing round in a ridiculous uniform'. She did, however, have her movements restricted to within a five-mile radius of her Cornwall home and was banned from using the telephone.

13 MARCH

Entertainer and actress, Tessie O'Shea was born in Cardiff on 13 March 1913.

As a young girl, Tessie was billed as the 'The Wonder of Wales' and, by her teens, she was regularly performing on Radio Wales. In the 1930s she adopted the name 'Two Ton Tessie from Tennessee' and was frequently a headline act at the London Palladium. She also appeared regularly on BBC television's variety show *The Good Old Days,* usually finishing her act by singing and playing a banjolele in the style of George Formby.

Tessie won a Tony Award for her portrayal of a cockney fish and chips peddler in the 1963 Broadway musical, *The Girl Who Came to Supper*. In 1964, she had already come to the attention of American audiences when her shared billing with the Beatles drew, what was then, the largest audience in the history of American television.

14 MARCH

On 14 March 1870, Frances Elizabeth Hoggan (née Morgan; 1843–1927) defended her thesis on progressive muscular atrophy in front of more than 400 spectators at Zurich University and was subsequently awarded a medical degree. She was the first British woman to receive a doctorate in medicine and the first female doctor to be registered in Wales.

Frances was born in Brecon, where her father was a curate, and she was raised in Aberafan and educated in Cowbridge and Windsor. She married Dr George Hoggan in 1874 and the couple then operated the first husband-and-wife medical practice in the UK. Francis was also a prominent supporter of women's rights and an active campaigner for social reform.

15 MARCH

On 15 March 2012, Leanne Wood from Penygraig, near Tonypandy, (born 13 December 1971) became the first female leader of Plaid Cymru. She was not only the first female leader of the party but the first Welsh language learner in the role, rather than someone already fluent in the language.

The decline of the mining communities of south Wales following the miners' strikes of the 1980s inspired Leanne to become involved in politics and, after studying at the University of South Wales in Pontypridd, she became a probation officer as well as being elected as a local councillor. She then worked for the Plaid MEP Jill Evans, and lectured in social policy at Cardiff University, before being elected to the Welsh Assembly in 2003. A staunch republican, she was once kicked out of the chamber for calling the Queen 'Mrs Windsor'.

16 MARCH

On Driving Instructor Day, we celebrate Maureen Rees, Britain's first reality television star. Maureen from Cardiff became a household name in 1997 following her appearances in the BBC docusoap *Driving School,* which followed the progress of a group of learner drivers who had repeatedly failed their driving test.

Maureen, nicknamed 'the driver from L (hell)', was the undoubted star of the show and became an instant celebrity. The series showed her furious verbal battles with her long-suffering husband, Dave, as he reluctantly acted as her instructor. In one episode. Dave screamed in terror and grabbed the steering wheel as Maureen moved into the overtaking lane of a dual carriageway and almost collided with another car. Another episode showed her accidentally running over her husband's foot.

Maureen eventually passed her driving test on the seventh attempt and her notoriety resulted in many subsequent television appearances. She was honoured with her own episode on Michael Aspel's *This Is Your Life* and released a well-remembered version of the Madness song 'Driving in My Car'. In 2000, Maureen appeared in a government video to promote road safety awareness.

17 MARCH ⚠

Brenda Chamberlain, award-winning artist and writer, was born on 17 March 1912. Her work was later defined by two lengthy periods of self-imposed isolation, first on Ynys Enlli (Bardsey Island) from 1947 to 1962, and then on the island of Hydra in Greece (1961 to 1967).

Brenda studied art at London's Royal Academy Schools from 1933 to 1936 where she met her husband, John Petts. The couple settled in north Wales and founded the Caseg Press under which Brenda published a collection of her poems. The couple divorced in 1944. In a search for solitude, she moved to Ynys Enlli in 1947, where she lived for a time with her partner, Jean Van der Bijl. The island is the supposed burial site of 20,000 saints and the community lived off the land. Brenda connected with the island's history and she was at her most productive here. In 1951 and 1953, she won the Gold Medal for Fine Art in the National Eisteddfod for her works encapsulating the uncompromising beauty of Ynys Enlli.

Brenda's self-illustrated portrayal of life on the island, *Tide-Race,* was published in 1962 and won many critical plaudits. However, it was extremely unpopular with the island's inhabitants and she was forced to leave. Brenda moved to the island of Hydra, where she stayed for five years until a military coup in 1967 forced her to flee. She returned to Bangor but suffered increasingly from depression which resulted in her death by suicide in 1971.

Her work can be found in the Amgueddfa Werin Cymru (National Museum of Wales), the Llyfrgell Genedlaethol Cymru (National Library of Wales), Cyfarthfa Castle and Royal Holloway University of London.

18 MARCH

A statue of Elaine Morgan was unveiled in Mountain Ash on the 18 March 2022. It was the second of two statues in Wales of a named, non-fictional woman commissioned as a result of the 'Hidden Heroines' campaign of 2019.

Elaine Morgan (7 November 1920–12 July 2013) was a coal miner's daughter born and brought up in Hopkinstown, near Pontypridd, who excelled in both the arts and science. She began writing plays for television. Her screenwriting credits include several dramatic adaptations of books, including Richard Llewellyn's 1939 novel *How Green Was My Valley* (1975), Vera Brittain's *Testament of Youth* (1979); and a miniseries on the Liberal prime minister *The Life and Times of David Lloyd George* (1981).

Elaine went on to be the author of several volumes on anthropology and evolution. They include *The Descent of Woman, The Aquatic Ape, The Scars of Evolution, The Descent of the Child, The Aquatic Ape Hypothesis* and *The Naked Darwinist*.

19 MARCH

On 19 March 1954, Laura Ashley (née Mountney; 7 September 1925–17 September 1985) first began trading. She became a designer and a businesswoman and founded the hugely successful fashion chain, Laura Ashley.

Laura was born in 1925. Her Welsh parents were living in London, but her mother returned to her own home in Dowlais, Merthyr Tydfil so that Laura would be born Welsh. Laura remained in Merthyr until 1932, when she was sent to the Elmwood School, Croydon, but she was evacuated back to Wales during the Second World War when she was thirteen and attended the Aberdare Girls' School. After school she served in the Women's Royal Naval Service and met her husband, engineer Bernard Ashley, in Wallington at a youth club.

Laura's breakthrough came when she looked for patches of Victorian fabric to make patchworks and, failing to find any, she decided to make her own. She used these to create Victorian-style headscarves. The scarves soon became popular with stores and high street chains and the couple established the Ashley Mountney Company. They moved back to Wales in 1961 and went into full-time production at Carno, near Newtown. The company grew rapidly in the late 1960s and early 1970s with shops opening in major cities across the world, and they changed the name. By 1981, when Laura Ashley moved into home furnishings, the company had 5,000 retail outlets throughout the world. In 1984 the opening of new company headquarters in Newtown, Powys, created 500 jobs.

In 1985, Laura Ashley died. She is buried in the churchyard of St John the Baptist, in Carno.

20 MARCH

The vernal equinox marks the beginning of spring and usually occurs in the Northern Hemisphere on 20 March. Historically, spring has been celebrated as a season of rebirth: a time when dormant plants and flowers begin to grow again. The iconic Welsh mythical character of Blodeuwedd ('Face of flowers') is closely associated with this time of year.

Blodeuwedd appears in the *Mabinogion*, a collection of medieval Welsh prose based on tales of mythology, folklore and heroic legends. This is her story.

The warrior hero Lleu Llaw Gyffes had been born to Arianrhod, much to her shame, during a test to demonstrate her virginity. Arianrhod cursed Lleu never to marry a mortal woman. Nevertheless, his magician uncles Gwydion and Math created a wife for him from the flowers of the oak, broom and meadowsweet and named her Blodeuwedd.

Blodeuwedd proved to be an unfaithful wife and contrived with her lover, a young huntsman named Gronw Pebr, to murder Lleu. She knew that, because of the magical nature of his birth, her husband could only be killed in a very specific way. Blodeuwedd tricked him into revealing the unlikely circumstances in which he could be killed. He could only be killed if he had one foot on a cauldron and one on a goat and if he was stabbed with a spear that took a year to make. With this, she set about planning his death.

When Gronw Pebr threw the spear at Lleu, striking him in the side, Lleu did not die but transformed into an eagle, and although badly injured, flew off into the night. Gwydion found Lleu perched high on an oak tree and healed his injury. Lleu then exacted his revenge by killing Gronw Pebr and turning Blodeuwedd into an owl, meaning that she was never able to show her face in the light of day ever again.

21 MARCH

21 March is World Down's Syndrome Day.

Sara Pickard, from Cardiff, has Down's syndrome and is a trustee of the Down's Syndrome Association as well as a former trustee of Learning Disability Wales. Sara attended Radyr Comprehensive School and Pontypridd College before joining Mencap Cymru in 2006 where she had the opportunity to prove that people with learning disabilities can have valued, skilled and, importantly, paid roles within organisations. She is very passionate about connecting with young people who have learning disabilities through her work and promotes the importance of their representation in public life.

In 2008 she was elected as an independent councillor for Pentyrch Community Council and was re-elected in May 2012. Sara also worked for four years on the Partners in Politics Project which aimed to help people with a learning disability to participate in the political process.

In 2022, Sara was appointed as Engagement Connector at Mencap Cymru. She is no stranger to the barriers that people with learning disabilities face as she had to suggest changes to the way council meetings were held to make them more accessible. She thinks the best way to approach these issues is to work with people – both abled and disabled – to show them how you can overcome problems and make things better together.

22 MARCH

Today is the feast day of St Darerca, the sister of St Patrick. Darerca is credited with one miracle: she blessed a poor man's barrel so that it provided endless ale for him but she also had as many as nineteen children, all of whom became saints or bishops and went on to play a significant a role in the establishment of Christianity in Ireland.

It is suggested that Patrick was born in Wales and, if this is true, then the likelihood is that Darerca was too. When he was about sixteen, Patrick was captured and carried off as a slave to Ireland. Some accounts suggest that his sister was with him. Darerca was certainly with him when he visited the place that is current-day Derry and met his sister's sons, the saints Reat, Nenn and Aedh. Darerca married at least twice and was also the mother of Gradlon Mawr, who became King of Brittany.

23 MARCH

Maud de Braose, Baroness Mortimer of Wigmore (born 1224) is thought to have died on this day in 1301. She was prominent in the politics of Wales during the thirteenth century.

Maud was born in Breconshire, the daughter of Marcher lord William de Braose and Eva Marshal. She was, therefore, the granddaughter of William Marshal, 1st Earl of Pembroke, regent of England and protector of the nine-year-old King Henry III. When Maud was six, her father was hanged on orders of Llywelyn ap Iorwerth, Prince of Gwynedd, for alleged adultery with Llywelyn's wife, Joan.

In 1247, Maud married Roger Mortimer of Wigmore Castle in Herefordshire and their union would go on to create an extremely powerful Marcher dynasty. Roger was a lifelong opponent of Llywelyn ap Gruffydd, Prince of Wales, and Maud organised the escape of Prince Edward (the future Edward I) after he had been taken hostage by Llywelyn ap Gruffydd's ally, Simon de Montfort, at the Battle of Lewes in 1264. The following year, Roger killed Simon de Montfort at the Battle of Evesham and sent his severed head and genitals as a gift to Maud.

Maud's sons Edmund and Roger were heavily involved in the ambush and death of Llywelyn ap Gruffydd in 1282. Through Roger, Maud is an ancestor of all the English monarchs from 1413 to the present day.

24 MARCH

Maudie Edwards (born 16 October 1906) died on this day in 1991. Maudie was an actress, radio broadcaster, comedian, dancer and singer, best remembered for speaking the first line of dialogue in the soap opera *Coronation Street* in 1960 in the role of Elsie Lappin.

Born into a show-business family in Neath, she first appeared on stage at the age of four and later formed her own repertory company, The Maudie Edwards Players, which performed at the Palace Theatre, Swansea.

She became a popular radio personality during the 1930s and became known as the 'the voice of Wales', on programmes including *Welsh Rarebit* (which attracted weekly audiences of ten million), *Workers' Playtime* and *Variety Bandbox*. She also worked for the Entertainments National Service Association (ENSA) during the Second World War. Her acting career stretched from 1936 to 1972, including appearances in *The Errol Flynn Theatre* series of films, *Dixon of Dock Green*, *Fraud Squad* and *Under Milk Wood*. She also provided the singing voice for film stars Diana Dors, Margaret Lockwood and Gene Tierney. In 1950, she performed with Frank Sinatra at the London Palladium on his first visit to Britain.

25 MARCH

On 25 March 2011, television presenter and extreme endurance runner Lowri Morgan was the only finisher of that year's, notoriously difficult, 380-mile non-stop 6633 Arctic Ultra race. In so doing she became one of only a handful of people to ever complete the event. She has also completed the Jungle Ultra Marathon in the Amazon rainforest.

The 6633 Arctic Ultra sees competitors attempt to cover either 120 or 380 miles through the Arctic in temperatures as low as -40°C and 70 mph winds. The runners are self-sufficient so they rest and eat when they choose. They can make use of checkpoints for water but they must sleep in the wilderness.

The Jungle Marathon is a 140-mile race along the Amazon River in Brazil in temperatures up to 40°C and 90 per cent humidity.

Born in Gowerton in January 1975, Lowri suffered a debilitating injury when she was nineteen that threatened her future sporting career. She would never be able to run again. She defied doctors' expectations, stepping up her regime and ultimately went on to represent Wales in both cross country and rugby.

In 2016, Lowri completed the Wales '333' when she ran 150 miles across the country via the highest peaks in Wales including Yr Wyddfa (Snowdon), Cadair Idris and Pen-y-fan. She completed the route in sixty hours, the fastest recorded time for the challenge.

26 MARCH

On 26 March 2000, Lindy Hemming, from Carmarthenshire, was the first Welsh woman to win an Academy Award, for Best Costume Design for the film *Topsy-Turvy* (1999).

Lindy trained as an orthopaedic nurse before enrolling at the Royal Academy of Dramatic Art, initially to study stage management but she later switched to design. She spent the first years of her professional career working in costume design for many notable theatre companies, including the Royal National Theatre, the Royal Shakespeare Company, and many others in London's West End. From the mid-1980s, Lindy began almost exclusively designing for film and she was the lead costume designer for the *James Bond* film franchise from 1995 until 2006. Her other design credits include *The Krays* (1990), *Four Weddings and a Funeral* (1994), *Lara Croft: Tomb Raider* (2001), *Harry Potter and the Chamber of Secrets* (2002), *Wonder Woman* (2017) and *Wonka* (2023).

27 MARCH

Sybil Christopher (born Sybil Williams), the actress, theatre director and New York nightclub founder was born in Tylorstown on this day in 1929. She was also known for being the first wife of the actor Richard Burton.

Sybil and Richard met in 1949 while filming *The Last Days of Dolwyn* and married later the same year. They divorced in 1963 following Burton's much-publicised affair with Elizabeth Taylor. In 1965, she founded Arthur, which became one of Manhattan's most popular celebrity nightclubs. It is claimed that DJ Terry Noel invented music 'mixing' at the club. She also founded the New Theatre in New York, and Bay Street Theater in Sag Harbor.

Sybil died on 7 March 2013. One of her daughters with Burton is Kate Burton, an award-winning actress, who made her film debut alongside her father in the 1969 film *Anne of the Thousand Days*.

28 MARCH

The funeral and memorial service of Elizabeth Williams Berry (1854–1969) was held at Resurrection Cemetery in Helena, Montana, US, on 28 March 1969. She was a highly respected horse-racing jockey. This was at a time when women jockeys were barred from riding at registered race meetings so she raced disguised as a man for more than twenty-four years under the name Jack Williams.

Elizabeth was born to Welsh parents in Melbourne, Australia, and began racing horses aged six, winning her first race aged ten. As she got older, Elizabeth maintained her disguise by wearing a bowler hat and smoking cigars. She became a jockey of great renown and claimed to have won over 4,000 races in Australia, England, South Africa, New Zealand, France and Italy. She moved to the US around 1900.

Elizabeth retired from jockeying in 1911 to become a horse trainer. She was given the nickname 'Mother' after she was awarded legal custody of a runaway boy she had taken in and taught horse-racing skills. Elizabeth lived to see women ride as licensed jockeys against men in 1969, just prior to her death at the age of 114.

DID YOU KNOW?

Joanna Morgan was born and raised in Crickhowell and became Ireland's first female professional jockey in 1974. She then became the first woman to ride at Royal Ascot and the first woman to ride in an Irish Classic Race.

29 MARCH

Today is the feast day of St Gwladys.

Gwladys was the daughter of King Brychan, the fifth-century founder and leader of the Kingdom of Brycheiniog (modern-day Breconshire). She was the queen of King Gwynllyw, the legendary founder of the city of Newport and the mother of Cadog, one of Wales's most important saints.

Legends differ on the details of how Gwladys and Gwynllyw got married. One suggests that the marriage was arranged by mutual consent; another that Gwynllyw, accompanied by 300 men, abducted Gwladys from her home in Talgarth.

The waterfall Sgwd Gwladys on the River Pyrddin at Pontneddfechan in Breconshire is named after Gwladys and her part in the mythical tale of 'The Lovers of Sgwd Gwladys'.

The story goes that a young Gwladys fell in love with a young man called Einion but because of his lowly birth, their union was forbidden by her father. Gwladys's tears of heartbreak formed a secluded pool into which her spirit poured in the form of a waterfall. Distraught at losing his true love, Einion threw himself into the river and immediately a second waterfall appeared. Sgwd Gwladys and Sgwd Einion Gam now flow together so that, although they could never be together in life, their spirits flow together forever in immortality.

30 MARCH

On 30 March 2017, Anna Hursey (born 22 June 2006) from Carmarthen became the youngest person to represent Wales at senior level in any sport, when she competed in a table tennis European Championship qualification match against Kosovo at the age of ten.

In 2018, Anna became the youngest competitor in Commonwealth Games history. At the 2022 Games, she and fellow Welsh native Charlotte Carey came third in the women's doubles event. It was the first time that two Welsh women had won a Commonwealth Games table-tennis medal. Anna is also a United Nations ambassador for climate change in sport and in 2021 she was invited to discuss the subject with US President Joe Biden.

31 MARCH

Born in Caerwys on this day in 1944, Myfanwy Talog was an actress. In 1966, while working together on the soap *Crossroads,* she met fellow actor Sir David Jason and the two became long-term partners.

Myfanwy worked as a teacher before taking up an acting career. She appeared in television shows *Ryan and Ronnie, The Magnificent Evans* with Ronnie Barker, *Bread, Within These Walls, A Sharp Intake of Breath, Butterflies, Yes, Prime Minister* and *Waiting for God.* She also narrated the Welsh-language children's animated television series *Wil Cwac Cwac* and did voice work for *SuperTed* and *The BFG.*

Myfanwy died of breast cancer in 1995.

1 APRIL

Mary Wynne Warner (née Davies; born 22 June 1932), died on this day in 1998. She was an internationally recognised mathematician and one of the world's leading experts in the field of fuzzy topology – used to calculate the best-estimated solution to complex problems using imprecise information, such as the prediction of earthquakes.

Mary was born in Carmarthen and raised in Llandovery. She graduated from the University of Oxford where she met and later married Sir Gerald Warner. Gerald became a diplomat and was recruited by MI6, which resulted in the couple travelling widely. Mary took up teaching and held research posts in Beijing, during China's Cultural Revolution, and Rangoon, where she was a first-hand witness to the student uprising that resulted in the execution of more than one hundred students and the arrest of more than 6,000 others. Mary earned her doctorate at the University of Warsaw, becoming the first wife of a diplomat to obtain a doctorate in a foreign country. She ended her career as a professor at City University in London.

Mary remained immensely proud of her Welsh identity and took a particular interest in the poetry of Wales. She also threw a cream pie at her husband during a diplomatic function for not intervening when some of the guests began making derogatory remarks about Wales.

2 APRIL

The British government undertook a census of everyone living in Wales and England on Sunday, 2 April 1911.

As part of the campaign for women's suffrage, women were encouraged to protest by boycotting the census. 'If women don't count, neither shall they be counted' was the rallying call on the night of the census. *Punch* magazine joked, 'The suffragettes have definitely taken leave of their census.'

There were many protests in which women gathered together to absent themselves from their homes and therefore avoid the counters from the census. One such gathering took place at 34 Albany Road in Cardiff and it was organised by Rachel Barrett, the secretary of the Women's Social and Political Union (WSPU) for south Wales. Over fifty women entered through a back lane to avoid suspicion, giving the password 'escape' to secure admission. To pass the time as they waited out the night, the women entertained themselves with talks, crochet work and playing cards. There was even a fortune-teller among them.

There were also lone protests: Emily Phipps, head-mistress of Swansea Municipal Secondary Girls' School, avoided the census by staying overnight in a sea cave on the Gower Peninsula.

3 APRIL

On 3 April 2019 Catrin Pugh from Wrexham became Welsh Woman of the Year.

In 2013 Catrin, who was then nineteen years old, was on a coach home from a skiing holiday in the French Alps when the vehicle crashed and burst into flames. Catrin was rescued by her boyfriend Shaun and put into an induced coma. She suffered third-degree burns to 96 per cent of her body and was given a one in 1,000 chance of survival. Catrin was flown to the specialist burns unit at Whiston Hospital on Merseyside, where she remained in the coma for three months and underwent 200 skin-graft operations. Catrin's case was extraordinarily hard to treat because her burns were so extensive that skin could only be taken from her scalp. The rest was taken from her brother and mother in operations that left both hospitalised for a fortnight.

Catrin is one of the few people in the world to survive such serious injuries. Her miraculous recovery has provided her with the opportunity to become an inspiration to many others. She has since become the face of the beauty brand Avon, focusing on the misrepresentation of beauty in the media. She is a motivational speaker and a physiotherapist for the Katie Piper Foundation (KPF) for people who have experienced serious burns.

4 APRIL

On 4 April 2024, Dr Sarah Beynon initiated an innovative series of guided bug explorations at her bug farm in St Davids, Pembrokeshire, where she was born and raised. Sarah is an internationally renowned entomologist, farmer and conservationist.

Dr Beynon's Bug Farm is a research and education centre that showcases the sustainable future of food, farming and wildlife conservation. The on-site Grub Kitchen is the UK's first edible insect restaurant, using cricket flour, an insect- and plant-based protein mince (which has now been included on school menus), bug burgers made with grasshoppers and mealworms, and carrot and cricket cake.

In 2018 she coordinated the creation of the St Davids Pollinator Trail, which led to St Davids becoming the first bee-friendly city in Wales.

Sarah has considerable experience as a media presenter, featuring in several radio interviews as well as appearing on BBC's *Springwatch* and *Countryfile*, as well as Channel 4 and the Discovery Channel.

Among numerous other accolades she was named as an emerging legend in 2017 's Welsh Year of Legends.

5 APRIL

On 5 April 2004, Katherine Jenkins released her debut album, *Première*. It charted at number one on the UK Classical Album Chart, as did her second album *Second Nature*, making her the first British classical artist to have two number-one albums in the same year.

Katherine was born in Neath in 1980 and first came to prominence in 2003 when she sang at Westminster Cathedral in honour of Pope John Paul II's silver jubilee. In 2005, she opened the charity concert Tsunami Relief Cardiff and in 2006, became the first female to win two consecutive Classical BRIT Awards. She is also the only artist in music history to simultaneously hold the top four positions on the classical album charts. In 2008, she signed the biggest-ever classical recording deal. After her thirteenth studio album *Guiding Light* reached number one in 2019, she became the first ever female classical artist to achieve a total of thirteen number one albums. Today, she is the UK's bestselling classical artist of the last twenty-five years.

Katherine has dedicated every award she's received to her late father, Selwyn, who passed away when she was only fifteen. She also completed the 2013 London Marathon in his memory, raising £25,000 for Macmillan Cancer Support. Katherine has appeared on many television programmes including *The Masked Singer* in the UK and *Dancing with the Stars* in the US.

6 APRIL

Opening on 6 April, the 1896 Summer Olympics was the first international Olympic Games held in modern history. Since then, six Welsh women have won Olympic gold medals.

The first was Irene Steer who, on 15 July 1912, swam the anchor leg for the world-record-breaking British swimming 4 × 100 metre relay team.

Irene Steer (10 August 1889–18 April 1977) was born and raised in Cardiff. She was keen on sport from an early age and regularly attended Cardiff RFC rugby matches with her father and learned to swim in Roath Park Lake when she was only eight years old. She won the first of seven consecutive 100-yard freestyle Welsh Championships in Swansea in 1907 when she was eighteen. In 1910, she won gold at the British Championships in a world-record-equalling time and was a strong prospect for the 1912 Olympics in Stockholm.

At the Stockholm Games, Irene was robbed of an individual medal due to a controversial collision in the semi-final with a German swimmer. Irene was comfortably leading but collided with her German rival during a turn. There were no lane markers so her disqualification following an objection by the German team seemed extremely harsh. However, putting the disappointment behind her, she went on to win the gold in the relay.

Irene retired in 1913 and switched her loyalties from rugby to football, becoming a lifelong fan of Cardiff City when she married the club chairman, William Nicholson.

DID YOU KNOW?

The other Welsh women to take home gold medals from the Olympics are Nicole Cooke (cycling, 2008), Jade Jones (taekwondo, 2012, 2016), Hannah Mills (sailing 2016, 2020), Elinor Barker (cycling, 2016) and Lauren Price (boxing, 2020).

7 APRIL

Clara Novello Davies was born in Cardiff on 7 April 1861. She was one of the first women to forge a career as a professional musician, singer, teacher and conductor. Her energy and charismatic personality enabled Clara to forge her musical career in Cardiff, London and New York. She was affectionately known to the Welsh public as 'Mam' and was the mother of Ivor Novello, one of the most popular entertainers of the first half of the twentieth century.

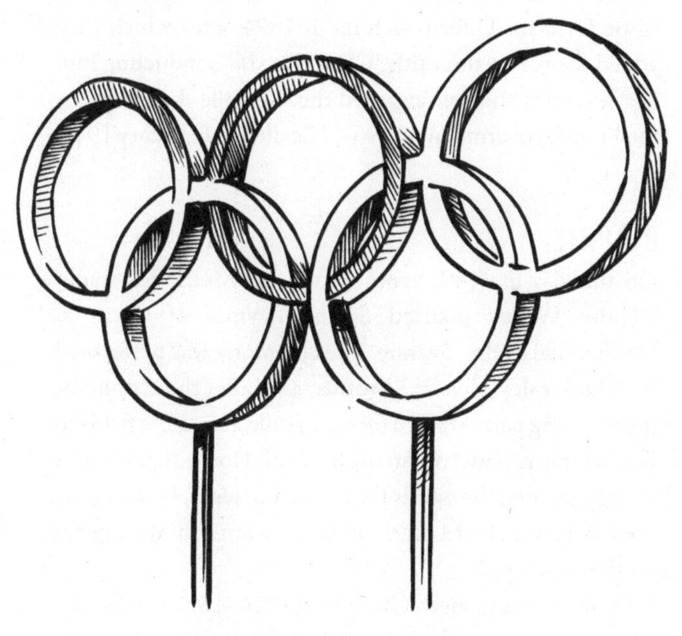

As a young woman, Clara was accompanist for the Cardiff United Choir and Cardiff Blue Ribbon Choir. In 1883, she founded and conducted the first Welsh Ladies' Choir, featuring over seventy voices from all over the country. They took first prize at the World's Fair in Chicago in 1893, which led to an invitation to tour Britain, France, South Africa and the United States. They were also commanded to perform for Queen Victoria in 1894, after which they added 'Royal' to their title. Clara was still conducting into her seventies and was awarded the Médaille du Mérite by the French government in 1937. She died in February 1943.

8 APRIL

On this day in 1749, hymn writer and Methodist leader Charles Wesley married Sarah Gwynne of Garth at Llanlleonfel in Breconshire. The ceremony was performed by John Wesley, Charles's brother, and, after the ceremony, the wedding party walked for half a mile across the fields to Garth House. It was reputedly in Garth House that Charles Wesley penned the words for the hymn 'Jesus, Lover of my Soul' as he watched a sparrow shelter from a thunderstorm on the windowsill.

Sarah Wesley, née Gwynne (1726–1822) was the daughter of Sarah and Marmaduke Gwynne. Her father was a wealthy lawyer who had been converted to Methodism by the evangelist Howell Harris. Marmaduke subsequently offered accommodation to travelling Methodist preachers and this is how Sarah and Charles's relationship began, even though Charles was seventeen years her senior. In 1753, Sarah suffered from a life-threatening episode of smallpox which left her horribly scarred and difficult to recognise. This did not prevent her from following Charles on his preaching circuit and she was loved dearly by the Methodist community.

9 APRIL

On 9 April 1649, Lucy Walter of Roch Castle near Haverfordwest gave birth to James Scott, 1st Duke of Monmouth. The boy's father was King Charles II of England, which made him a significant claimant to the throne of England.

Roch Castle had declared for Charles's father, Charles I, during the English Civil War, but it was captured and burned by the Parliamentarians in 1644. Lucy was forced to flee to London and then to The Hague, which is where she met Charles and where they became lovers. James Scott was their only child and it was Charles who made him Duke of Monmouth. During the Exclusion Crisis of James II between 1679 and 1681, many Protestants wanted to name James Scott heir to the throne, claiming that Lucy and Charles had secretly married. The truth is less edifying. When Charles ended the affair in 1651, Lucy's life spiralled into a series of scandals and ill-fated love affairs. She died in Paris in 1658.

10 APRIL

Born on this day in 1893, Rosa Ward OBE, JP was a pioneer and significant early member of the Girl Guide movement.

Rosa was born in Pakistan, where her father was serving as a brigadier general in the British Army. By 1912, her family had returned to their home in Denbigh, and it was here that she founded a Girl Guide company – the first in north Wales. In 1916, Rosa organised what is thought to be the first camp for Girl Guides in Wales at Segrwyd, Denbigh. By 1931, she was the National Guide Commissioner for Camping.

During the First World War, Rosa was a member of Denbigh's Voluntary Aid Detachment, providing nursing care for military personnel. When war broke out again in 1939 she was Chief Commissioner for Wales's Girl Guides. Rosa agreed to be the temporary chair of the Guide International Service (GIS) which was formed to provide on-the-ground assistance to continental Europe. In the same year, she was appointed Justice of the Peace for Denbighshire and from 1961 to her death in 1984 she was vice president of the Girl Guides Association.

Rosa received many awards and honours including the Guides' Silver Fish award in 1928 which is the movement's highest adult honour. In 1948, she was awarded an OBE for her work with GIS. In 1997, two stained-glass windows were commissioned and dedicated to Rosa in the main hall of Tŷ Clwyd, Girlguiding Clwyd's centre in Llanfair Talhaearn. In 2017, her outstanding commitment to Guiding in Wales and the GIS was recognised in the Welsh Year of Legends.

11 APRIL

Cerys Matthews, singer, songwriter, broadcaster and author, was born in Cardiff on 11 April 1969. Cerys is best known for being the lead singer of the rock band Catatonia.

She was also a leading figure in the period of the 1990s referred to as Cool Cymru. This was a time when many Welsh music artists, actors and sporting events highlighted the culture of Wales to an international audience. It also brought a sense of pride in their identity to Welsh people and culminated with Wales voting for a democratically elected Assembly in 1997, for which Cerys had been an enthusiastic campaigner. The period is epitomised in the chorus of Catatonia's hit song 'International Velvet', which not only included lyrics in the Welsh language but a chorus where Cerys declared that she thanks god every day that she is Welsh.

Cerys famously duetted with fellow Welsh legend Tom Jones on the 1999 Christmas hit 'Baby, It's Cold Outside'. She became a regular voice on BBC Radio 6 Music from 2009, eventually hosting her own Sunday show. In 2012 she joined the judging panel for the Dylan Thomas Literary Prize and, in 2013, she became the artistic director for the opening ceremony of the international world music event, Worldwide Music Expo (Womex). In 2014, she co-founded the Good Life Experience Festival and was also involved in BBC's Ten Pieces education scheme, which helped introduce a generation of schoolchildren to classical music.

For her services to Welsh culture, Cerys was awarded an inaugural St David Award in 2014. The awards recognise exceptional achievements by Welsh citizens and are the highest accolade awarded by the Welsh Government.

12 APRIL

Lady Diana Noel, 2nd Baroness Barham (born 18 September 1762), abolitionist and eccentric philanthropist died on this day in 1823.

Diana was the heiress to her parents' estate of Barham Court, Teston in Kent and an extremely wealthy woman. She was also a leading abolitionist of the slave trade and a financial supporter of the campaigns of Thomas Clarkson and William Wilberforce. In 1813, she left her 'profligate' husband and moved to Fairy Hill on the Gower peninsula. The Baroness was a devout Christian and became concerned about the spiritual well-being of the local people of Gower. She established Lady Barham's Connexion, a body of six chapels and free schools connected with the Welsh Calvinistic Methodists.

Lady Barham was also considered to be somewhat eccentric and would be carried to the Sunday services at Bethesda Chapel in Burry Green in a sedan chair. She had her own room behind the pulpit, warmed by an open fire, and, if she grew tired of the sermon, the door of the room would close and Lady Barham would go home.

13 APRIL

Dame Margaret Price, one of the most internationally successful and popular British operatic singers of her generation, was born on this day in 1941.

Although her father was a talented pianist, he discouraged Margaret from pursuing a musical career and she initially intended to become a biology teacher. However, when she was fifteen, noticing Margaret's undoubted singing ability, her music teacher at Pontllanfraith Grammar School brought her to the attention of the organist and choral conductor Charles Kennedy Scott, who persuaded her to study at Trinity College of Music in London.

Margaret made her stage debut in 1962 with the Welsh National Opera as a mezzo-soprano before successfully auditioning for the Royal Opera, Covent Garden. Margaret then successfully moved into the soprano repertoire which brought her international acclaim, especially in Mozart and the lighter Verdi roles. She made her American debut in 1968 and appeared in Köln for the first time in 1971, where she subsequently based her career.

Margaret was appointed DBE in 1993 and retired to north Pembrokeshire in 1999, where she taught a small number of students and bred golden retrievers.

14 APRIL

Dorothy Squires (born Edna May Squires on 25 March 1915) died on this day in 1998. Dorothy was an extremely successful and charismatic popular singer of the 1950s and 60s and, at one time, was one of the highest-paid female singers in the UK. She is best remembered for her versions of 'I'm in the Mood for Love' and 'If You Love Me (Really Love Me)'.

Dorothy was born in Pontyberem and raised in Dafen near Llanelli. She began to perform professionally at sixteen in the working men's club of Pontyberem and the Ritz Ballroom in Llanelli. When she was twenty, she moved to London and changed her name. She became romantically involved with the leader of a band she worked with, Billy Reid, whose connections were very helpful to her career. Dorothy's big break came in 1945 when she became a resident artiste at the BBC's *Variety Bandbox* programme and performed at the London Palladium.

Dorothy met the, then-unknown, actor Roger Moore and the couple married in 1953. In Hollywood, Dorothy was instrumental in establishing Moore's career. However, as his career took off, his infidelities increased and they divorced in 1968. Dorothy's career subsequently slumped and she embarked on a series of litigations that were financially draining and resulted in her being declared bankrupt in 1987. She was given a home in the Rhondda village of Trebanog by Esme Coles, a dedicated fan and friend, and it was here that she lived for the remainder of her life.

15 APRIL ⚠

On 15 April 1805, Mary Morgan became the youngest woman ever known to be executed in Wales.

Mary was a servant at Maesllwch Castle, just outside Glasbury which was the home of the wealthy MP for Radnorshire, Walter Wilkins. Mary had fallen pregnant at the age of sixteen. It was strongly rumoured that the father of Mary's child was Wilkins's son who had forced himself upon her.

A cook gave evidence that, in September 1804, Mary became unwell and retired to her room. The cook later found a dead baby girl inside Mary's mattress and a penknife hidden under the pillow. Mary was arrested and taken to the county gaol at Presteigne, where she awaited trial for murder at the Radnorshire Great Sessions in April 1805.

Her trial was presided over by George Harding, a cousin of the Wilkins family, and Mary was found guilty and condemned to death by hanging. It was accepted at trial that Mary, initially, had every intention of keeping the child. She displayed genuine remorse over the fate of her daughter and it seemed likely that she had suffered a severe mental breakdown when she realised that she and her child faced a life of shame and poverty in the workhouse. She told the court, 'I determined, therefore, to kill it, poor thing! Out of the way, being perfectly sure that I could not provide for it myself.'

Harding's refusal to show mercy and his lack of empathy towards Mary was much criticised. When the sentence was delivered, many of those in court were in tears. Harding called infanticide 'the vice of the poor', especially of those in service, and blamed their 'lack of religion and of education'. Mary's short life has since been commemorated by a gravestone in the churchyard at Presteigne.

16 APRIL

Gladys Morgan (born 7 November 1898) died on this day in 1983. Gladys was a popular radio and television comedian, whose career ran from the 1930s to the 1960s. She was billed as the 'Queen of Comedy' and was recognisable for her diminutive frame (she was just four foot ten inches tall), and her toothless, unmistakable and rousing laugh. At the peak of her career, she was one of the country's best-loved performers.

Gladys was born in Swansea and began her show-business career locally, primarily as a singer. However, her popularity soared when she started performing comic roles. During the Second World War, she formed a family comedy group with her husband Frank Laurie and their daughter Joan. They were also employed by the Entertainments National Service Association (ENSA) to entertain the troops.

Gladys's big break came in 1940 with the popular BBC radio variety show *Welsh Rarebit* where she became the resident comedienne, sharing top billing with a rising young star, Harry Secombe. Her success led to many variety tours around the UK and appearances on television shows such as *The Good Old Days*, *Educating Archie* and *The Frankie Howerd Show*.

17 APRIL

In Easter week 1093 (17–23 April), Rhys ap Tewdwr, the last king of Deheubarth, was killed at the Battle of Brecon. His death marked the beginning of significant Norman expansion into south Wales and was a life-changing event for his daughter, Nest ferch Rhys.

After her father's death, Nest was taken into captivity by King William Rufus, where she became the subject of the lustful attentions of his brother Henry (later Henry I) which probably resulted in the birth of her son, Henry FitzHenry. She was married twice. Once to Gerald of Windsor, the governor of Pembroke Castle, and then to Stephen, constable of Cardigan Castle.

In homage to Greek mythology, Nest has become known as the 'Helen of Wales'. At a gathering while she was married to Gerald, was Owain ap Cadwgan who immediately fell in love with her. Owain tried to abduct Nest and set fire to the castle. In one version of the story, Nest persuaded her husband to escape via a latrine shaft while she stayed to deal with Owain. Nest subsequently left with Owain. According to some sources, she bore him two sons. Nest later returned to Gerald, who got his revenge by killing Owain.

Nest's children were central figures in the subsequent Norman conquest of Ireland. Nest and Gerald were also the grandparents of Gerald of Wales (*Giraldus Cambrensis*), the celebrated cleric, chronicler and royal clerk to Henry II. They were also the progenitors of the FitzGerald and de Barry families of Ireland.

DID YOU KNOW?

When the Norman lover of Alice 'the Vicious' of Abergavenny was killed during the Norman conquest of Ireland, Alice reputedly took her revenge by beheading seventy prisoners with an axe before throwing their corpses over a cliff edge.

18 APRIL

On 18 April 2015, a slate memorial was unveiled in memory of Gwen John (22 June 1876–18 September 1939), the renowned Welsh artist, at her burial place in Janval Cemetery in Dieppe, France. For many years, her place of rest was unknown but it was rediscovered following extensive research for the S4C documentary series *Mamwlad gyda Ffion Hague* (*Mother Country with Ffion Hague*).

Gwen was born in Haverfordwest in 1876, but, following the death of her mother, her family moved to Tenby. After leaving the Slade School of Art in London, she moved to Paris, where she was regarded as an eccentric, modelled for Rodin – who became her lover – and studied with Whistler. In 1910 Gwen moved to the outskirts of Paris, where she led an increasingly reclusive lifestyle.

She was overshadowed by her brother, Augustus John, during her lifetime but her reputation has steadily grown since her death. Her paintings are mainly portraits of anonymous female sitters. Some of the best examples of her work are held at Amgueddfa Werin Cymru (National Museum of Wales) and in Tate Britain, London.

The memorial in Dieppe is inscribed '*Mae pobl fel cysgodion i mi ac fel cysgod ydwyf innau*' ('People are like shadows to me and like a shadow I am to them'), which is a translation of a sentence Gwen wrote in one of her letters to Rodin.

19 APRIL

On 19 April 1850, Mary Cornelia Vane-Tempest inherited the mansion and estate of Plas Machynlleth following the death of her father, Sir John Edwards, MP for Montgomery.

In 1846, Mary had married George Vane-Tempest, who would become the 5th Marquess of Londonderry and one of the largest and richest landowners in the UK. When Mary inherited the Plas, they made it their principal residence and carried out extensive improvements and alterations.

Mary was very highly regarded by the locals for her charitable work in the community. The grounds of Y Plas were often turned over for public events and *eisteddfodau* and Mary regularly distributed food and clothing to the poor. The couple founded Machynlleth's first infants' school which, in 1892, they converted to the Londonderry Cottage Hospital, the town's first hospital. At Mary's bequest and under her patronage, the Vane almshouses were constructed to house local widows and the poor.

To mark their appreciation, the local community funded and built Machynlleth's iconic town clock to celebrate the coming of age of Mary and George's son, Charles Vane-Tempest (the future 6th Marquess of Londonderry), with the foundation stone being laid on 16 July 1874. The community also commissioned a bust of Mary which can still be seen in the grounds of Y Plas.

In 1948, the mansion and estate of Y Plas, Machynlleth was gifted to the town of Machynlleth by the Vane-Tempest family.

20 APRIL

Born on this day in 1979, Professor Haley Gomez (née Morgan) from Barry is a world-leading expert in astrophysics and cosmic (star) dust. Her groundbreaking research shows that cosmic dust is formed in the huge explosions of stars known as supernovae, and it also plays a key role in increasing the understanding of how many galaxies there are in the Universe.

She serves on the WISE (Women into Science and Engineering) in Wales campaign committee. The campaign aims to encourage girls to pursue courses and careers in science, technology, engineering and mathematics.

In 2014, Haley won the Inspire Wales award for the most inspirational Welsh person in the Science and Technology category. She was elected a Fellow of the Learned Society of Wales in 2017 and awarded an MBE in 2018. In 2023 she was appointed as Head of the School of Physics and Astronomy at Cardiff University.

21 APRIL

Ann Griffiths (née Thomas, 1776–1805) was baptised on 21 April 1776. She is considered to be one of Europe's leading religious poets and Wales's most prominent female writer of hymns.

Ann was born in Llanfihangel-yng-Ngwynfa, north Powys, and brought up as a member of the Anglican Church. Her family were heavily involved in the social and cultural life of the predominantly Welsh-speaking community. Ann was described as being intelligent, witty, mischievous and single-minded. When she was seventeen, her mother died, and she became the mistress of the household.

She followed her brothers into the Calvinist Methodist movement after hearing the preacher Benjamin Jones speak in 1796. In 1802, she began writing hymns and poetry, reciting them to her maid as they walked to chapel in Bala. Ann married in 1804 and gave birth to a daughter, Elizabeth, the following year. However, Elizabeth died within a fortnight and Ann, less than a fortnight later, died aged just twenty-nine.

Her work, published after her death, expresses her fervent Christian faith and reflects her considerable intellect and detailed scriptural knowledge. It makes her a significant figure in Welsh nonconformism as well as a national icon. Her hymn '*Yr Arglwydd Iesu*' ('The Lord Jesus') was sung at the enthronement of Dr Rowan Williams as Archbishop of Canterbury in 2003.

22 APRIL

Megan Lloyd George, the first female MP for a Welsh constituency, was born in Criccieth on 22 April 1902.

Megan's selection to stand for the safe Liberal seat of Anglesey in 1929 initially caused controversy. She was the daughter of David Lloyd George who had served as British prime minister from 1916–1922. The accusations of nepotism faded as Megan enjoyed a career that would span thirty years.

In 1944, Megan Lloyd George opened the first Welsh

Affairs debate at Westminster. In 1949, she became deputy leader of the party and began championing many Welsh causes including the establishment of a Welsh Parliament and a Secretary of State for Wales.

She defected to Labour in 1951 and returned to parliament in 1957 after winning Carmarthen for Labour. She was a prominent voice in the Tryweryn Defence Committee, the body formed to attempt to resist the controversial flooding of a village near Bala to provide water for English consumers which, nevertheless, went ahead in 1965. She remained an MP until her death in 1966. Megan was appointed a Member of the Order of Companion of Honour five days after her death. In 2016, she was included in the 'Fifty greatest Welsh men and women of all time'. And a Purple Plaque was installed on her family home in Criccieth in 2019.

23 APRIL

On 23 April 2005, in honour of world-famous actress Siân Phillips, the British Academy of Film and Television Arts Cymru (BAFTA in Wales) inaugurated the Siân Phillips Award. The award would go to a Welsh man or woman who had made a significant contribution in either a major feature film or network television programme.

Siân was born on 14 May 1933 in Gwaun-cae-gurwen. She was christened with the name Jane but her Welsh teacher at school called her Siân (the Welsh version of her name) and the name stuck. Siân's family spoke Welsh for the majority of her childhood and she only learned English by listening to the radio.

From the age of eleven, she was working as an actress for BBC Radio in Wales. She made her first television acting appearance at seventeen. Siân joined the National Theatre Company, making her first appearance on the London stage in 1957 and her film debut in 1964 in the film *Becket*.

She is perhaps best known for her roles in the television dramas *I, Claudius* (for which she won a BAFTA), *Tinker, Tailor, Soldier, Spy* and *Smiley's People*. She also starred in the films *Goodbye, Mr Chips* and *Murphy's War*. She was nominated for an Olivier and a Tony award for her West End and Broadway performance as Marlene Dietrich in *Marlene*.

Siân has been married three times. Her second husband was fellow actor Peter O'Toole. Their tempestuous relationship ended in 1979. She later recalled that her mother had warned her that 'marriage wouldn't suit me and she was right'.

Siân was made a Dame Commander of the Order of the British Empire (DBE) in 2016 for her services to drama.

24 APRIL

Television and radio presenter Gabby Logan was born in Leeds on 24 April 1973. She is a former Welsh international rhythmic gymnast and the daughter of Wales soccer international Terry Yorath.

Her father was the manager of Bradford City in 1985 and she was in the crowd at Valley Parade just before the stadium fire occurred. The young Gabby watched the tragedy unfurl. Then in 1992, she and her family suffered the tragic loss of her brother, who passed away from a heart defect while playing football at home with their father.

Gabby competed for Wales as a rhythmic gymnast at the 1990 Commonwealth Games. After graduating in law from Durham University in 1995, she began presenting on local radio in Newcastle, before joining Sky Sports in 1996. She worked there until 1998, when she joined ITV, fronting *On the Ball* and presenting their UEFA Champions League coverage. She was one of the few women sports presenters on terrestrial television at the time. Gabby left ITV for BBC Sport in 2006. There she has hosted *Final Score* and *Match of the Day* as well as fronting coverage for many live sports events including the London Marathon, rugby's Six Nations tournament and the BBC Sports Personality of the Year.

25 APRIL

On 25 April 2017, Sheila Morrow (born in Bangor in 1947) was appointed as the President of Great Britain Hockey.

Sheila is a former Wales and Great Britain hockey international and captain, who played in five World Championships during her seventeen-year international career. She combined her playing career with working as a PE teacher in Cardiff and, after retiring from playing, she became a well-respected umpire and Olympic judge, as well as taking up development positions with the Sports Council for Wales and Sport England. In 1990, Sheila was one of the inaugural inductees into the Welsh Sports Hall of Fame.

DID YOU KNOW?

Leah Wilkinson's 204 international hockey caps (183 for Wales and 21 for Team GB) make her Wales's most-capped sportsperson of all time.

26 APRIL

Lady Emma Hamilton (born Amy Lyon) was born on this day in 1765 in Ness, near Neston, Cheshire. She was a maid, a model, a dancer, an actress and – through her love affairs – one of the most influential women of her time. Emma's mother was from Hawarden in Flintshire and when Emma was just two months old she moved back there.

Emma received no formal education and her life was hard in Wales. So, aged twelve, she left for London where she worked as a maid to various actresses at the Drury Lane theatre in Covent Garden then as a performer herself. Emma became the mistress of many powerful men including Charles Francis Greville, the Lord of the Treasury and the founder of the town of Milford Haven, who introduced her to the painter George Romney. Emma became the subject of many of Romney's portraits.

In 1791, she married Sir William Hamilton, the British envoy at Naples. The naval hero Horatio Nelson visited in 1793. He was also married but he and Emma became lovers. After her husband died in 1803, Emma lived with Nelson in Merton, Surrey, and they had a daughter together. Although she inherited money from both Nelson, upon his death in 1805, and Hamilton, she squandered most of it and was imprisoned for debt in 1813. Emma fled to Calais in 1814 to avoid her creditors and died there the following year.

27 APRIL

On 27 April 2013, Angela Kwok was awarded a Welsh Asian Women Achievement Award in recognition of her work as a champion for the Chinese community in Cardiff.

Angela arrived in Cardiff from Hong Kong in the early 1970s when she was sixteen. Her family established the Rice Bowl, Cardiff's first Chinese restaurant, and Angela worked there. She was married with a daughter by the age of nineteen and she and her husband were running a takeaway in Pontcanna. Angela spoke little English when she came to Wales. She realised that her long working days left her isolated from both the Chinese and Welsh communities, and that this was a common problem for many other Chinese women. She organised regular meetings for the women to build support networks, improve their English and computer skills and make friends.

In 1984, she established the South Wales Chinese Women's Association and later, the Cardiff Chinese Community Service Association for men and women. She worked with the South Wales Police as a translator and became a member of the Race Equality Council. Angela passed away in 2016 but the work that she did has left an engaged and diverse community in Cardiff, and was further recognised in 2020 when a Purple Plaque was installed on her family home in Cardiff.

28 APRIL

On 28 April 2006, Hayley Parsons from Cwmbran founded the financial services comparison website Go.compare.com. The company rapidly became a multi-million-pound success and won Hayley many accolades and awards, including the South Wales Chamber of Commerce 'Woman in Business Award' in 2009.

Hayley left school at sixteen to work for a local insurance company. She joined Admiral Insurance in 1992 and set up their car insurance comparison site, Confused.com. She left Admiral in 2006 to found Go.compare.com.

In 2014, Hayley joined a panel to advise the Welsh Government on the development and promotion of entrepreneurship in Wales. She is also a member of the Inspire Growth Wales investment consortium, which mentors and invests in technology-focused start-ups and businesses in Wales. Hayley is a huge supporter of Welsh rugby and in 2019 became a non-executive director at Cardiff Blues, and the first woman to join the region's board.

29 APRIL

Today is the feast day of St Endelienta. She is recognised as a Cornish saint but was also believed to be a daughter of Brychan, the fifth- century king of Brycheiniog.

Endelienta is believed to have travelled from Wales to north Cornwall to join her brother St Nectan and spread the word about Christianity. On her way, she stopped on Lundy Island where she founded a church. In Cornwall, she settled at Trenteny, described as being near St Endellion, where she lived a very austere life, subsisting only on the milk of a cow. Legend has it that she was the goddaughter of King Arthur and, when her cow was killed by the Lord of Trenteny for wandering onto his land, Arthur killed the lord in revenge. However, Endelienta considered that this was too high a penalty and miraculously restored the lord to life.

Endelienta requested that, on her death, her body was to be put on a cart pulled by two bullocks and that she was to be buried wherever they took her. These instructions were carried out and the bullocks came to a rest at the top of a hill. It was here that she was buried and a church was built over her grave. The church and the subsequent settlement that grew up around it are now named St Endellion in her memory. There are also two wells nearby which are named after her.

30 APRIL

Today is International Jazz day and we celebrate the life of Patti Flynn (born Patricia Maude Young, 1937–2020), a renowned jazz singer, author and social activist. In 2023, she became the first Black woman to be awarded a Purple Plaque, which acknowledges notable women in Wales, celebrating their achievements and honouring their legacies.

Patti was the youngest child of seven in a family from Tiger Bay in Cardiff. Her father was a merchant seaman from Jamaica who had come to Cardiff during the 1920s and her mother was a white woman from Cardiff.

Patti developed her love of music as a child listening to popular jazz artists of the day. She was encouraged to explore music by Vic Parker, the legendary Cardiff jazz guitarist. She went on to have a career as a jazz singer and international cabaret artiste and later moved to Spain, where she became a respected music producer and radio presenter. On her return to Cardiff, Patti and her friend Humie Webbe established the Butetown Bay Jazz Heritage Festival. As well as celebrating the music heritage of Tiger Bay, the festival also showcased up-and-coming musical talent.

Patti was passionate about researching Black history and culture and, in 2017, was one of the founding members of the Black History Month movement in Wales.

Losing her father and two brothers during the Second World War inspired her to campaign for a monument marking the contributions made by the Black, Asian and minority ethnic people who had served during the world wars. The memorial, unveiled in 2019, now stands in the Welsh National War Memorial, Cardiff. That year, Patti was also honoured with the Ethnic Minority Welsh Women Achievement Association's (EMWWAA) Lifetime Achievement Award.

1 MAY

Also known as May Day, Beltane or, in Wales, Calan Mai, 1 May is associated with the legendary figure of Creiddylad who is described in the *Mabinogion* tale of '*Culhwch ac Olwen*' as 'the most majestic maiden who ever lived'.

She had two suitors: Gwyn ap Nudd and Gwythyr ap Greidawl, who was one of the knights of King Arthur. Creiddylad and Gwythyr were betrothed, but before they were married, Gwyn ap Nudd forcefully abducted her. In the ensuing battle between the rivals, Gwyn perpetrated acts of such cruelty on his prisoners that Arthur himself was forced to intervene. He decreed that Gwyn and Gwythyr would fight for Creiddylad every year on 1 May until Doomsday. Whoever won the fight on Doomsday would claim Creiddylad for his bride.

It has been suggested that Creiddylad is a fertility goddess and the battle between the rivals is one that establishes the strongest and most virile and will guarantee

Hester continued to write and to cultivate literary and artistic company, notably with lifelong friends Sarah Siddons, Fanny Burney, Oliver Goldsmith, David Garrick and Joshua Reynolds. Hester's seminal work *Retrospection* deconstructs masculine discourses and establishes a feminine viewpoint of history and culture. She remains a central figure in early British feminism. She retired to Brynbella, a house at Bach y Graig, before the end of her life.

DID YOU KNOW?

Hester Thrale was a member of the bluestocking circle: a women's social movement that encouraged women to fill their social gatherings with intellectual pursuits that emphasised education and the arts.

3 MAY

The 1926 General Strike was called on 3 May and it had a major effect on the mining communities of the Rhondda Valley. It also hugely influenced Annie Powell (1906–86), who became Britain's first female Communist mayor when she became Mayor of Rhondda in 1979.

In solidarity with the strikers, large numbers from other industries went on strike, too. On the first full day of action, there were over 1.5 million people on strike. The government reacted aggressively and brought in the armed forces and the police, and the media helped to turn public opinion against the strikers. The TUC held secret talks the fertility and renewal of the earth in the ensuing season. Her story may also be connected with the annual battle between summer and winter and the cyclical changing of the seasons, with Creiddylad as the eternal May Queen, always seeking peace and stability between the opposing forces of light and dark.

2 MAY

Hester Thrale (Hester Lynch Thrale Piozzi), diarist, author and socialite, died on 2 May 1821.

She was born at Bodfel Hall, Caernarfonshire, the only daughter of Hester Lynch Cotton and Sir John Salusbury of the powerful and wealthy Anglo-Welsh Salusbury family.

Hester and her first husband Henry Thrale became close friends with the prominent literary figure Samuel Johnson. Unlike her husband, Johnson took Hester's literary ambitions seriously. She became his literary collaborator, friend and confidante for more than ten years, and he travelled with her to Wales on several occasions.

Her husband's death in 1781 left Hester an extremely wealthy widow, and there was speculation that she would marry Johnson. However, to Johnson's open dismay, Hester married Italian musician and teacher Gabriel Mario Piozzi and left with him for Europe.

She and Johnson reconciled their friendship before his death in 1784, after which she published *Anecdotes of the Late Samuel Johnson* and *Letters to and from the Late Samuel Johnson*, both of which were successful and remain among the best-regarded personal accounts of Johnson's life and personality.

with the mine owners which resulted in the strike being called off after nine days without a single concession being made. Some of the miners struggled on alone, relying on food banks and fundraising campaigns but, by the end of November, most had drifted back to work.

During the strike, Annie was a trainee teacher at Trebanog and witnessed first hand the great hardship and poverty of the schoolchildren and their mining families. Her despair at the government's indifference to the challenges faced by the mining community led her towards becoming an active Communist Party member. She also became an active member of the National Union of Teachers.

In 1955, after thirteen attempts, Annie was elected as a Communist councillor for Penygraig and played a key role in the campaign for more council houses to be built in the Rhondda.

Annie died in 1986; 700-plus mourners attended her funeral, including representatives from parties across the political divide.

4 MAY

On 4 May 1725, according to tradition, Ann Thomas, the 'Maid of Cefn Ydfa', was forced to marry lawyer Anthony Maddocks against her wishes. She reputedly died pining for her true love, Wil Hopcyn.

Ann was born in 1704, a cousin of philosopher Richard Price. Her father died in 1706 and she was placed in the wardship of Anthony Maddocks from Cwmrisga, who persuaded her family that Ann should marry his son, also called Anthony. However, legend tells us that Ann had previously fallen in love with the poet and thatcher

Wil Hopcyn. When their love was discovered, they were forbidden to see each other.

The couple continued sending love letters to each other in secret but these were discovered by Ann's mother who confiscated her writing materials. Hopcyn left the area and the wedding went ahead, but she is said to have pined so badly for her lover that she fell seriously ill. On her death bed, she requested to see Hopcyn one last time. He arrived in time for Ann to die in his arms. Ann was buried on 6 June 1727 in St Cynwyd's Church, Llangynwyd, near Maesteg.

5 MAY

The centenary edition of *Vogue* magazine was issued on 5 May 2016. It features Marjorie 'Bo' Gilbert from Aberdare, the first centenarian model to pose for *Vogue*'s pages.

Bo was always interested in style and couldn't resist when she was approached by the magazine for the Harvey Nichols shoot. She told *WalesOnline* that she never went out without her heels and make-up. 'You've got to keep the standards up, although I do it to suit myself. I certainly don't dress up for the boys.'

Other notable Welsh faces who have appeared in *Vogue* include Grace Coddington from Anglesey. In 1959 aged eighteen, Grace won a modelling competition run by *Vogue* which led to a successful career in fashion. Having always shown an interest in styling shoots, she began working for British *Vogue* in 1968 and became the magazine's photo editor. For many years she collaborated closely with top photographers, creating fantastical and theatrical narratives for the magazine's fashion pages. After working for Calvin Klein in New York in the 1980s, she returned to *Vogue* in

1988 to become the creative director of American *Vogue*.

Callie Thorpe, who describes herself as a 'sassy Welsh girl', is a plus-size fashion model and blogger who appeared in *Vogue* in 2017. Despite receiving a horrible backlash from some about her size, Callie continues to work and to speak out to promote body confidence and to question conventional beauty standards.

6 MAY

Wrexham's Elizabeth Randles (born 1 August 1800) died on this day in 1829. She was a musical child prodigy who started playing the piano at the age of sixteen months – although, because of her small size, she needed to use the side of her hand to press each key.

Elizabeth, also known as Bessy, first performed in public playing *Ar Hyd Y Nos* at Wrexham Theatre. She subsequently came to the attention of Sir Watkin Williams Wynn, MP for Denbighshire, which led to a performance for King George III and the royal family when she was three-and-a-half years old. During her time at the court, Elizabeth met George III's granddaughter Princess Charlotte. The eight-year-old princess said to Elizabeth, 'Do you know that my grandfather is King of England, and my father is Prince of Wales?' 'Well,' replied Elizabeth, 'my father is the organist at Wrexham.'

The royal recital caused such a sensation that a tour of the UK was organised between 1805 and 1808, with Elizabeth presented as the 'Little Cambrian Prodigy'. In 1818, Elizabeth took lessons from the German composer Friedrich Kalkbrenner, who also taught Chopin, before moving to Liverpool and becoming a teacher herself.

Elizabeth's health, however, was described as 'delicate' and she died in 1829 without fulfilling her undoubted potential.

7 MAY

Cwmdonkin Rescue Shelter in Swansea was opened on 7 May 1886.

The shelter was set up as a temporary refuge for 'fallen women' – those who were often pregnant or with a child, poor and unmarried – with the stated aim of teaching them practical skills to help them integrate back into their communities. Women were encouraged to abstain from alcohol and to stay away from the docks where thousands of sailors passed through the town. The shelter also organised emigration to Canada, Australia and New Zealand as a way for some young women to start new lives.

One of Cwmdonkin's most incorrigible inmates was Margaret Rogers. She made an astonishing 275 appearances in court for drunken and disorderly behaviour during her turbulent life.

Maggie was originally from Haverfordwest and, along with many others, was attracted to Swansea which had become a booming industrial centre in the 1860s. However, Maggie's downfall was alcohol and she soon became a regular in the drinking dens of Victorian Swansea, and in the courtroom and newspapers. She was described as 'an unfortunate', 'a prostitute' or 'the famous Swansea drunkard' and local police came to refer to her as 'Mad Maggie'.

Like so many of the women who must have passed through Cwmdonkin, Maggie was a victim of her circumstances and of a society where women had little protection if they were poor or suffering from addictions. But she turned her life around. When she died at Swansea Union Workhouse in 1908, the same newspapers noted that she was 'cleanly and industrious', had a 'pretty wit and much intelligence' and that 'had her life in its earlier years been ordered differently' she may have had an easier life.

8 MAY

When Natasha Asghar assumed office as a member of the Senedd for South Wales East on 8 May 2021, she became its first female ethnic minority member. Natasha, who holds a BA in Politics and Social Policy and a Master's in Contemporary British Policy and Media, had previously worked successfully as a banker, a television presenter and a radio DJ. She decided to enter politics following the death of her father, Mohammad Asghar, who represented the same constituency and became the Shadow Minister for Transport and Technology.

Natasha is passionate about improving the public transport network throughout Wales and in 2021 she was named as one of the BBC's 100 Women, highlighting the achievements of women in society. In 2024, she also won the Devolved Politician of the Year Award for her campaigning against the controversial 20 mph speed-limit policy in Wales.

9 MAY

Born in Bangor in 1895, Mary Dilys Glynne died on this day in 1991. She was a scientist of international repute and a mountaineer at a time when there were not many women in either field.

Mary began her scientific career as a voluntary worker in 1917 at Rothamsted Experimental Station (now known as Rothamsted Research), an agricultural research centre. She was soon given a position as assistant botanist. She was a founding member of the plant pathology department. Her early work concerned wart disease in potatoes but her other main interest was in cereals. She showed that the flattening of some crops before they are harvested is often caused by fungal diseases rather than by wind and rain, and that these diseases are increased by monoculture (growing only one crop on a piece of land). As a result of her research, preventative measures, including rotation of crops, were promoted.

Mary recalled that she was introduced to rock climbing in 1925 'by two young men who found me on the top of Great Gable' where she was fell-walking. After a preliminary season in the Alps, she went climbing in Australia where she travelled on a fellowship in 1928–9. She also climbed in New Zealand and South Africa. She conquered the Matterhorn, Aiguille du Grépon, Aiguille des Petits Charmoz, Dent du Requin, the Aiguille du Midi and Mont Blanc. Among this long list of peaks ascended, she recorded the second ascent (and the first by a woman) of Mount Spencer. She was elected a member of the Ladies' Alpine Club, and subsequently became vice president. She also joined the Pinnacle Club.

10 MAY

On 10 May 1778, Eleanor Butler and Sarah Ponsonby arrived in north Wales. Here they chose Plas Newydd, a cottage near the Denbighshire town of Llangollen, as their home and became known as the 'Ladies of Llangollen'.

The two women had met in Ireland in 1768 and had fallen in love. As was typical of the time, their respective aristocratic families had vehemently disapproved of their mutual attachment and had sought to coerce them into unwelcome marriages. The women defied their parents and fled to start a new life together funded only by modest incomes from their disgruntled relatives.

Having established themselves in Plas Newydd, Sarah and Eleanor's unconventional lifestyle both fascinated and scandalised the locals. They were known as excellent hosts and conversationalists. They made changes to Plas Newydd in the Gothic style and their home soon became a destination for their many guests. The ladies cultivated their celebrity status, welcoming distinguished visitors who included the Duke of Wellington, William Wordsworth, Percy Shelley and the young Charles Darwin.

Eleanor and Sarah died within two years of each other and are buried together in the graveyard of St Collen's church in Llangollen. A memorial still stands in the churchyard, and the carefully preserved house and gardens at Plas Newydd survive as a testament to their love and their bravery in defying the conventions of their time.

DID YOU KNOW?

The diaries of Anne Lister (1791–1840), the English landowner from West Yorkshire known as the 'first modern lesbian' thanks to her diaries detailing her love affairs, show that she visited the Ladies of Llangollen in 1822.

11 MAY

On 11 May 1896, the Empire, Queen Street, Cardiff became the first commercial entertainment venue in Wales to project silent films, just one year after Lumière cinematography was developed.

Lily Haggar, born in Brynmawr in 1891, was probably Wales's first silent movie actress. She was the daughter of William Haggar from Essex, who, along with his wife and eleven children, toured across south and west Wales filming local events. William went on to make over thirty films between 1901 and 1908 and opened a cinema chain in 1909 which expanded across south Wales.

Lily's best-known films are *The Life of Charles Peace* (1905) and *The Squire's Daughter* (1905).

Other notable Welsh silent film actresses include:

- **Eleanor Daniels** was born in 1886 in Llanarthne and she was raised in Llanelli. She began performing at thirteen. By 1907, she had won three National Eisteddfod chairs. She toured the United States with the Welsh Players in 1914 and later emigrated there, where she went on to enjoy a successful career in silent films. She died in 1994.

- **Mary Glynne** was born Mary Aitken in 1895 in Penarth. She appeared in twenty-four films between 1919 and 1939 but died relatively young in 1954 in London.

- **Queenie Thomas** was born Marjorie Violet Queenie Thomas in 1898 in Cardiff. She was billed in America as 'England's Mary Pickford' and starred in *The School for Scandal* (1923) opposite Basil Rathbone.

- **Pauline Peters**, from Cardiff, was born in 1895. She appeared in over thirty films during the silent movie era. She reached the peak of her career in the 1920s working with the prolific actor and director, Walter Forde. Her last role was a sound picture: *Deadlock* (1931).

12 MAY

The newly elected National Assembly for Wales (now known as the Senedd) met for the first time on 12 May 1999. Among the cabinet ministers unveiled on that day was Jane Hutt who was appointed as Minister for Health and Social Services.

Jane, the member of the Senedd (MS) for the Vale of Glamorgan, has been re-elected at every subsequent election since 1999 and has served in every administration to date. She holds the record for the longest-serving Welsh Government minister. Jane was one of the founder members of Welsh Women's Aid, a feminist organisation campaigning on behalf of women who are victims of domestic violence, and she is a director of the equal opportunities organisation, Chwarae Teg (Fair Play).

On International Women's Day 2023, Jane issued the following statement on behalf of Senedd Cymru: 'I believe our focus on intersectionality, equality of outcome and social justice is how we will move towards our vision of a gender equal Wales. No woman or girl can be left behind. Across Wales, we will work with and for Black, Asian and minority ethnic women, disabled women, LGBTQ+ women, women in poverty, older women, girls and others to deliver equality and social justice.'

13 MAY

On 13 May 2007 Kirsty Jones from Pembrokeshire, a professional kitesurfer and pioneer in the sport of kitesurfing, completed a solo non-stop 140-mile kitesurf crossing from the Canary Islands to the Western Sahara in Morocco. It took nine hours and it was a world first. Her efforts raised money for equipment for a disabled charity in Morocco and for a windsurfing centre in Tarfaya established by Youths United.

Kirsty is a three-time British Kitesurf Champion, a three-time Kitesurf World Wave Champion, a two-time Master of the Ocean Champion and the first person to kitesurf from Ireland to Wales. This feat, in 2002, raised funds for the Tŷ Hafan Children's Hospice near Cardiff.

14 MAY

Nansi Richards – known also by her bardic name Telynores Maldwyn or as 'the Harpist of Montgomeryshire' – was born on 14 May 1888 at Pen-y-bont-fawr, Montgomeryshire. She was the most distinguished figure in traditional harp-playing in Wales in the twentieth century and is credited with bringing harp-playing back into popularity and prominence.

Nansi won the National Eisteddfod harp competition on three consecutive occasions between 1908 and 1910. In 1911 she played for the royal family when they visited Plas Machynlleth as part of the investiture of Edward VIII, and was able to call herself the 'Royal Harpist'. Nansi then made a tour of the music halls of Britain in the company of comic entertainer Fanny Fields, who encouraged her to perform tricks while performing, such as playing with her back turned, or playing two harps simultaneously.

During the First World War, Nansi volunteered to entertain the troops. In 1923, she toured America, where she performed for President Calvin Coolidge, Henry Ford and Will Kellogg the cereal manufacturer.

DID YOU KNOW?

Will Kellogg was looking for advertising ideas for his cornflakes when he met Nansi Richards. She suggested using the similarity between the Welsh word for cockerel '*ceiliog*' and Kellogg's own name, and the iconic Cornelius Rooster was born.

15 MAY

Merched y Wawr was established on 15 May 1967. It is an organisation for women in Wales similar to the Women's Institute but with Welsh as the lead language of the movement. Its aims are to promote women's issues and to support culture, education and the arts in Wales.

Merched y Wawr came into being as a result of a decision made by the WI in 1967 to use only the English language throughout its organisation. The exclusion of the Welsh language caused outrage in many of the WI branches in Wales and many members elected to break away from it. Zonia Bowen of Y Parc near Bala worked with Sulwen Davies and others to found a new organisation which would operate solely in Welsh.

Today, Merched y Wawr has thousands of members and hundreds of branches. Members raise money for charities, develop new skills, participate in cultural and informative events and celebrate their Welsh identity.

16 MAY

Amy Dillwyn, one of Britain's first female industrialists, was born on this day in 1845.

Born in Sketty, Amy was educated at home near Killay, Swansea, and grew up to be a rebellious young woman. Her father Lewis Llewelyn Dillwyn was MP for Swansea and owner of one of the largest steelworks in the world. Amy occupied herself by writing popular novels. Her work explored women's roles in Victorian society, as well as regularly touching on themes surrounding her own sexuality and what it was like being a gay woman at the time. Amy never conformed to Victorian society: she wore a trilby hat and was rarely seen without a cigar. She never married but she did fall in love with a woman called Olive Talbot who she would often refer to as her 'wife'.

Amy's life changed when her father died in 1892. The family faced financial ruin. Amy took over the debt-ridden works at Llansamlet and turned the ailing enterprise around. By 1905 she was able to sell her shares to a German company and dedicate the rest of her life to local politics. She campaigned for better education and votes for women. In 1911, she called for a boycott of a department store in Swansea, where seamstresses were on strike in protest at their working conditions.

Amy died on 13 December 1935. Her ashes are buried in the churchyard of St Paul's Church, Sketty.

17 MAY

Twm Siôn Cati is a famous figure in Welsh folklore and 17 May is the day his stories are celebrated. Tales abound of the banditry, trickery and showmanship of the legendary sixteenth-century Welsh outlaw who is known as the Welsh Robin Hood. However, in later life, he relinquished his life of crime and became a well-respected landowner, historian and poet. And it was all because of one woman.

Joan was the wealthy widow of Thomas Williams and therefore the heiress to the Ystradffin estate. Legend has it that Joan was extremely reluctant to respond to Twm's advances, but he persisted in his courtship. One night she opened her window and told him to leave and never return. He asked her to extend her hand for a farewell kiss. When she did so, he grasped her hand and refused to let go. He threatened to cut off her hand and keep it as a memento and even drew blood from her wrist with his dagger. Joan conceded and agreed to marry him.

After they were married, Joan purchased a pardon for Twm, or Thomas as he was thereafter known. She persuaded him to give up banditry and he became an upstanding member of society and, ironically, a Justice of the Peace.

18 MAY

International Museum Day is 18 May. It is the day when museums take the opportunity to promote the important role they play in collecting and curating objects and materials of cultural and historical importance.

Amgueddfa Werin Cymru (National Museum of Wales) acquired a fascinating collection in 2023. It was the legacy of Jessie Knight, widely considered to be the UK's first female tattoo artist. Jessie's collection comprises nearly 1,000 pieces including tattoo designs, photographs and the tools she used during her sixty-year career.

Jessie (1904–92) was born in Croydon into a circus family who toured the UK. As a child, she acted as a sharpshooter's dummy for her father, which resulted in her being shot twice. She later became a bareback horse rider. The family settled in Barry. Her father, who had learned to tattoo when he was a sailor, opened a shop. He taught Jessie the trade and, when he returned to sea, she took over the business at age eighteen.

This was at a time when tattoos were considered vulgar by many and were certainly not associated with young women. When Jessie got married, her husband disapproved of her work and this led to tensions within the relationship. Her family tell of a night when a diminutive Jessie shot her abusive husband for kicking her beloved dog down the stairs. He survived and Jessie ended the marriage.

Jessie opened up tattoo shops in Portsmouth and Aldershot. As the popularity of tattooing increased, her bold colourful designs meant her business boomed. In 1955, even though the industry was almost entirely dominated by men, Jessie was runner-up Champion

Tattoo Artist of All England, for her depiction of a Highland fling on a man's back.

Jessie returned to open a business in Barry in 1968, where she continued to work until the 1980s.

19 MAY

On 19 May 2006, two *Big Brother* contestants, Imogen Thomas and Glyn Wise, were told not to use the Welsh language in private conversations. The ruling was reversed after a formal complaint from Cymdeithas yr Iaith Gymraeg (The Welsh Language Society).

Imogen, from Llanelli, was a former glamour model who won the Miss Wales contest in 2003. She was later involved in many *Big Brother* spin-off programmes.

Other notable Welsh female *Big Brother* housemates include:

- **Helen Adams** from Cwmbran, came second in the second series in 2001. Before entering the house, she worked as a hairdresser and part-time dance instructor. She was notable for her spontaneous and often illogical comments which were jokingly called 'Helenisms'. Helen struck up a relationship with fellow housemate Paul Clarke which captivated the nation's interest and gained them celebrity status.

- **Rachel Rice** came from Pontypool and won the ninth series in 2008. Rachel was a television and film actress, notably appearing alongside Hugh Grant in the 1993 Gothic horror *Night Train to Venice* when she was eight. She was also second runner-up in the Miss Wales contest in 2003. Rachel has a degree in English and Drama and is now a schoolteacher.

20 MAY

Born on this day in 1870, Sarah Winifred Parry was one of Wales's finest short story writers. Writing as Winnie Parry, she became a household name in Wales with her serialised fiction in the raft of Welsh-language magazines and periodicals that existed at the turn of the twentieth century.

Sarah was born in Welshpool and, shortly after her birth, the family moved to Port Dinorwic (now known as Y Felinheli) Caernarfonshire. There, after her mother's death in 1876, she was raised by her grandparents. She had little formal schooling but spoke both Welsh and English and received tuition from her grandfather.

Her most acclaimed work, *Sioned,* was first published as a serial between 1894 and 1896 in the journal *Cymru* and then as a complete novel in 1906. In 1908, she went to Croydon to live with her father and became editor of the popular children's Welsh-language magazine *Cymru'r Plant.* Around 1915, she gave up writing, and worked as a secretary firstly for her father's engineering firm and then for the Liberal MP for Anglesey, Sir Robert Thomas, 1st Baronet.

Several attempts were made to republish *Sioned*, but it was not until well after Sarah's death in 1953 that the Welsh publisher Honno reissued it, in 1988.

21 MAY

'Myfanwy', arguably the most famous love song in Wales, was first performed on 21 May 1875, at the opening concert of the Aberystwyth and University Musical Society. The occasion was the thirty-fourth birthday of the song's composer, Joseph Parry, who at the time was Professor of Music at the University.

The lyrics, written by Richard Davies, are a retelling of a fourteenth-century love story: the tragic story of the unfulfilled love of a poor young poet called Hywel ab Einion for a beautiful young noblewoman, Myfanwy Fychan.

Castell Dinas Brân, the remains of which still stand above the Welsh town of Llangollen, is the setting for the sad love story. Myfanwy was the daughter of the Norman earl of Arundel and was, according to sources at that time, the most beautiful woman in Powys. Proud of her beauty, Myfanwy rejected many suitors, believing them unworthy of her. When Hywel, a poor bard, plucked up the courage to climb the steep hill to Dinas Brân to sing for her and declare his love, she was temporarily captivated by the beauty of his voice. However, the arrival of a rich, handsome and more articulate suitor thwarted Hywel's romantic aspirations and he was cruelly spurned. His lamentation of unrequited love is encapsulated in the lyrics of the song.

22 MAY

The feast day of St Elen is on 22 May.

According to legend, Elen was the daughter of British King Octavius and the wife of Macsen Wledig (Magnus Maximus), who briefly served as the Emperor of the Western Roman Empire. Her story is recounted in 'The Dream of Macsen Wledig', which is one of the tales in the *Mabinogion*.

In the tale, Macsen dreams of a lovely maiden in a wonderful far-off land. He sends his men all over the earth in search of her. Eventually, they find her in a castle in Wales. The maiden is Elen of Segontium, the Roman base now known as Caernarfon. She loves him and becomes his wife.

Elen inspired Macsen to construct roads across Wales, including the famous Sarn Helen, which is named after her and stretches from Aberconwy to Carmarthen. Many parts of Sarn Helen are integrated into the modern road network, and Elen is regarded as the patron saint of British road builders and the protector of travellers.

Elen is also credited with introducing the Celtic form of monasticism to Wales from Gaul, and is the patron of the churches of Llanelen in Gower and Penisa'r-waun near Caernarfon.

23 MAY

A memorial to Gwenllian ferch Gruffydd was unveiled at Kidwelly Castle on 23 May 1991.

She is thought to have been born around 1106, and she was the daughter of Gruffydd ap Cynan, Prince of Gwynedd. Gwenllian was also the wife of Gruffydd ap Rhys, Prince of Deheubarth in southwest Wales.

In 1136 Gwenllian's husband travelled north to seek support against the Norman Lord of Kidwelly, Maurice de Londres, who was threatening war against the Welsh. Gwenllian received news that a large force of Norman reinforcements had been dispatched to swell de Londres' army at Kidwelly. She realised that she could not wait for her husband's return. She donned chain mail and armed herself with a sword and set out with her two sons and a small army.

Gwenllian and her soldiers could not take on the might of the Normans in battle. So a group approached Kidwelly Castle stealthily, while she sent half of her men ahead to attack the Norman ships. However, they were betrayed by Gruffydd ap Llywelyn to the enemy and the small army was ambushed.

Gwenllian's forces were outnumbered. One of her sons was killed while defending his mother. Gwenllian, her other son and her surviving men were taken captive. She was beheaded by de Londres in front of her son on the battlefield.

It is claimed that Gwenllian's headless ghost, unable to rest until her head is returned to her grave, walks across the field beside Kidwelly Castle where her final battle took place to this day.

24 MAY

On 24 May 2007, record-breaking adventurer Tori James from Pembrokeshire became the first Welsh woman to reach the top of Mount Everest. She was also just twenty-five years of age, making her the youngest British woman to achieve the feat.

Tori was also a member of the first all-female team to complete the Polar Challenge, a 360-nautical-mile race to the Magnetic North Pole. She set the record for the longest open sea kayak crossing in UK waters (200 km) and has cycled the length of New Zealand, a distance of 2,400 km.

Tori is now a motivational speaker who challenges people to learn about themselves in her adventure-inspired training sessions. She is president of Girlguiding Cymru, a Fellow of British Exploring and an ambassador for the Duke of Edinburgh's Award in Wales.

25 MAY

The first national gathering in support of establishing a Welsh League of Nations was convened on 25 May 1920 in Llandrindod Wells and resulted in the Welsh League of Nations Union (WLNU) being founded in 1922.

During its conference at Aberystwyth University in 1923, the head of the WLNU's women's committee, Annie Hughes-Griffiths, from Llangeitho, suggested sending a petition from the women of Wales to the women of the USA asking them to persuade their government to join and lead the League of Nations. The petition was distributed to every household in Wales, and was signed by 390,296 women – 30 per cent of Wales's female population at the time.

Annie headed up the delegation in 1924 that took the petition to America with the financial backing of philanthropists Gwendoline and Margaret Davies (see 31 July). She was joined by Mary Ellis, a prominent educationalist from Dolgellau; Elined Prys, a leading psychologist from Trefeca; and her friend and travelling companion, Gladys Thomas.

In the US, the press noted that if the signature sheets were laid end-to-end they would go on for seven miles. Annie travelled all over the country and then presented the petition to US President Calvin Coolidge.

Although America did not sign up to the League of Nations, American women's organisations were inspired to form The National Committee on the Cause and Cure of War, which held its first conference in 1924. This organisation continued until 1939, when it was effectively ended by the start of the Second World War. However, the vision shared by the women's movements of Wales and America was finally realised in 1945, with the founding of the United Nations, in which America has played a leading role.

26 MAY

On 26 May 1568 a congress of bards and musicians took place at Caerwys on the orders of Queen Elizabeth I. Wales has a long history of bardic tradition that is mainly dominated by male figures. But there is one female medieval poet whose substantial body of work survives to this day: Gwerful Mechain from Powys.

Unfortunately, little else is known about Gwerful's life. We think that she was from the *cantref* (medieval Welsh land division) of Mechain, situated north of Welshpool.

Gwerful wrote her verses in strict metres and used *cynghanedd* (a way of arranging sounds within a single line commonly used in Welsh-language poetry). Her subject material was far from conventional, though. She composed some of the most direct and sexually uninhibited poetry in the Welsh language, even directly addressing female sexuality in her 'Ode to the Vagina', as well as a range of domestic issues affecting medieval women.

Gwerful was regarded as an equal by her male contemporaries. She worked within the poetic culture of her day while at the same time challenging and subverting it.

27 MAY

Today is the feast day of St Melangell, the patron saint of hares and rabbits.

In AD 604, Prince Brochwel Ysgithrog of Powys was hunting in the Tanat Valley when his hounds chased a hare into a thicket. There they found a beautiful maiden at prayer. The hare sheltered under the hem of her garment for protection, and the dogs fled despite their master's urging.

The Prince discovered that the lady was Melangell, a king's daughter who had fled Ireland to escape a forced marriage. He gave her the valley as a place of sanctuary. Melangell remained there, where she founded a nunnery. There is a shrine honouring her at St Melangell's Church in the former village of Pennant Melangell.

28 MAY

Australian pop singer, songwriter, and actress Kylie Minogue was born in Melbourne, Australia on 28 May 1968.

Kylie's role in the television soap series *Neighbours* brought her widespread recognition, but it was as a pop artist that she became globally popular. She has sold over eighty million records and she is the only female vocalist to have topped the UK album chart in five consecutive decades.

Kylie's mother Carol Jones was a dancer born in Maesteg, where her family ran the local post office, and her great-grandmother Megan Hughes was born in Blaenau Ffestiniog. Kylie's grandmother, Millie, celebrated her 101st birthday in 2020. Kylie and her sister, Dannii, both refer to Millie as *nain*.

29 MAY

On 29 May 1953, journalist Jan Morris was the first to report that Edmund Hillary and Tenzing Norgay had reached the summit of Everest.

Jan Morris (born James Humphry Morris; 1926–2020) was an acclaimed historian, author and travel writer. She was born in Somerset to an English mother and a Welsh father. Despite being born and largely raised in England, she always identified as Welsh and became a dedicated Welsh nationalist.

After graduating from Christ Church, Oxford, Morris served during the Second World War before becoming a newspaper correspondent covering high-profile stories such as the Suez Crisis (1956) and the trials of Francis Gary Powers, the US spy plane pilot in Moscow (1960) and the Nazi war criminal Adolf Eichmann (1961). She also interviewed Che Guevara and the British intelligence defector Guy Burgess.

In 1949, Jan married Elizabeth Tuckniss and the couple settled in Llanystumdwy. Jan began transitioning from a man to a woman in 1964. In 1972 she underwent sex reassignment surgery, becoming one of the first high-profile figures to do so. She detailed her transition in *Conundrum* (1974), her first book under her new name.

Morris received honorary doctorates from the University of Wales and the University of Glamorgan, was an honorary fellow of Christ Church, Oxford, and was a fellow of the Royal Society of Literature. She was elected to the Gorsedd Cymru in 1992 as well as receiving the Glyndŵr Award for Outstanding Contribution to the Arts in Wales in 1996. Jan died in 2020 at the age of ninety-four and was survived by her wife Elizabeth and their four children.

30 MAY

Some think that 30 May AD 542 was the date of the death of King Arthur. Arthur is one of the most famous characters in Welsh legend, and his exploits have been written about for centuries. An important figure in the world of Arthurian legend is Arthur's queen, Guinevere.

Although there is scant evidence to link Guinevere to a real historical figure, the earliest mention of Guinevere is in Geoffrey of Monmouth's twelfth-century *History of the Kings of Britain* which refers to her as Guenhuvara (in Welsh, Gwenhwyfar). Some stories from Welsh mythology focus on her infidelity and fickleness. However, in Monmouth's version, she is described as a queen of great beauty descended from the Romans. In Arthur's absence, she is seduced by his traitorous nephew, Mordred, who seizes Arthur's kingdom.

Other later versions see Guinevere either as a sultry seductress who seeks revenge when her amorous advances are spurned, or as a hapless victim of kidnapping who becomes infatuated with her rescuer, Sir Lancelot.

Perhaps the most famous example of a more Christianised version of the legend is Thomas Malory's *Le Morte d'Arthur* (1485). Here Guinevere, though not in love with Arthur, was his loyal, dutiful wife until she met Lancelot. They fell passionately in love but tried to conceal their affair from Arthur. When discovered, Guinevere elected to join a convent to spend her life in penitent devotion to God and the service of others, and Lancelot renounced the life of a knight to live a humble Christian existence.

31 MAY

On the 31 May, for many years, the people of Coventry commemorated the ride Lady Godiva of Mercia made on horseback, naked, through the marketplace of the city in 1043.

Lady Godiva's granddaughter, Ealdgyth, became Queen Consort of all of Wales from 1057 until 1063 when she married Gruffydd ap Llywelyn, the only Welsh King who ruled over the entire territory of Wales.

Ealdgyth (Edith) was the daughter of Ælfgar, Earl of Mercia, who formed an alliance with Gruffydd ap Llywelyn to resist the growing power of the Godwinsons. However, by 1063, both Gruffydd and Ælfgar had been killed and Ealdgyth had become the wife and queen consort of Harold Godwinson, King of England. Harold was killed at the Battle of Hastings in 1066 during the invasion by the Normans.

1 JUNE

On 1 June 2013, the Wales national women's netball team won the European Netball Championship for the first time.

Liz Nicholl from Barry, a former Wales netball international, has held many high-profile roles in British sport including, from 2010–19, chief executive of UK Sport and president of World Netball. She has been awarded numerous awards including the *Sunday Times* Sports Administrator of the Year Award, the Sports Journalists Association (SJA) Gold Medal for services to elite sport, and the British Sport Industry Lifetime Achievement Award. In 2023 Liz was appointed as Dame Commander of the Order of the British Empire (DBE).

Helen Weston from Cwmbran is a former captain and the record holder for the most Wales netball caps (112). In 2007 she became the only netball player, to date, to be inducted into the Welsh Sports Hall of Fame.

2 JUNE

The Merthyr Rising of 1831 was the result of simmering unrest against unjust and unfair working and living conditions. On 2 June 1831, a critical and ultimately defining flashpoint occurred during the rising when an angry crowd were confronted by soldiers who opened fire. In the resulting melee, at least sixteen of the protestors were killed and hundreds were seriously injured, including a soldier who was stabbed with a seized bayonet.

There was a notable female presence at the uprising. Many women were actively involved and others made pikes for an anticipated siege. When order had finally been returned and the soldiers were marched out of Merthyr, women are reported to have lined the road, jeering the kilt-wearing Highlanders with cries of, 'Go home and put some trousers on.'

Twenty-six people were arrested and put on trial in the aftermath. The sentences issued by the judge included periods of hard labour, imprisonment and penal transportation to Australia. Two were sentenced to death by hanging: Lewis Lewis (Lewsyn yr Heliwr) whose sentence was later commuted to one of transportation for life, and Dic Penderyn (born Richard Lewis) who was controversially hanged on 13 August 1831. Also on trial were two women. Joan Jenkins was identified as one of the leaders of the rising, and Margaret Davies, was thought to have been involved in an attack on the house of a court official. Both Joan and Margaret were sentenced to hard labour with the judge saying they should not be spared punishment because they were women.

3 JUNE

Rose Mary Crawshay (née Yeates) organised the first public meeting in Wales to discuss the issue of alcohol at the Temperance Hall in Merthyr Tydfil on 3 June 1870. Rose was a philanthropist and an early promoter of women's rights.

Rose was born in Caversham Grove in Oxfordshire. In 1846, she married the twenty-nine-year-old Robert Thompson Crawshay, the owner of Cyfarthfa ironworks and often referred to as the 'Iron King of Wales'. Cyfarthfa ironworks was, at one point, the biggest in the world and made the Crawshays extremely wealthy. Their home was the lavish seventy-two-room Cyfarthfa Castle of which Rose became the mistress.

Rose displayed a genuine social conscience and organised soup kitchens for the iron workers and set up classes to encourage women to make their own clothes. In 1862, when forty-nine men and boys were killed following the Gethin Pit explosion in Abercanaid, Rose personally visited every family affected. Rose was also a supporter of women's rights and suffrage and used her wealth to support campaigns to get women the vote.

Rose financially supported the establishment of Vaynor and Penderyn High School and was also one of the first women to sit on a local education board. She helped form the Swansea Training College which was the first facility in Wales where women could train to be qualified teachers, and established seven free cottage libraries to promote the benefits of literacy in south Wales. She created the Byron, Shelley, Keats In Memoriam Prize Fund in 1888, the only UK literary prize, at the time, for female scholars. In the same year the British Academy established The Rose Mary Crawshay Prize for non-fiction women writers.

4 JUNE

One of the many extraordinary feats in the life of Vulcana, at the time known as the strongest woman in the world, took place in Edinburgh on 4 June 1921, when she risked her life to save another act's horses at the Garrick Theatre when the venue caught fire.

Miriam Kate Williams (6 May 1874–8 August 1946), better known by her stage name 'Vulcana', was born in Abergavenny, where her father was a Baptist minister.

Kate performed extraordinary feats of strength from a young age. In school she astonished her friends by carrying the school organ. She became a professional strongwoman at the age of fifteen. Together with her partner William Hedley Roberts,who went under the stage name Atlas, she toured music halls throughout the UK and Ireland and travelled extensively in Australia, France and Spain. She juggled with a 56 lb dumbbell in each hand, used a 224 lb barbell and could raise and hold above her head at arm's length a man weighing over twelve stone. On 29 May at Haggar's Theatre in Llanelli, Vulcana lifted a challenge ball that rival strongwoman Athelda (Frances Rheinlander) had failed to raise after twenty-five minutes of trying.

As well as weightlifting, Vulcana was a talented wrestler, swimmer and fencing champion, winning hundreds of medals for her achievements. She was also involved in many acts of heroism, for which she received awards for bravery. As well as rescuing the horses in Edinburgh – which caused her serious burns – she rescued two children from drowning in the River Usk in July 1901.

> **DID YOU KNOW?**
> Vulcana was passionate about promoting women's fitness, and advocated for 'sensible clothing and vigorous exercise for all young women'. She was vehemently opposed to corsets and advised girls not to wear them.

5 JUNE

HIV Long-Term Survivors Day is observed on 5 June, the day in 1981 when the first reports of what would become known as AIDS were made by doctors in Los Angeles.

Cardiff-based Lisa Power came out as a lesbian in the 1970s, a time when homosexuality was still controversial in British society. As a volunteer in the 1980s at the London Lesbian and Gay Switchboard, Lisa saw at first hand the devastating impact that the disease was having on people's lives. She channelled her anger at the discrimination faced by the gay community into relentless campaigning.

Lisa was one of the founding members of the lesbian and gay rights charity Stonewall, established in 1989, and the first openly gay person to speak at the United Nations in 1991. She was a director of the Terrence Higgins Trust and introduced National HIV Testing Week in the UK and then in Europe.

Lisa continued to work and volunteer as an LGBTQ+ and sexual health activist with groups such as Fast Track Cardiff and Vale. She is also a trustee of Pride Cymru and was named on the 2017 Pinc List of leading Welsh LGBTQ+ figures.

Another Welsh woman who has had a massive impact in the battle against HIV was Margaret Tisdale (née Breeze; 1950–2015), from Welshpool. Margaret was an internationally renowned clinical virologist who, during a thirty-three-year career with GlaxoSmithKline, was instrumental in developing treatments for HIV and AIDS as well as drugs to prevent the development of influenza.

6 JUNE

Susan Caroline Williams-Ellis was born on this day in 1918, and went on to create the iconic Portmeirion Pottery brand.

Susan was the daughter of Sir Bertram Clough Williams-Ellis, architect and creator of the holiday resort of Portmeirion. At sixteen, she was sent to Dartington Hall School in Devon, where she was taught pottery by Bernard and David Leach. It was an interest she returned to after working as a map-maker during the Second World War. After the war, she returned to Wales. Alongside her husband, she built up the Portmeirion Pottery business, developing her own ranges and designs which have become well loved worldwide. She also worked as a book illustrator and painter, before retiring in 2005.

7 JUNE

Gwenllian ferch Llywelyn (born 1282) died on this day in 1337. Her father was Llywelyn ap Gruffydd, Prince of Wales. Her mother was Eleanor de Montfort (see 8 July), the daughter of Simon de Montfort, 6th Earl of Leicester and granddaughter of King John of England.

Eleanor died during or shortly after giving birth to her and Gwenllian was raised by her father at the royal home in Abergwyngregyn.

This was a time when Wales was struggling to maintain its independence. When Edward I invaded Wales, Llywelyn was killed and Wales subsequently became subjugated by England. Gwenllian's guardianship was then assumed by her uncle, Dafydd ap Gruffydd. Dafydd, his wife Elizabeth Ferrars and daughter Gwladys were being pursued by the forces of Edward I. When they were eventually captured, Dafydd was executed and Gwenllian was abducted by Edward. She was confined for life to the convent at Gilbertine Priory at Sempringham to stop her from becoming a focus for Welsh discontent but also to prevent her from having heirs who might lay claim to her native Welsh royal legacy. Gwladys was sent to Sixhills convent in Lincolnshire where she died in 1336.

Elizabeth's fate is not known for certain, but she would never see any of her children again and is thought to have been buried at the parish church in Caerwys.

There is a memorial stone of Welsh blue slate in Gwenllian's name in Sempringham.

8 JUNE

On 8 June 2008, Helen Jenkins from Bridgend won her first Triathlon World Championship, an achievement she repeated in 2011. She is one of the sport's most decorated athletes, achieving more World Triathlon Series podium finishes than any other British woman and representing Team GB in three Olympic Games (2008, 2012 and 2016).

Other notable Welsh women triathletes include:

- **Leanda Cave** was the 2002 World Triathlon Champion. She also won the 2012 Ironman Triathlon and the Ironman 70.3, becoming the first woman in the history of the sport to win both these titles in the same year.

- **Rachael Bland** was a journalist and presenter from Cardiff. After she was diagnosed with breast cancer, she created a podcast *You, Me and the Big C*. Rachel competed in many triathlons to raise funds for Breast Cancer Care, prior to her death from the disease in 2018, aged forty.

- **Anneliese Heard** comes from Bassaleg near Newport. She completed her first triathlon at the age of eight and became British Juvenile Champion at the age of twelve. She was crowned World Junior Champion in both 1999 and 2000.

- **Holly Lawrence** is a triathlete who competed for Wales in the mixed relay event at the Commonwealth Games in 2014. She went on to win the 2016 Ironman 70.3 World Championship.

- **Non Stanford** was born in Bridgend. She was World Triathlon Champion in 2013 and, despite struggling with recurrent injuries, she became European Champion in 2022, her final year of competing.

9 JUNE

The town of Milford Haven was founded on 9 June 1790, when Sir William Hamilton obtained, by Act of Parliament, permission to develop the land on the northern shore of the Milford Haven waterway. Situated in a natural harbour, the town was intended to be a whaling centre. By 1800 it had developed into a Royal Navy dockyard.

Julie-Anne Wood began her coastguard career as a watch assistant in Milford Haven in 1999. In 2017 she made history when she became the UK's Head of Maritime Operations at the Maritime and Coastguard Agency and the first woman to hold the role since the establishment of the coastguard in 1822.

DID YOU KNOW?

William Hamilton was able to establish Milford Haven as he and his wife Catherine had inherited the Slebach estate from her father. William became British Ambassador to Naples in 1764, he and Catherine entertained on a grand scale. Among their guests in 1770 were none other than Wolfgang Amadeus Mozart and his father, who complimented Catherine's skill at the harpsichord as 'uncommonly moving'.

10 JUNE

The opening of the railway line connecting Newtown to Oswestry on 10 June 1861 was instrumental in transforming the local drapery business of Eleanor and Pryce Pryce-Jones from a small rural concern into a booming global business.

Eleanor, a local dressmaker, married Pryce, a draper's assistant, in 1859. They set up a shop selling drapery. Access to the rail network enabled them to supply Welsh flannel to markets in England, the rest of Europe, the United States and Australia. They are credited with establishing the world's first mail-order catalogue which boasted Queen Victoria and Florence Nightingale as customers. They invented a combination of a rug, shawl, blanket and pillow, which later became known as the sleeping bag and was used by the German Army during the Franco-Prussian War of 1870–1. They went on to build the iconic Royal Welsh Warehouse, which had its own post office, next to the railway line in the centre of Newtown.

Eleanor became a central figure in community life in Newtown. She was president of the Newtown Needlework Guild that supplied clothing and textiles to British troops and was the driving force behind both her husband's and son's subsequent political careers. She and her husband also funded the construction of the All Saints Church in Llanllwchaearn, which was presented to the parish in 1888.

The success of the Newtown woollen industry was short-lived. By the 1880s, the absence of local supplies of coal to power the machinery and competition from the larger mills in the north of England caused it to decline.

11 JUNE

Born on this day in 1863, Millicent Hughes Mackenzie was the first female professor in Wales and the first woman to stand for a Welsh seat in parliament when she was a candidate in the general election held on 14 December 1918. There were seventeen women candidates in Britain that year, but only Millicent stood for a Welsh constituency.

Millicent Mackenzie was born in Bristol and became the professor of education at the University College of South Wales and Monmouthshire (later Cardiff University) in 1908. She was not only the first female professor in Wales but the first appointed to a fully chartered university in the entire United Kingdom. She was the author of many books on teacher training. Much of her work focused on methods for preparing teachers for working in schools and she advocated for coeducational education, where male and female students are taught together.

Millicent became a founder member of the Cardiff branch of the suffragette movement in 1912. She was also a supporter of the humanist movement and promoted moral, rather than religious, education. In 1915, she retired and embarked on lecture tours with her husband through India, Burma (Myanmar), Ceylon (Sri Lanka), Europe and America.

Millicent died in 1942. In 2023 a public park behind the Amgueddfa Genedlaethol Caerdydd (National Museum Cardiff) was opened and named in her honour.

12 JUNE

Margaret Haig Mackworth (née Thomas) was born on this day 1883. She was raised at Llanwern House, near Newport, by her parents David Alfred Thomas, 1st Viscount Rhondda, prominent politician and industrialist, and Sybil Haig, a noted suffragette, feminist and philanthropist. Along with her father, she famously survived the sinking of RMS *Lusitania* in 1915.

Margaret became the secretary of the militant Women's Social and Political Union (WSPU) and was involved in many suffragette activities, especially in the Newport area. Most famously she set fire to a postbox and, when she was subsequently given a prison sentence, she went on hunger strike. In 1917 she became the commissioner of the Women's National Service for Wales and Monmouthshire which worked to recruit women to work in agriculture, and went on to fulfil a major new role in London as Chief Controller of women's recruitment in the Ministry of National Service.

In 1918 her father died and Margaret inherited his title and became Lady Rhondda. She fought a famous test case in an attempt to take her father's seat in the House of Lords, citing the Sex Disqualification Act of 1919 which allowed women to take positions on professional bodies. Her request was ultimately refused but she lived to see the passage of the Life Peerages Act in 1958, which allowed for the creation of female peers and also entitled women to sit in the House of Lords. Unfortunately Margaret died just three months before she was able to take her seat.

13 JUNE

National Sewing Machine Day is 13 June and celebrates the invention of one of the world's most important innovations. Asmaa Al-Allak, from Cardiff, was named as Britain's best home seamstress when she won the BBC reality show *The Great British Sewing Bee* in 2023.

Asmaa, a consultant breast surgeon with the Cwm Taf Morgannwg University Health Board, was born in Iraq but has made Wales her home. Her family left war-torn Iraq when she was fourteen. She met her husband while studying medicine in Cardiff. She then decided to settle in the city with her husband and two children. Asmaa found her love of sewing by watching and learning from her grandmother, who was a seamstress. She now specialises in making underwear and has made post-op bras for her breast-cancer patients.

She said after winning the show, 'I have always counted myself as adopted Welsh, my children were born in Wales and I have lived most of my life in Wales. I really hope I have made them proud because I am proud of Wales.'

14 JUNE ⚠

The Battle of Naseby, fought on this day in 1645, resulted in a decisive victory for the Parliamentarian New Model Army, commanded by Sir Thomas Fairfax and Oliver Cromwell, over the Royalist army under Charles I and Prince Rupert during the first English Civil War.

In the aftermath, the Parliamentarian cavalry were in pursuit of fleeing Royalists when they came across a large group of women. On hearing them speak in an unfamiliar language, the English soldiers assumed that the women

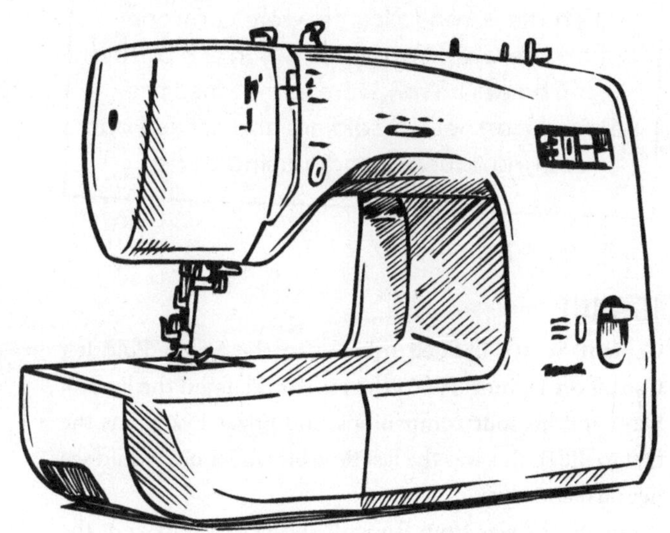

were Irish Catholics and, given Cromwell's antipathy towards Catholicism, they killed over a hundred and mutilated many others. The women were, in fact, camp followers of the Welsh Royalist regiments and the language they were speaking was Welsh.

DID YOU KNOW?

Female camp followers were common during the Civil War, especially in the armies of Charles I. They were sometimes the wives or partners of soldiers and carried out cooking, laundry and nursing duties.

15 JUNE

Captain Scott's ill-fated mission to the South Pole left Cardiff on 15 June 1910. The mission claimed the lives of Scott and his four companions, and Edgar Evans was the first to die so this was the last time his wife, Lois, would see her husband alive.

Lois Evans was from Rhossili and her parents kept the Old Ship Inn at Middleton. She campaigned tirelessly to restore her husband's reputation after he was blamed for the failure of the mission.

She had married Edgar on his return from Scott's first Antarctic exploratory expedition from 1901–4. The couple had made their home in Portsmouth where they had three children and where Edgar completed his Royal Navy training.

Edgar was part of the five-man team that attained the Pole on 17 January 1912. He was the first of the team to die on 17 February. His comrades all perished the following month and their bodies were not discovered for a further eight months.

While her husband was away, Lois and her three young children had been forced to move back to Gower. It was here, before confirmation of their loved ones' deaths had reached the families, that she was doorstepped by journalists. Unlike the other widows, Lois was a working-class woman and therefore didn't have the protection of high society or financial security and she was hounded by reporters. They wanted someone to blame for the tragic outcome of the expedition and Edgar was the target of their ire. Lois showed great resilience and strength in defending her husband's reputation.

Lois had a memorial plaque to Edgar placed in the church at Rhossili and he is also remembered with the Edgar Evans Building at the naval establishment on Whale Island, Portsmouth. Lois never remarried. An official memorial to Edgar Evans was raised in 1994 and presented to the city of Swansea.

16 JUNE

On this day in 2008, actress and singer Sue Jones-Davies, from Dinas Cross, near Fishguard, became Mayor of Aberystwyth. Upon taking office, she was able to lift a long-standing local ban on the film *Monty Python's Life of Brian* in which she had played the part of Judith Iscariot.

When it was released in 1978 the film was considered to be controversial and some religious groups accused it of being blasphemous. Thirty-nine local authorities in the UK banned the film, as did entire countries such as Ireland and Norway.

The film was eventually screened at the Aberystwyth Arts Centre on 28 March 2009 with cast members and the co-writers of the film, Michael Palin and Terry Jones, in attendance.

17 JUNE

On 17 June 1928, American aviator Amelia Earhart left Trepassey Harbor, Newfoundland with pilot Wilmer Stultz. When they arrived at Pwll near Burry Port, twenty hours and forty minutes later, she became the first woman to fly across the Atlantic Ocean. Their historic flight is commemorated by the Amelia Earhart Gardens in Burry Port.

In 1933, Britain's most famous woman pilot, Amy Johnson, and her husband Jim Mollison (the 'Flying Sweethearts'), took off from the Pendine Sands beach, south Wales, in their attempt to fly non-stop across the Atlantic. Huge crowds congregated on the beach during the three weeks of preparations for the flight. They were blown off course and crash-landed at Bridgeport, Connecticut, after flying for thirty-nine hours and covering a distance of 3,300 miles at an average speed of 85 mph. However, both were uninjured.

Three Welsh women served as pilots during the Second World War. They were Pamela Duncan, Katie Doreen Williams and Suzanne Ashton. Suzanne continued to work as a commercial pilot after the war.

18 JUNE

The Battle of Waterloo took place on 18 June 1815. Few people know that this famous battle has a historic connection to two Welsh women.

Jenny Jones from the hamlet of Tal-y-llyn, near Machynlleth was certainly a camp follower responsible for cooking, laundry and nursing the wounded but she may also have fought at the battle.

Jenny was born in Ireland (probably in Granard in County Longford) and met Lewis Griffiths from Tal-y-llyn when he was stationed there with the Royal Merionethshire Militia. The couple were married, apparently against the wishes of Jenny's family, and returned to live in Wales.

In 1814, Lewis joined the 23rd Regiment (Royal Welch Fusiliers) and travelled with the army to fight Napoleon in Europe, accompanied by Jenny and their six-month-old daughter. During the fierce fighting, Lewis was injured and the chapel in which Jenny was sheltering suffered a direct hit, killing many but sparing her. The couple were separated. After the battle, Jenny searched for Lewis and eventually found him in a Brussels hospital.

Lewis and Jenny rejoined the regiment for the rest of the campaign, after which they returned home to Tal-y-llyn, where Lewis found work in Aberllefenni quarry. But their lives were to end in tragedy. Lewis received no pension, his Waterloo Medal was stolen and he was then killed in a quarry accident in 1837. Jenny remarried, but when her second husband died, leaving her with nine children, she became dependent on the Dolgellau Poor Union. She died in poverty in 1884 and is buried in Tal-y-llyn parish churchyard.

19 JUNE

On 19th June 2024, the Welsh Assembly voted to support plans to introduce a dedicated British Sign Language Bill for Wales.

Instrumental in raising the profile of BSL in the UK is nineteen-year-old Hafwen Clarke from Aberystwyth, who made history on 13 May 2024 by becoming the first person to deliver a speech using BSL at Buckingham Palace as she received her gold Duke of Edinburgh Award.

In her speech she paid tribute to the support her family has given her over the years, encouraging her to push herself. She is keen to encourage other deaf and disabled young people to get involved and participate in social, cultural and educational activities.

Hafwen is trilingual with BSL being her first language followed by Welsh and English. She is now a Duke of Edinburgh ambassador in Wales, and has said that she wants to be 'a voice for young people with disabilities'.

20 JUNE

Born this day 1974 in Swansea, Non Evans is a sportswoman who has represented Wales in four different sports: rugby union, wrestling, weightlifting and judo. She is the first woman to have competed at the Commonwealth Games in two different sports.

She is a former captain of the national women's rugby team and Wales's all-time leading points scorer, having scored sixty-four tries. In judo, Non won a silver medal at both the 1992 and 1996 Commonwealth Judo Championships and competed for Wales at the 2002 Commonwealth Games. In weightlifting, she competed at the 2002 Commonwealth Games and in wrestling, she came second at the 2010 British Championships, which earned her selection for the 2010 Commonwealth Games.

21 JUNE ⚠

Rhiannon, the goddess of horses, forgiveness, rebirth, the moon and fertility is an important figure in Welsh mythology and early Celtic religion. She is also closely associated with the summer solstice that nearly always falls on 21 June.

The summer solstice is the first day of astronomical summer and the longest day of the year for people in the Northern Hemisphere. In ancient times, solstices and equinoxes were important in helping people to develop calendars and grow crops. It has been a special moment of the annual cycle of the year since Neolithic times and, over the centuries, has been marked by festivals and celebrations.

Rhiannon, a beautiful goddess, is featured in the stories from the *Mabinogion*. She first appears near Gorsedd Arberth (Narberth), the chief court of Pwyll the Prince of Dyfed. She is riding a shining white horse and Pwyll immediately falls in love with her. Riding his own horse, he tries to catch up to Rhiannon and even though her horse does no more than amble, he is unable to. After three days, when he can ride no more, Pwyll appeals to Rhiannon to stop, which she duly does, telling him that all he had to do was ask.

Rhiannon and Pwyll are married and she gives birth to a son, Pryderi, who mysteriously goes missing. The servants, fearing they will be blamed, come up with an elaborate deception by killing a puppy and smearing Rhiannon's face with its blood as she is sleeping. They then scatter the bones all around her making it look as though Rhiannon has eaten her baby. Their deception works and Rhiannon is thought to have murdered her own son. As punishment, she is forced to act as a horse, carrying visitors into the royal court. However, seven years later, Pryderi arrives at the gate of the court. He and his mother immediately recognise each other. And Rhiannon's good name is restored.

22 JUNE

The Windrush Generation are commemorated on 22 June, which is Windrush Day.

On 22 June 1948, the passenger liner HMT *Empire Windrush* arrived at Tilbury Docks, Essex. The vessel carried 1,027 Afro-Caribbean immigrants who had come in response to a government campaign to attract workers to rebuild Britain in the aftermath of the Second World War. They were followed by many more large groups of Commonwealth citizens who came to live and work in Britain between 1948 and 1971. They are referred to as the Windrush Generation and, despite having made an invaluable and lasting contribution to life in Wales, many have encountered hostility, racial discrimination, threats of detention and deportation as well as being denied access to healthcare. These injustices began to be revealed as part of the Windrush Scandal in 2017.

That same year, Roma Taylor, who had emigrated from Antigua to Cardiff in 1959 when she was fifteen, launched Windrush Cymru Elders to advocate for the now-ageing Windrush Generation and promote an understanding of ethnic minority concerns and needs while also celebrating key milestones and marking the contribution of people of African descent.

Roma recalled that her first memories of Cardiff were a far cry from the lush foliage and fresh blue waters of Antigua. She remembers 'all these chimneys'. She embraced her new home immediately: a 1959 photograph shows a fifteen-year-old Roma in full Welsh costume on the national day in Butetown. She served in the army nursing corps and later became a foster parent to over twenty children, even though she had a big family herself (seven children, twenty-five grandchildren and eighteen great-grandchildren).

Roma said of her decision to establish Windrush Cymru Elders: 'I wanted to look after these elders who were at home alone twiddling their thumbs with no one to take them to go shopping or to the hospital, no one to ask them if they needed anything and so on. Some of them have no one, some of them have no families, and that is very sad.'

Roma was awarded a British Empire Medal in 2024 for her tireless efforts and dedication in helping others in her Welsh community.

23 JUNE ⚠

Born on this day 1984 in Bangor, Duffy (Aimée Anne Duffy), is a singer-songwriter, best known for her hit songs 'Mercy' and 'Warwick Avenue'.

Duffy and her twin sister Katy were raised in Nefyn on the Llŷn Peninsula and moved to Pembrokeshire with their mother when their parents divorced. Returning to Nefyn at the age of fifteen to live with her father, Duffy started singing with various local bands. She got her big break in 2003 when she finished second on the Welsh television talent show *Wawffactor* (*Wow Factor*). Her debut album *Rockferry* reached number one in the UK charts and was also 2008's bestselling album, bringing her international acclaim and a Grammy award in 2009. In 2010, she made her acting debut in the film *Patagonia*.

In 2011, Duffy disappeared from the spotlight. After many years of silence and avoiding the media, she revealed in 2020 that she had been the victim of an abduction and rape. She told reporters that she had disappeared so she could recover. That year she also posted two unreleased songs. 'I can tell you in the last decade, the thousands and thousands of days I committed to wanting to feel the sunshine in my heart again,' she told an interviewer, 'the sun does now shine.'

24 JUNE

Following the death of her brother Gilbert at the Battle of Bannockburn on 24 June 1314, Eleanor de Clare inherited the Lordship of Glamorgan based at Caerphilly Castle. Eleanor, the 6th Lady of Glamorgan (3 October 1292–30 June 1337) was a remarkable and prominent figure in Welsh politics in the early fourteenth century.

Eleanor was the daughter of the infamous Gilbert de Clare, Lord of Glamorgan, who built Caerphilly Castle and was a leading military commander in Edward I's campaigns to subjugate Wales. Eleanor's mother was the daughter of King Edward I.

In 1306, when she was thirteen, Eleanor married the highly ambitious and infamous Hugh le Despenser the Younger. The couple rose to prominence as favourites. Hugh was even rumoured to be the King Edward II's lover. When the king was deposed in 1326 by his estranged wife, Queen Isabella and her lover, Roger Mortimer, Hugh was executed for high treason. Eleanor was imprisoned in the

Tower of London and only released on the agreement that she sign over her titles and lands to Roger Mortimer. She was released and her lands restored to her in 1328.

In 1329, Eleanor was abducted by, or according to some sources she eloped with, the knight William la Zouche. Although William was one of Eleanor's first husband's captors, they married. However, she was imprisoned again, accused of stealing jewels from the Tower of London. Although she was released in 1330 she was only restored to her titles and land again when Edward III overthrew and executed Roger Mortimer later that year.

25 JUNE

Mary Rose Tudor (born 18 March 1496) died on this day in 1533. She was the daughter of Welsh-born King Henry VII and his wife Elizabeth of York. She was, by most accounts, the favourite sister of King Henry VIII: he named his first surviving daughter after her and it is likely he named his famous warship the *Mary Rose* in her honour.

Mary was described as one of the most beautiful princesses in Europe. In 1514, as part of a peace treaty with France, she married King Louis XII. Louis was fifty-two and died less than three months later. Rumours were that he was reputedly worn out by his efforts in the bedchamber, but it's more likely from the effects of gout.

Mary was deeply in love with Charles Brandon, the Duke of Suffolk, and the couple defied the king and got married in secret in 1515. Henry eventually forgave his sister but their relationship came under further strain when Mary disapproved of his divorce from his first wife, Catherine of Aragon.

26 JUNE

Mary Williams, born in Aberystwyth on 26 June 1883, was a pioneering academic in the fields of modern languages and medieval literature. She was the first woman to be appointed as head of department at a British university.

Mary studied French and German at University College of Wales and then spent two years as a secondary schoolteacher, while studying for a master's degree. She studied at both the National University of Ireland in Dublin and the Sorbonne University in Paris as part of her doctorate. In Paris she began research into the origins of the French Arthurian Romances – a subject which became her lifelong passion.

During the First World War, Mary was a lecturer of French and German at King's College London. This was despite anti-German sentiment driving most schools and universities to stop teaching German. Mary's argument was that a knowledge of the enemy's tongue was of service in the struggle against them.

In 1921, despite opposition from established (and likely male) members of the college council, Mary was appointed to the new post of Professor of French Language and Literature in the Department of Modern Languages at University College Swansea.

In 1934, the French government awarded Mary the Officier d'Academie, a distinguished academic award, and Chevalier de la Legion d'Honneur, the highest French order of merit, for promoting French language and literature to the Welsh nation.

Mary served as president of the Folklore Society between 1961 and 1963 and, throughout her life, she remained an enthusiastic promoter of Wales. She was the first president of the University of London's Welsh Society, president of the London Society of Old Aberystwythians, president and founder of the South Wales Branch of the Modern Language Association and an active member of the International Celtic Congress, as well as being a keen supporter and benefactor of Llyfrgell Genedlaethol Cymru (National Library of Wales).

27 JUNE

On this day in 2018, Nicola Davies, born in Llanelli in 1953 and raised in Bridgend, was appointed as a Lady Justice of Appeal or a judge of the Court of Appeal. She was the first Welsh woman to hold the title but, before that, she was also the first Welsh woman to hold the appointments of QC and High Court Judge.

She is now acknowledged as the most experienced medical defence KC in the UK. In 2021, she chaired the first all-female Court of Appeal session in Wales, sitting alongside Mrs Justice Jefford and Mrs Justice Steyn.

28 JUNE

On 28 June 1940, as the Second World War intensified, Rosalind Rusbridge (née Bevan), a well-known peace campaigner from Swansea, refused to sign the Declaration of Allegiance in support of the war. As a result, she lost her job as a teacher and her stall selling the publication *Peace News* in Swansea market was closed by the council.

Rosalind was educated at Swansea High School for Girls and later studied at the University of Cambridge. She obtained a Diploma of Education from the University of

Oxford before returning to Swansea to teach at Glanmôr Girls' School.

Rosalind was greatly affected by her father's experiences during the First World War. He had been awarded a Distinguished Conduct Medal for evacuating wounded soldiers but he had been exposed to poisonous gas on the battlefields and he died as a result of the effects in his fifties. She defined herself as a socialist and Christian pacifist she formed a pacifist group in Swansea. She also was one of the first women to become a member of the Peace Pledge Union. When the Second World War broke out she became a conscientious objector. She rented the stall at Swansea market, from where she distributed anti-war literature and spoke publicly about her support for pacifism.

After protests from teaching unions and civil liberty groups, the requirement to sign the declaration was reversed but, by then, Rosalind had already left Swansea to teach at Chester Boys' Grammar School and later Clifton High School for Girls, where she worked until she was nearly seventy. She continued to be a human rights and peace activist until her death. She was a representative for the southwest at the national body of the Christian Campaign for Nuclear Disarmament (CCND) and protested at United States military bases at Aldermaston and Greenham Common.

Rosalind's story is recorded in the film, *Swansea Conchie Controversy* (1988) and in the book, *Parachutes and Petticoats* (1992).

29 JUNE

On 29 June 1812, at Covent Garden, Sarah Siddons took to the stage as Lady Macbeth and gave what has been credited as the most extraordinary farewell performance in theatre history.

After the famous 'sleepwalking' scene in Shakespeare's *Macbeth* – which sees a guilt-ridden Lady Macbeth washing invisible blood from her hands and is the last time she appears in the play – the applause from the audience was so intense and prolonged that the play could not continue. When the curtain eventually reopened it revealed Sarah Siddons in her own clothes, no longer in the costume of her stage character. She delivered a highly emotional speech of farewell which lasted for a reported eight minutes before the curtain closed on her for the final time.

Sarah Siddons (née Kemble; 5 July 1755–8 June 1831), was born in the Shoulder of Mutton public house (now called the Sarah Siddons Inn) in Brecon. She would grow up to become reputedly the best actress of the eighteenth century.

Sarah was the eldest of twelve born to Roger and Sarah Kemble, a couple who were actor-managers for a company of travelling players. She received an education as a result of her mother's insistence on her attending school in the towns the company travelled to. She fell in love with and married, despite the disapproval of her parents, William Siddons, an actor in her father's troupe.

She made her first appearance on the London stage at Drury Lane in 1782, and was hailed as a 'sensation'. This sparkling debut was the beginning of a twenty-year career and she was dubbed the 'queen of Drury Lane'.

Many anecdotes testify to the power she had over her

audiences. While performing *Tamburlaine*, her cries of agony as she fell lifeless on the stage were so convincing that the audience believed she was actually dead, and it took the intervention of the theatre manager to persuade them that it was just part of her performance.

30 JUNE

Today is the feast day of St Eurgain, thought to be Britain's first female Christian saint. Her name has been linked to two Welsh churches through the work of the bard Iolo Morganwg so historical evidence of her life is limited.

According to one legend, Eurgain was the daughter of Maelgwn Gwynedd, a sixth-century King of Gwynedd. She married Elidyr Mwynfawr from the kingdom of Alt Clut (later known as Strathclyde). When Maelgwn died in c. AD 560, his illegitimate son Rhun claimed the throne of Gwynedd. This prompted Elidyr to invade Gwynedd with a large army to enforce Eurgain's claim to the throne. Rhun, however, was able to repel the invading force and Elidyr was defeated and killed at Llanbeblig near Caernarfon.

Eurgain is then thought to have begun spreading the word of Christianity in northeast Wales. The church of St Eurgain and St Peter in Llaneurgain (Northop) is dedicated to her and she is said to be buried on a hill near Criccin near Rhuddlan.

1 JULY

A series of reports on the state of education in Wales, were presented to the UK Government on 1 July 1847. The reports – which came to be known as 'The Blue Books' – concluded that the use of the Welsh language was impeding children's learning. They also resulted in the introduction of the Welsh Not: a wooden token hung around the necks of schoolchildren as a punishment for speaking in Welsh. The report also criticised poor social conditions in Wales, the Welsh Nonconformist religion and singled out what it considered to be the immorality of young Welsh women for particular criticism. It concluded that Welsh women, had a tendency to engage in hard physical work alongside men which meant that they lacked housewifely skills and this consequently made them poor wives. The reports were written by three English commissioners.

There was a furious reaction in Wales where the reports became known as *Brad Y Llyfrau Gleision* (The Treachery of the Blue Books). The outrage was especially felt by Welsh women and led to the publication of Wales's first magazine for women, *Y Gymraes* (*The Welsh Woman*). Elinor Evans (as Elen Egryn) wrote a poetic introduction to the first issue, in which she called for Welsh women to rise 'above shame and hateful mockery'. In 1850, Elinor's collection of poems *Telyn Egryn* (*Egryn's Harp*) was the first Welsh-language book to be published by a Welsh woman.

2 JULY

On this day in 1928, the Representation of the People (Equal Franchise) Act received Royal assent. It meant that all women, regardless of property ownership, could vote from the age of twenty-one bringing their rights in line with those of men. Millicent Fawcett wrote in her diary that day: 'It is almost exactly sixty-one years ago since I heard John Stuart Mill introduce his suffrage amendment to the Reform Bill on 20 May 1867. So I have had extraordinary good luck in having seen the struggle from the beginning.'

The following year, Edith Picton-Turbervill, a great supporter of Millicent Fawcett, was elected as the Member of Parliament for The Wrekin division in Shropshire.

Edith's father inherited the wealthy Turbervill estate of Ewenny Priory in Glamorgan in 1892. It was here that she first became politically aware after witnessing the squalid living conditions of workers building the Vale of Glamorgan Railway.

Edith's deep religious beliefs led her to join the Young Women's Christian Association (YWCA). She worked for them in India in 1900 before returning to Britain due to ill health. During the First World War, she rejoined the organisation and worked providing hostels and canteens

for the women munitions workers and members of the Women's Army Auxiliary Corps in France. She later served as national vice president for the YWCA. Edith was also a fervent campaigner for women to enter the priesthood and was the first woman to be invited to preach a sermon in a Church of England service.

As an MP, she was the first woman to sit on the Ecclesiastical Committee of Parliament and successfully campaigned for a law enacting that no pregnant woman should be executed.

3 JULY

Born this day 1958 in Maesteg, Siân Lloyd is the UK's longest-serving female weather forecaster, appearing on *ITV Weather* for twenty-four years.

Siân is the daughter of teachers and attended Ysgol Gymraeg Ystalyfera Bro Dur bilingual school, before graduating from University College, Cardiff. She then gained a meteorology qualification from the Met Office College.

She started her television career as a researcher at *BBC Wales Today* before working for S4C. While working for Worldwide Television News in London she was one of two hundred candidates who were screen-tested for *ITV Weather*. She fronted the show from 1990 to 2014. She has appeared as a contestant in television shows including *I'm a Celebrity… Get Me Out of Here!* and *Total Wipeout*. She published her autobiography *A Funny Kind of Love* in 2008.

Siân is proud of her Welsh roots and, in 1995, she helped to establish SWS (meaning 'kiss', and standing for 'Social, Welsh and Sexy'), a networking group for Welsh people living away from home.

4 JULY

Alice in Wonderland Day is 4 July, marking the day when author Lewis Carroll first told his story to Alice Liddell, the young girl who inspired him to write the famous novel.

Alice first came to the resort of Llandudno, with her family, in 1861 when she was eight. They stayed at the Tudno Villa Apartments, now the St Tudno Hotel on Llandudno's north shore. Later, the family built a holiday home named Penmorfa on the west shore.

Carroll was a close friend of the family and it is believed that it was hearing tales of Alice and her sisters' holiday adventures in Llandudno that inspired him to write *Alice in Wonderland*. Two rocks that sit prominently on Llandudno's west shore were known locally as the Walrus and the Carpenter, which were the names Carroll gave to characters in the sequel, *Alice Through the Looking Glass*.

Llandudno has always been proud of its *Wonderland* connection through Alice and has established the Alice Town Trail of locations that were thought to have inspired Carroll. There are wooden statues of *Wonderland* characters scattered around the town, a floral clock on the promenade and a jam-tart-eating competition is held during the town's annual Victorian Extravaganza.

5 JULY

Aneira Thomas, from Loughor, was born in Amman Valley Hospital at one minute past midnight on 5 July 1948. This was also the day the National Health Service was launched, making Aneira the first NHS baby.

Aneira was the youngest of seven and the only one of her siblings not to be born at home. Had she been born a day earlier, her mother would have had to pay for a hospital stay.

She was named after Aneurin Bevan, the Minister for Health and the driving force behind the idea that quality healthcare should be available to all, regardless of wealth or social status.

Aneira later had a career working in the NHS as a mental health nurse. Her two children were born in NHS hospitals as were her grandchildren. After her retirement she continued to be an active supporter of the NHS, speaking out on a range of issues in the media and at public rallies.

6 JULY

On 6 July 2016, Lydia Hall, from Bridgend, won the Welsh National PGA Championship, becoming the first woman golfer to win a PGA national tournament.

Other notable Welsh women golfers include:

- **Vicki Thomas** is probably Wales's greatest amateur golfer of either sex. She was Welsh Ladies Amateur Champion on eight occasions and played in every Curtis Cup against the Americans between 1982 and 1992. She was inducted into the Welsh Sports Hall of Fame in 1998.

- **Tegwen Matthews** from Cardiff was the first Welsh woman to compete in the Curtis Cup in 1974 and was the non-playing captain of the side that won the event in 2012.

7 JULY

The foundation stone for the telescopic observatory built at the Penllergare Estate is dated 7 July 1851. It was built by John Dillwyn Llewelyn as a gift for his scientifically minded daughter's sixteenth birthday. Her name was Thereza Dillwyn Llewelyn (1834–1926), and she was born at the Penllergare Estate, near Penllergaer, Swansea. Thereza would go on to become a prominent astronomer and a pioneer of scientific photography.

Thereza's family was interested in the fields of science and photography. Her father was a notable botanist and pioneering photographer. Her aunt, Mary Dillwyn, was one of Wales's earliest female photographers. And her mother's cousin, Henry Fox Talbot, was a famous scientist, inventor and photographic pioneer.

Although an unusual endeavour for women at the time, Thereza's father encouraged her interest in astronomy. From the Penllergare observatory, they produced some of the earliest photographs of the moon in the mid-1850s. It is also thought that Thereza may have observed Donati's Comet in 1858 before it was officially announced by the Italian astronomer credited with identifying it.

DID YOU KNOW?

Thereza was also a keen naturalist and corresponded with Charles Darwin, who was interested in her observations of birds taking nectar from flowers.

8 JULY

On 8 July 1279, Eleanor de Montfort penned a letter to her cousin Edward I in an effort to secure peace between Wales and England.

Eleanor de Montfort (1252–1282), was Princess of Wales, Lady of Snowdon and the wife of Llywelyn ap Gruffydd.

Eleanor was born at Kenilworth Castle, the only daughter of Simon de Montfort who was leader of the baronial revolt against the rule of Henry III and an ally of Llywelyn. Her mother was Eleanor of England, the daughter of King John.

In 1264, it was agreed that Eleanor (aged thirteen) and Llywelyn (aged forty-two) would marry, but her father was killed before the union could happen and Eleanor and her mother were forced to flee to France. When relations between Llywelyn and Edward I broke down in 1277, Edward invaded Wales and captured Eleanor on her way from France to marry Llywelyn.

Edward released Eleanor following the signing of a treaty with Llywelyn and the couple were married at Worcester Cathedral in 1278. Eleanor proved to be a key negotiator in trying to maintain peace between Wales and England evidenced by the 8 July letter where she assures Edward of Llywelyn's good intentions. However, the period of relative peace was shattered in March 1282 when Llywelyn's younger brother, Dafydd, attacked Hawarden Castle.

Eleanor died during or shortly after giving birth to her and Llywelyn's only child, Gwenllian (see 7 June) in 1282. Llywelyn was devastated and dispirited by his wife's death and was killed in an ambush at Cilmeri in December 1282, allowing Edward to complete the subjugation of Wales.

Eleanor is buried at the Franciscan Friary of Llanfaes on Anglesey.

9 JULY

On 9 July 1941, British cryptologists at Bletchley Park broke the secret Enigma codes used by the German army to direct ground-to-air operations. The subsequent intelligence gleaned made a significant contribution to the eventual Allied victory and the end of the Second World War.

Mair Russell-Jones from Pontycymer was among the code breakers hand-picked to serve at Bletchley Park. She was studying music and German at Cardiff University in August 1941 when she was headhunted by 'a man from the Foreign Office' to work in Hut Six at Station X (known now as Bletchley Park).

Mair worked eight-hour shifts every day with scientists, musicians, mathematicians and inventors. The work was intense – with up to 6,000 messages being dealt with daily.

She had signed the Official Secrets Act and so did not talk about her war work until 1998 when her son Gethin recognised her in a photograph of the women in front of Hut Six. He said of his mother: 'The fact she knew German … was a dab hand at crosswords and her knowledge of music … helped in her ability to see patterns in passages that needed to be decoded.' Mair's memoir *My Secret Life in Hut Six* was published in 2014, the year after she passed away.

10 JULY

Cymraeg 2050, the Welsh government's language strategy to achieve a million Welsh speakers by 2050, was published on 10 July 2017.

Notable women who have made contributions towards this vision are:

- **Philippa Gibson** is a Welsh tutor at Aberystwyth University, and was presented with the Inspire! Tutor Award for her exceptional contribution in helping adult learners to speak Welsh in 2020. Philippa learned Welsh as an adult after moving from Bristol. She has dedicated thirty years to developing the university's Welsh learning programme.

- **Christine James** was the first woman to be appointed Archdruid of the National Eisteddfod of Wales. She was also the first Welsh learner to be appointed to that role.

- **Eve Myles** is a Welsh actress with a long and successful career in television. She learned to speak Welsh for her role in the S4C drama *Un Bore Mercher (Keeping Faith).*

- **Carol Vorderman** spent two months learning the language as part of the reality show *Cariad@iaith (Love4language).* Carol then presented the weather on S4C in fluent Welsh.

- **Nushin Chavoshi-Nejad** is from Iran and Farsi is her first language. She became a fluent Welsh speaker after starting evening classes. She is now a Welsh tutor for Dysgu Cymraeg Morgannwg

(Learn Welsh Glamorgan), based at the University of South Wales, teaching the *Croeso i Bawb* (*All are Welcome*) course.

- **Alina Shestak** arrived from Kharkiv, Ukraine, as a refugee to stay with a host family in Merthyr Tydfil in 2022. She decided to learn Welsh after becoming a teaching assistant in a primary school. Alina took the *Croeso i Bawb* course in her local library and has now joined a choir and learned to sing '*Calon Lân*'.

11 JULY

Caitlin Macnamara (8 December 1913–31 July 1994) married the poet Dylan Thomas on 11 July 1937. Their marriage was a turbulent one but the couple remained together until Dylan's death in 1953 and she protected his legacy in later years.

Caitlin was introduced to Dylan in 1936 by the artist Augustus John. The attraction was immediate and that summer Dylan travelled to Laugharne, where Caitlin was staying at Castle House. By the end of 1936 the two were a couple and corresponded regularly.

After they married, they spent time in Chelsea, Oxford, Ireland and Italy before moving back to Laugharne and settling at the Boat House, which was purchased for them by Margaret Taylor, one of Dylan's benefactors. Dylan was keen to portray himself as a bohemian but many contemporaries thought that it was Caitlin who was the more rebellious character.

After Dylan's death, friends in Swansea set up a trust to administer the income from his writings for the benefit of Caitlin and their three children. Initially, Caitlin stayed at Laugharne, but by her own account, she experienced severe emotional and psychological distress, exacerbated by alcoholism, which forced her to move. She relocated to Sicily with Giuseppe Fazio, a director's assistant, with whom she had a son. Caitlin died in Catania in 1994 but she is buried next to Dylan in Laugharne.

12 JULY

On 12 July 1798, Elizabeth Smith, a renowned linguist, translator and poet from Piercefield, near Chepstow, wrote a letter to a friend that cemented her in history as the first named woman to climb Snowdon (Yr Wyddfa). An ascent had been recorded in 1775 by a team that included women but no names were specified. In the letter Elizabeth described 'a view, of which it is impossible to form an idea from description. For many miles around it was composed of tops of mountains, of all the various forms that can be imagined; some appeared swimming in an ocean of vapour; on others the clouds lay like a cap of snow, appearing as soft as down. They were all far below Snowdon, and I was enjoying the finest blue sky, and the purest air I ever breathed.'

Elizabeth's beautifully written accounts of her pioneering mountain climbing were an inspiration to women climbers who came after her. The Pinnacle Club, the UK's only national rock-climbing club for women, was officially inaugurated in 1921 at a meeting in the Pen-Y-Gwryd Inn at the foot of Snowdon.

13 JULY ⚠

On 13 July 1955, Ruth Ellis was executed by hanging at HM Prison Holloway. She was convicted of the murder of her lover, David Blakely, and she was the last woman in the United Kingdom to be executed.

Ruth was born in Rhyl in 1926. In her teens she moved to London where she found work as a nightclub hostess and model and later an escort. Ruth had two children and married once but her life was turbulent and some of her relationships were violent.

In 1953, Ruth was the manager of The Little Club in Knightsbridge and in a relationship with David Blakely. It was another volatile relationship and she also began seeing Desmond Cussen. This led to intense jealousies and drunken rows between Ruth and David and she was frequently beaten. In early 1955 Ruth suffered a miscarriage after being punched in the stomach by Blakely.

On 10 April 1955, Ruth followed Blakely to a local pub with a pistol allegedly given to her by Cussen. She fired five shots, killing him. She then calmly told bystanders to call the police to whom she surrendered, allegedly saying 'I am guilty. I am rather confused.'

At her trial, Ruth told the court: 'It's obvious when I shot him I intended to kill him.' However, it was thought that there were considerable grounds for the charge to be reduced to manslaughter. The jury were not informed of her miscarriage and there was a campaign for a reprieve – which Ruth refused to be a part of – supported by a petition signed by over 50,000 people and sent to the Home Secretary. The request was denied.

Ruth's case sparked a debate about the morality of the death penalty, which was eventually abolished in Britain in 1965.

14 JULY

On 14 July 1959, the town of Llandudno was granted a town crest emblazoned with the adopted motto *Hardd Hafan Hedd* (Beautiful Haven of Peace). It is the description given to the town by Queen Elisabeth of Romania following her five-week stay in Llandudno in 1890, during a period of 'convalescence and contemplation'.

Elisabeth was fluent in four languages and a prolific writer of poetry, novels and essays. She had been introduced to Welsh poetry from an early age by her tutor, the polyglot Georg Sauerwein. This was acknowledged at the National Eisteddfod in Bangor when she was admitted to the Gorsedd of Bards under the pseudonym she used for writing: Carmen Sylva.

Elisabeth regularly attended Llanrhos church and was entertained at Gloddaeth Hall by the artist Lady Henrietta Augusta Mostyn, who promoted Llandudno as a premier seaside resort and was a supporter of the Gwynedd Ladies' Arts Society. Henrietta also commissioned the Mostyn Art Gallery in Llandudno, which is thought to be the first art gallery in the world dedicated to exhibiting work by women.

Elisabeth's visit is commemorated by the naming of three streets in Llandudno: Carmen Sylva Road, Roumania Drive and Roumania Crescent.

15 JULY

Legendary actress Julie Christie won an Academy Award and came to international attention for her performance in *Darling*, a film released on 15 July 1965.

Julie was born at Singlijan Tea Estate, Chabua, Assam, British India, on 14 April 1940. Her father Frank ran the tea plantation but her mother was a Welsh-born painter called Rosemary.

At the age of six, Julie was sent to stay with a foster mother to be educated in England. She became upset and rebellious and was asked to leave two convent schools before becoming more settled at boarding school in High Wycombe. Here, she became involved in theatrical performances.

Julie's parents separated when she was young and her mother returned to live in rural Wales where Julie made regular trips to stay with her. After finishing school, Julie studied drama in Paris and London before embarking on an acting career.

Julie's breakthrough film appearance was in *Billy Liar* in 1963 and she gave a memorable performance in *Doctor Zhivago* in 1965.

Julie dated fellow actor Warren Beatty on and off between 1967 and 1974 and they were celebrated as the most high-profile couple in show business. However, Julie was never comfortable in the glare of the public eye. In 1977, she bought a farm near Montgomery. To date, Julie has starred in more than forty films as well as supporting many causes such as animal rights, environmental protection and the anti-nuclear-power movement.

16 JULY

Actress Angharad Rees was born on 16 July 1944. Her life began in Edgware, Middlesex but her Welsh parents moved back to live in Rhiwbina, Cardiff, when she was still a baby.

Angharad is best known for her starring role as Demelza in the 1970s BBC television costume drama *Poldark*, which captivated the hearts of millions of viewers. Angharad also starred in the 1972 film version of *Under Milk Wood*, and was an accomplished stage actress, appearing in several West End productions in London.

Angharad married actor Christopher Cazenove in 1973 and together they had two sons. She and Christopher divorced in 1994 but remained close friends. When their son, Linford tragically lost his life in a car accident in 1999, aged twenty-five, Angharad retired from acting. In recognition of her acting career she was made an honorary fellow of the Royal Welsh College of Music and Drama in 2004.

In 2005 she married Sir David McAlpine of the famous construction family and they remained together until her death. Angharad was diagnosed with pancreatic cancer in 2009 and died on 21 July 2012.

17 JULY

Betsi Cadwaladr (born 24 May 1789) was a Welsh nursing pioneer and died on this day in 1860. Unrecognised for her achievements at the time, she was buried in a pauper's grave at Abney Park Cemetery, London. In 2012, her life and work were celebrated with the unveiling of a memorial stone and a bench near her grave. Today, her name is also synonymous with the largest health organisation in Wales.

Born in Llanycil, near Bala, Betsi was one of sixteen children. She was not happy working as a maid in Wales and she travelled to Liverpool to find work at fourteen where she would go by the name Betsi Davies as it was easier for the English to pronounce. Betsi resisted calls from her sister who expected her to settle down and marry and instead travelled widely. She claimed that she visited South America, Africa and Australia as a maid to a ship's captain. She even claimed to have been at the Battle of Waterloo. Whatever the truth of Betsi's claims, it was on board ships that she began nursing.

When Betsi learned of the conditions suffered by the British soldiers wounded in the Crimean War (1853–6), she joined the military nursing service. Her first post was in a hospital run by Florence Nightingale. Betsi and Florence crossed swords over working practices. Betsi was independent and outspoken whereas Nightingale was more reserved and described Betsi as having a 'foul tongue' and a 'cross temper'.

After working there for many weeks, Betsi ran out of patience with Nightingale's bureaucracy and made her way nearer to the front line at Balaclava. There, she became an unsung heroine of the Crimean War, saving countless lives as she worked tirelessly to improve the unhygienic conditions. Eventually, she even gained the respect of Nightingale who acknowledged Betsi's valuable contribution to nursing in the Crimea.

Betsi died in 1860. The Betsi Cadwaladr University Health Board was founded on 1 October 2009. It is the largest health organisation in Wales and provides health services for the six counties of north Wales, parts of mid-Wales, Cheshire and Shropshire.

18 JULY ⚠

On 18 July 1864, a petition challenging the death sentence given to Mary Prout of Amroth for the murder of her newborn baby was presented.

Mary became pregnant out of wedlock and was sent by her family to the workhouse in Narberth, where her baby daughter Rhoda was born. When Rhoda was ten weeks old, Mary was evicted. Mary walked eight miles with her child to her grandmother's house in an increasing state of desperation. When Mary arrived she was alone and told her grandmother that Rhoda had died in the workhouse. Rumours began to circulate and after the baby's body was found at the bottom of a disused mineshaft, Mary was arrested for murder.

At her trial, Mary wasn't allowed to address the court. Character witnesses came forward to plead that she was not of sound mind and that the crime was not premeditated but committed in a moment of madness. This was at a time when the impact of post-natal depression was entirely unknown. The jury returned a guilty verdict, even though they accepted that it was not a premeditated act. The judge sentenced Mary to death. There was widespread sympathy for Mary, and the local vicar launched a petition for clemency which was signed by 1,120 people. Mary's sentence was eventually commuted to twenty years in jail by consent of Queen Victoria.

Mary was released from prison in 1878 and returned to Pembrokeshire, where she married and had two children. Mary died in 1921. She is buried in St Elidyr Church in Amroth, where her children erected a memorial stone. Baby Rhoda is said to be buried in St Issel's churchyard near Saundersfoot in an unmarked grave.

19 JULY

Angharad Tomos, author and Welsh-language campaigner from Dyffryn Nantlle in Gwynedd, was born in Bangor on 19 July 1958. She is a fervent activist for the Welsh language, and was chair of Cymdeithas yr Iaith Gymraeg (The Welsh Language Society) from 1982 to 1984. She was imprisoned for attempting to climb the Crystal Palace television transmitter to draw attention to the lack of broadcasting in the Welsh language. She is also a vocal supporter of the Wales is Not For Sale campaign which aims to highlight housing inequality in Wales and the number of properties bought for holiday lets at the expense of locals.

Angharad has written and illustrated many Welsh-language books for children and has twice won the crown at the National Eisteddfod. She also won the Mary Vaughan Jones prize in 2009 for her contribution to Welsh Children's Literature. She has written several novels for adults, and a play which was staged by the Welsh National Theatre in 2012.

20 JULY

Novelist Iris Gower died on this day in 2010.

She was born Iris Davies in Swansea in 1935 and wrote under the pen name Iris Gower. Iris was known for her historical romances, most of which are set in the seaport of Swansea and the nearby Gower Peninsula – the inspiration for her nom de plume.

As a young woman, Iris worked as a nursery teacher and took other part-time jobs, but she also began writing in her twenties and had several stories published in popular magazines, such as *Jackie* and *Woman's Own*. Her debut novel, *Tudor Tapestry*, was published in 1974, but it was the success of her novel

Copper Kingdom in 1983 that introduced her to a worldwide audience. It was one of many of her novels set in the copper industries of Swansea or in the rural life of its hinterland.

21 JULY

Ann Clwyd Roberts (née Lewis) died on 21 July 2023. Born in Denbigh in 1937, Ann was brought up in Pentre Halkyn, and became the first female MP to represent a seat in the south Wales valleys. She was the longest-serving and – at one point – the only female Welsh Labour MP. When she stood down in 2019, after thirty-five years representing Cynon Valley, she was the oldest woman to have sat as an MP.

Ann was educated at Holywell Grammar School, Queen's School, Chester and Bangor University, before training as a journalist. She worked for BBC Wales as a studio manager, and then as Welsh correspondent for the *Guardian* and *Observer* newspapers.

She was elected as the MEP for Mid and West Wales in 1979 and a Westminster MP in 1984. Over her career, Ann served as chair of the Parliamentary Labour Party, Shadow Secretary of State for National Heritage and for Wales as well as Shadow Minister for Overseas Development. Ann was a passionate campaigner on a range of causes, including compensation for miners suffering from pneumoconiosis, the Kurdish people of Iraq and the outlawing of female genital mutilation. She was also a great champion for the promotion of the Welsh language.

Following her death in 2023, Wales's then First Minister Mark Drakeford described her as 'a fearless campaigner, a defender of human rights and a trailblazer for female politicians.'

22 JULY

Jessica Leigh Jones, multi-award-winning engineer and astro-physicist, was born in Cardiff on this day in 1994. In 2012, she designed a portable uterine contraction monitor for pregnant women and became the first female to win the UK Young Engineer of the Year Award. She also won the Institution of Engineering and Technology (IET) Intel Inspiration Award for Entrepreneurship.

Jessica was educated in Tremorfa and attended Cardiff University before taking up a post with Sony UK Technology Centre at Pencoed. After her big breakthrough in 2012 she went on to win many more awards and accolades. In 2017 she was in *The Daily Telegraph*'s Top 50 Women in Engineering under 35, Aviva's Woman of the Future for Technology and Digital and was given the Freedom of the City of London. In 2018 she was named in the *Forbes* 30 under 30 lists for Europe and Europe's Youngest.

In 2020, Jessica co-founded iungo Solutions, aimed at upskilling and retraining people affected by Covid-19. Jessica was also appointed an MBE for services to women in engineering in Wales in 2020 and has been appointed to roles encouraging young people to participate in engineering with the United Nations and the Welsh Joint Education Committee (WJEC). She is director of Engineering Education Scheme Wales and visiting professor at the University of Wales Trinity St David. She also as serves on the board of directors of the Institute for Apprenticeships and Technical Education.

23 JULY

On 23 July 1949, the Welsh Folk Dance Society was founded.

In the sixteenth century, the opportunity for the community to meet and dance in the open air to music provided by a musician sat on the *twmpath* (a tump of raised ground) was an important part of Welsh life. However, when the Nonconformist Church became dominant in the 1730s, dancing was discouraged. This resulted in folk dancing almost vanishing in Wales by the twentieth century.

This decline was reversed in the 1930s when Lois Blake, an Englishwoman who had moved to Denbighshire, took it upon herself to reintroduce the historic dance steps and music. She revived dances such as Lord of Caernarvon's Jig from 1652, the Llangadfan Set of 1790 and the Llanover Reel which had been popular at the Llanover estate until the late nineteenth century.

The establishment of the Welsh Folk Dance Society and the establishment of the Lois Blake trophy for folk dancing at the National Eisteddfod have ensured that the tradition of Welsh folk dancing continues.

24 JULY ⚠

On 24 July 2007, at the age of twenty-four, Abi Carter founded Forensic Resources Ltd, a forensic science consultancy firm that recovers evidence from crime scenes using archaeological techniques to provide expert advice to legal firms, fraud investigators, insurers, HR departments and private clients. Her work has also played a key role in high-profile criminal cases such as the Raoul Moat killings and the murder of Joanna Yeates.

Abi's dad was from Monmouth but she grew up in the Middle East. She returned to Wales to study and graduated in forensic archaeology from Cardiff and then Bournemouth universities. She then went to work with a team on the mass graves of the 1995 genocide in Srebrenica, Bosnia and Herzegovina. The task was to identify victims and give closure to their families. Since 2017, Abi has been heavily involved with the charity Remembering Srebrenica. In 2019, she was recognised by the gender-equality charity Chwarae Teg (Fair Play) in its Womenspire Awards.

25 JULY

Catherine Glynne (6 January 1812–14 June 1900) is regarded by many as being the driving force behind her husband, William Gladstone, who served as prime minister of the United Kingdom for twelve years. They were married in Hawarden Church on 25 July 1839 and set up home at Hawarden Castle, her ancestral home in Flintshire.

In contrast to her husband, Catherine was known to be famously untidy and would leave letters and papers strewn across the floor in her wake. She also didn't care for fancy attire. A friend described her as 'like a fresh breeze'. While Queen Victoria loathed Gladstone she loved Catherine. She would tease William by saying, 'What a bore you would have been if you had married someone as tidy as you are.' Catherine also had a social conscience and used her contacts as the wife of the prime minister to found convalescent homes and orphanages both locally in the Hawarden area and in London. She is buried alongside her husband in Westminster Abbey.

William Gladstone's greatest political opponent, Benjamin Disraeli, was also married to a Welsh woman: Mary Anne Disraeli, 1st Viscountess Beaconsfield (born Mary Anne Evans, 1792–1872) from Tongwynlais near Cardiff.

Mary was an unconventional and outspoken character who often scandalised Victorian society with her outrageous remarks, although the Queen is said to have been often amused by her witticism. She assisted her husband in writing and editing his books. She is buried with Disraeli in the Church of St Michael and All Angels at Hughenden, close to the Disraeli family home in Buckinghamshire.

26 JULY

Baroness Tanni Grey-Thompson was born in Cardiff on 26 July 1969. She was christened Carys Davina Grey, but her sister described her as 'tiny' when she first saw her, pronouncing it 'tanni', and the name stuck.

Tanni, who has spina bifida, is one of Britain's most successful Paralympians ever, winning eleven Paralympic gold medals, as well as six London Marathons.

When her sporting career ended, she was made a peer and has become a champion in the House of Lords for the rights of disabled people. Alongside other sporting legends like Jack Nicklaus, Boris Becker and Pelé, Tanni is a member of the Laureus World Sports Academy, which strives to improve the lives of disadvantaged children through participation in sport.

27 JULY

On 27 July 1865, the clipper ship *Mimosa* anchored at New Bay (later Porth Madryn) in the Chubut Region of Argentine Patagonia. On board were 153 Welsh emigrants who had travelled with the aim of creating a society free from religious persecution where they could preserve the Welsh language and culture. With the help of the local Tehuelche people, their community flourished and became known as Y Wladfa.

Eluned Morgan (20 March 1870–29 December 1938) was born aboard a subsequent sailing to Y Wladfa. Her father was Lewis Jones, one of the founders of the colony, but she was given the surname Morgan because *Môr-ganed* means 'born at sea'.

Eluned was taught to speak both Welsh and Spanish and was sent back to Wales to Dr Williams' School in Dolgellau to learn the English language. There, she led student protests against the school's English-only policy, which prohibited the speaking of Welsh by students. Eluned returned to Patagonia in 1918 and is remembered primarily for her books: *Dringo'r Andes* explores life in Patagonia; *Gwymon y Môr* describes the voyage from Wales to Patagonia and *Plant yr Haul* is about the Indigenous people of Peru.

DID YOU KNOW?

Rachel Jenkins, one of the early settlers of Y Wladfa, saved the community by suggesting simple irrigation and water management techniques that boosted the fertility of the Chubut valley and ensured the survival of its Welsh inhabitants.

28 JULY

On 28 July 1896, the cartoon character Dame Wales (*Mam Cymru*) first appeared in the *Western Mail*. The image depicted a weeping woman dressed in traditional Welsh costume, grieving the death of Arthur Linton, a nationally celebrated cyclist from Aberaman.

Dame Wales was the creation of the cartoonist J. M. Staniforth (1864–1921). She was a working-class woman dressed in Welsh national costume. She embodied Wales in a similar way that John Bull was used to symbolise Britain. Dame Wales was usually portrayed as the voice of reason, standing up against the out-of-touch elite in authority.

In one cartoon, she is shown being led away by a policeman during the 1908 Welsh Coal Strike telling him, 'Not so fast, young man; you are here to keep the peace – not to break it.'

29 JULY

On 29 July 2006 Connie Fisher, from Hayscastle near Fishguard, first appeared on the reality television talent show *How Do You Solve a Problem like Maria?*. The show covered the search for a performer to fill the role of Maria von Trapp in Andrew Lloyd Webber's West End production of *The Sound of Music*.

Connie won the competition and has subsequently gone on to star in many other roles. She has played the recurring role of Amanda in the television drama series *Casualty* and starred in the television drama *Caught In A Trap*. In August 2009, she was made a member of the Gorsedd at the National Eisteddfod in Bala.

Connie was born in Northern Ireland, in 1983. She and

her mother moved to Hayscastle when she was four. She considers herself to be Welsh and is a fluent Welsh speaker.

30 JULY

Harriet Windsor-Clive was born in London on 30 July 1797. She was the daughter of the 5th Earl of Plymouth and, in 1855, she was granted the title of 13th Baroness Windsor. The estate, known as the Plymouth Estate, included the town of Penarth and the family's seat at St Fagans Castle.

Harriet lived in Cardiff for a time where she saw the new Cardiff Docks which were being constructed by the Marquess of Bute. In 1855, she formed the Penarth Harbour Company to build a dock between Penarth Head and the River Ely. The docks were completed by 1865 and the Taff Vale Railway immediately took the lease, much to the annoyance of the Marquess of Bute who had offered incentives to the company to build the railway to Cardiff instead.

Penarth Docks' annual coal exports peaked in 1913, when 4,660,648 tonnes were exported in a year. There was then a slow decline until the docks closed in 1963. The site has since been redeveloped to become Penarth Marina, which now opens into Cardiff Bay.

In 1857, Harriet developed the housing in what is now known as Grangetown and was also known for her charitable donations in the area. She paid for the construction (in 1852–3) and the reconstruction following a fire (1856) of the Church of St Fagan, Trecynon. She paid for the restoration of St Mary's Church at St Fagans; Radyr's St John the Baptist, and the cathedral at Llandaff. She also financed the national schools at Aberdare and Penarth.

31 JULY

On 31 July 1920, the Davies sisters, Gwendoline (1882–1951) and Margaret (1884–1963) purchased Gregynog Hall, near Newtown. They are recognised as two of Wales's most famous philanthropists and established Gregynog as a centre of excellence for art and music in Wales.

Gwendoline and Margaret inherited immense wealth from their grandfather David Davies, a mining and railways entrepreneur. The sisters were both born at Llandinam and educated at Highfield School in Hendon. They were brought up as strict Nonconformists and never married. As young women, they travelled widely across Europe which gave them a passion for the art of France and Italy. They amassed the largest collection of French Impressionist and post-Impressionist works in the country. They also collected Chinese and Islamic ceramics and commissioned contemporary handmade furniture.

During the First World War, the sisters worked as volunteers with the Red Cross in France. They also helped a number of refugee Belgian artists and their families to move to Wales. After the war, the sisters purchased Gregynog to house their impressive collection. They also funded many charities and educational and cultural initiatives such as Prifysgol Cymru (University of Wales), Amgueddfa Werin Cymru (St Fagans National Museum of History) and LLyfrgell Genedlaethol Cymru (National Library of Wales). They established Gregynog Press in 1922, producing limited-edition books with fine hand-coloured illustrations which were revered by collectors the world over.

The sisters bequeathed their art collection to Llyfrgell Genedlaethol Cymru. Gregynog Hall was left to the University of Wales.

AUGUST

1 AUGUST

Gwyl Galan Awst (*Lughnasadh* in Celtic) is the Celtic festival that marks the beginning of the grain harvest – a highly significant time in the agricultural calendar. In Wales, this time is associated with the mythological enchantress Ceridwen.

In Welsh legend, Ceridwen lived beneath the waters of Llyn Tegid (Bala Lake). She was the wife of the giant Tegid Foel, and bore a son, Morfran, who was exceptionally ugly. Ceridwen sought to compensate her son's hideous appearance with a magic potion to endow him with wisdom and creative inspiration.

A servant, Gwion, was tasked with stirring the cauldron, which required simmering for a year and a day. The boy accidentally consumed a drop of potion from Ceridwen's magical cauldron and, to escape her wrath, he shapeshifted into a grain of wheat. Ceridwen, however, transformed herself into a black hen who gobbled up the grain. The grain

grew inside her, and she gave birth to a son who, according to legend, became the great bard and sorcerer Taliesin.

Ceridwen has come to represent transformation and rebirth. For many, she symbolises the cycles of the seasons in nature, the interconnectedness of all living beings and the bond between humans and the natural world.

The Christian Church, most likely in an attempt to convert followers of the old Celtic tradition, introduced the feast of Lammas and on 1 August it became customary to bring to church an offering of a loaf of bread made from the new crop of grain. Shops and houses would often be decorated, and there were fairs and craft festivals, marches, plays and dancing. Later, Christian communities moved the celebration to the end of the harvest in September. Harvest hymns helped to popularise the festival, as did the growing custom of decorating churches with home-grown produce for the harvest festival service.

2 AUGUST

Hollywood actress Myrna Loy was on 2 August 1905 in Montana. She became one of the most highly paid actors in the film industry.

Myrna's Welsh grandparents had emigrated to America in 1856 and she often spoke of her Welsh heritage. 'My father's family was Welsh, they have a great heritage,' she is recorded as saying. 'My father was a great storyteller … My Welsh grandfather was a pioneer – I weep every time I see *How Green Was My Valley* [a 1941 film about a Welsh mining family] because that's him.'

Myrna became known as 'The First Lady of Film' and her remarkable career spanned six decades. It began with silent film roles where she was cast primarily as a femme fatale. Later, she starred as Nora Charles in *The Thin Man* series. In 1936 she was voted 'Queen of the Movies' to Clark Gable's 'King' in a nationwide audience poll.

Myrna was politically active, and an outspoken critic of the film industry's racist attitudes. She is quoted as saying, 'Why does every Black person in the movies have to play a servant? How about a Black person walking up the steps of a courthouse carrying a briefcase?'

Although never nominated for an Academy Award, she received an Academy Honorary Award in 1991 for her lifetime's achievement.

DID YOU KNOW?

In 1948 Myrna Loy became a member of the US National Commission for UNESCO, the first Hollywood celebrity to do so.

3 AUGUST

The 2014 Commonwealth Games took place in Glasgow and ended on 3 August. Wales gained a record medal total of thirty-six.

Among the gold medal winners were five Welsh women:

- **Natalie Powell** is from Beulah in Powys won a gold medal in Judo. In 2017 she became the first female British *judoka* to be ranked number one in the world.

- **Jazz Carlin and Georgia Davies** are Swansea-based swimmers who both won gold medals in their sport. Jazz won gold in the 800 metre freestyle and Georgia in the 50 metre backstroke.

- **Francesca Jones**, whose father is from Neath, won the ribbon event in rhythmic gymnastics. Francesca was also awarded the David Dixon Award which is awarded to the outstanding athlete of each Games based on their performance but also their fair play and contribution towards their team.

4 AUGUST

The Mines and Collieries Act, passed on 4 August 1842, banned females of any age from working underground and required the boys hired by mines to be no younger than ten years old.

Following this, women and girls took to carrying out surface work at the mines in Wales. They would load carts, sort coal from stone and haul materials from the pit face. They became known as 'patch girls'.

The name refers to the near-surface deposits of coal or iron ore which were called patches. Patches could be dangerous. In 1860, Diana Llewellyn, aged twenty-two, was killed by a landslide working on patches at Twyn Carno, Rhymney, and in 1898, Mary Ann Canniff, aged twenty-eight from Tredegar, was buried under a tonne of rubble working the Sirhowy patches below an overhanging cliff.

Tredegar was central to the Industrial Revolution – having both a coal mine and an ironworks – and was particularly associated with patch girls. In 2013, the six-mile Homfray Trail at Bedwellty Park in Tredegar was opened in honour of the town's industrial past. Among its fifteen sculptures is a memorial to the patch girls. The memorial statue depicts the sisters Margaret and Rebecca Lewis, as they would have looked in 1861 when Margaret was eighteen and Rebecca ten. It represents the many women and girls who gathered from the patches in the Heads of the Valleys region.

5 AUGUST

Helen Wyn Thomas was only twenty-two when she was killed in an accident involving a police vehicle on 5 August 1989. Helen was a Welsh peace activist renowned for her dedication to championing peace and rejecting violence. She had been part of a protest group protesting against nuclear weapons at Greenham Common Women's Peace Camp.

The Greenham Common Women's Peace Camp was a series of protest camps that were initiated in 1981 by a group of women marching from Newport, Cardiff and the south Wales valleys to a base in Greenham, Berkshire, where the UK government planned to allow the US to store cruise missiles. Led by Ann Pettitt, the organisers were a small core group of mainly women and children calling for disarmament and appealing for a peaceful world.

When the government ignored their requests for consultation, the women remained at Greenham and the peace camp was established. For nineteen years it acted as a focus for many thousands of people to express their opposition to cruise missiles and weapons of mass destruction.

Greenham has become an intrinsic part of Wales's history of peace protests, and Helen Wyn Thomas remains one of the movement's most prominent figureheads.

6 AUGUST

On 6 August 2024, Eluned Morgan was confirmed as the sixth First Minister of Wales and the first woman to hold the position.

Eluned (born in Cardiff on 16 February 1967) has served as a Welsh Assembly member in the Senedd since 2016 and was elected as leader of Welsh Labour in July 2024 having previously served as Minister for the Welsh Language from 2017 to 2021 and Minister for Mental Health and Wellbeing from 2020 to 2021.

Eluned was previously a Member of the European Parliament (MEP) from 1994 to 2009 and was granted a life peerage in the House of Lords, as Baroness Morgan of Ely, in 2010. She was educated at Ysgol Gyfun Gymraeg Glantaf, Atlantic College and the University of Hull where she gained a degree in European Studies. She previously worked as a television researcher and as the Director of National Development for SWALEC (South Wales Electricity and now known as OVO Energy).

Eluned is a Fellow of Trinity College Carmarthen and an Honorary Distinguished Professor and Fellow of Cardiff University.

7 AUGUST

Eigra Lewis Roberts, one of the foremost Welsh-language writers of our time, was born on this day in 1939 in Blaenau Ffestiniog. Her work includes short stories, novels and poetry and also works for radio and television.

After graduating from the University College of North Wales, Bangor, Eigra worked as a teacher in Holyhead and Llanrwst before turning to writing. In 1959, she won the open novel prize at the National Eisteddfod with her first novel *Brynhyfryd*. After this she was the recipient of multiple awards. She won the Prose Medal in 1965 and 1968 at the National Eisteddfod and the Drama Medal in 1974. In 1995 she was awarded the BAFTA Cymru award for the best screenwriter and in 2006 she won her first Crown at the Swansea National Eisteddfod.

8 AUGUST

On 8 August 2021, at the Tokyo Olympic Games, Lauren Price from Ystrad Mynach became the first Welsh boxer to win an Olympic gold medal. She is also the first Welsh woman to become a boxing World Champion and to win a Commonwealth Games gold medal.

Lauren was born in Newport in 1994 and raised by her grandparents in Ystrad Mynach. In her youth, she excelled in many sports: she was the youngest-ever competitor in the British Kickboxing Championships and won a silver medal at the World Championships at the age of thirteen. She later became a four-time world champion and six-time European champion in the sport. Lauren also played football for Wales and was named the Football Association of Wales Club Player of the Year in 2013.

In 2014, Lauren started to concentrate on her boxing and, after her success at the Tokyo Olympics, she turned professional and became the first British women's welterweight champion in 2023, as well as the first woman to receive a Lonsdale Belt. In 2024, Lauren claimed the WBA, IBO and *The Ring* magazine women's welterweight world titles to become Wales's first female world champion boxer.

9 AUGUST ⚠

On 9 August 1211, Marcher lord William de Braose also known as 'The Butcher of Abergavenny' died in ignominious exile in France. His wife Maud (sometimes known as Matilda), known as 'The Lady of Hay' in many Welsh legends, was a formidable woman who also came to a bad end.

Maud was a strong-willed, intelligent woman. When her husband was fighting a campaign for King John, he left her to safeguard their seat at Hay Castle in Herefordshire. In 1198, Maud defended another of their estates at Painscastle from a sustained Welsh attack, holding out for six weeks until reinforcements arrived. Over a thousand Welsh soldiers were killed during the siege, and it came to be known as Matilda's Castle.

In 1208 the king demanded their son as a hostage to ensure the family's obedience after he had met with criticism from them and other barons. Maud refused. She and her son fled to Ireland but were quickly captured. They were brought back in chains, first to Windsor Castle and then to Corfe Castle in Dorset. Locked in a dungeon, Maud and her eleven-year-old son were left to starve to death.

Legend has it that, when their bodies were recovered, William's cheek bore his mother's bite marks.

Many other legends grew up around Maud. She was said to have supernatural powers and that she built Hay Castle herself in one night, carrying the stones in her apron. When one fell out and lodged in her slipper, she picked it out and flung it. It landed in St Meilig's churchyard three miles away across the River Wye. The nine-foot-high standing stone can still be seen inside the church.

10 AUGUST

Amy Dowden, born in Caerphilly on 10 August 1990, is a professional dancer best known for her appearances on the television show *Strictly Come Dancing*. Amy and her husband and dancing partner, Ben Jones, are former British National Latin Dance Champions and she holds the world record for the most back-Charleston kick-steps in thirty seconds.

Amy's successful dancing career is all the more remarkable due to the considerable health issues she has had to overcome. She has suffered from Crohn's disease since she was a child. In 2021 Amy was awarded the 2021 Best Documentary BAFTA Cymru award for *Strictly Amy: Crohn's and Me,* in which she shared her experiences.

In May 2023 Amy was diagnosed with an aggressive form of breast cancer and underwent a mastectomy and chemotherapy. She continued filming her BBC show *Dare to Dance* during her treatment, and documented her treatment and recovery process on Instagram to raise awareness of the disease and to encourage young women to undergo regular checks.

In 2024, she was named on *The Independent*'s Influential Women list and in the same year was awarded an MBE for services to fundraising and raising awareness of inflammatory bowel disease.

11 AUGUST

Berta Ruck, a prolific writer of romance novels, died, aged a hundred, on this day in 1978. From 1914 to 1972, she published over ninety books, which earned her the epithet of the 'Queen of Romance'. Her work frequently challenged the strict pre-First World War attitudes towards femininity and masculinity.

Born in 1878 in Punjab, British India, Berta moved to Wales when she was two to live with her grandmother in Merioneth. Later, her whole family settled in Caernarfon where her father was appointed chief constable of Caernarfonshire. Berta attended St Winifred's School in Bangor and studied at the Lambeth School of Art, the Slade School of Fine Art and the Académie Colarossi in Paris, before marrying the writer Oliver Onions, best known for his ghost stories.

Berta began a career as an illustrator for magazines for which she then began to contribute short stories. Her first novel, *His Official Fiancée,* was published in 1914 and became a bestseller. During the 1920s and 1930s, she spent much of her time in Vienna and produced up to three books every year. At the outbreak of the Second World War, she and her husband settled in Aberdyfi where she spent the remainder of her life, writing and publishing until the 1970s.

12 AUGUST

Eileen Beasley (born Eileen James on 4 April 1921) died on this day in 2012. She was from Henllan Amgoed near Whitland and is regarded by Welsh-language campaigners as the 'mother of direct action' and the inspiration for the creation of Cymdeithas yr Iaith Gymraeg (the Welsh Language Society).

Eileen met her husband Trefor Beasley through Plaid Cymru and, in 1952, they settled in Llangennech near Llanelli. They came to prominence when they refused to pay their council rate bills, as they were only provided in English. Llanelli Rural District Council would only communicate with the Beasleys in English, so their missives were ignored. Eileen and Trefor's continued refusal to comply led to them being taken to court sixteen times. Trefor was imprisoned for a time and their personal belongings were taken by bailiffs. Local support for their campaign, however, was demonstrated in 1955 when both Eileen and Trefor were elected as Plaid Cymru councillors for the same district council that they were in dispute with. This resulted in the council grudgingly issuing a bilingual rate demand in 1960, which the Beasleys promptly paid.

The Beasleys' stand inspired other Welsh nationalists including Saunders Lewis who gave a radio speech entitled 'Tynged yr Iaith' ('The Fate of the Language') in 1962 in which he predicted the extinction of the Welsh language unless action was taken. He specifically praised the actions of Eileen and Trefor. Lewis's speech subsequently led to the creation of Cymdeithas yr Iaith Gymraeg. In 2006, the society honoured Eileen's commitment to the Welsh language at a special ceremony in Aberystwyth, describing her as the 'Rosa Parks of Wales'.

13 AUGUST ⚠

On 13 August 1905, Annie Gwen Jones gave birth to a son in her home in Barry in the Vale of Glamorgan. He was named Gareth Richard Vaughan Jones.

Annie, an accomplished and intelligent woman, had spent three years as tutor to the daughters of Arthur Hughes in Hughesovka, modern-day Donetsk in Eastern Ukraine, a colony of Welsh migrants which was founded by Arthur's father, the Welsh industrialist John Hughes. Annie's account of her wonderful adventures and experiences in Ukraine, published as *Life on the Steppes of Russia*, instilled in her son a desire to visit that country and also Russia.

Gareth became a journalist and he was the first to bring the existence of the Holodomor, or the great Ukrainian famine, to the attention of the Western World. The famine affected the grain-producing areas of what was, at the time, the Soviet Union. This included Ukraine where it became known as the Holodomor. Between 1932 and 1933, millions of Ukrainian deaths were caused by famine that was, by the consensus of historians, man-made. Numerous documents have been discovered ordering the starvation of areas of the Union. Gareth wrote: 'Everywhere was the cry "There is no bread. We are dying. We are waiting for death."' His reporting was denounced and met with denials from the Soviet Union, and he was banned from ever visiting again.

Described as 'the unsung hero of Ukraine' he was kidnapped and murdered on the eve of his thirtieth birthday, in Mongolia in 1935. Many have claimed that the Soviet secret police engineered his execution in an act of revenge for revealing the truth about the Holodomor.

14 AUGUST ⚠

Rhoda Willis, also known as Leslie James, was executed by hanging at Cardiff prison on 14 August 1907 and was the last woman to be hanged in Wales.

Born in Sunderland, Willis had been found guilty of 'baby farming': placing-out infants for money or selling them for profit. Many of the children came from unwed mothers, sex workers and destitute or deserted wives who couldn't care for their own children.

In Rhoda's case, she had already engaged in several transactions involving babies when she placed an advertisement in Cardiff's evening newspaper seeking a baby to adopt. She received a reply on behalf of a pregnant lady and it was agreed that Rhoda would collect the baby when it was born.

Rhoda collected the infant at Hengoed railway station, along with the pre-agreed fee of £8. She returned to her lodging very drunk. As her landlady helped her into bed, she found a bundle containing the body of the baby girl. The landlady immediately sent for the police who arrested Rhoda at the scene.

Subsequent legislation, including the Children Act 1908, gradually placed adoption and foster care under the protection and regulation of the state.

15 AUGUST

On 15 August 1929, Edith Parnell, at age sixteen, became only the second person to swim the Bristol Channel and remains the youngest person to have achieved this feat. Sustained by Bovril and sips of tea and accompanied by a support boat carrying a team of supporters, including the president of Penarth's Swimming Club on his ukulele, Edith completed the crossing from Penarth to Weston-super-Mare in ten hours and fifteen minutes.

Edith later became a successful journalist. She was not only the first woman reporter for the Reuters News Agency in Paris and London but also the first woman editor of a Sunday newspaper. She died in 1938, aged only twenty-five years, after complications from a Caesarean section.

The first person to swim the Bristol Channel was also a young woman from Penarth. On 5 September 1927, twenty-one-year-old Kathleen Thomas swam the treacherous eleven-mile stretch in seven hours and twenty minutes. She was then taken to a nearby hotel, where she had both a warm and cold bath, took a half-hour rest and ate a fish lunch before returning to Wales as a hero.

DID YOU KNOW?

Jenny James from Rhydyfelin, near Pontypridd, was the first Welsh person to swim the English Channel. She completed the swim on 16 August 1951, in a time of thirteen hours and fifty-five minutes.

16 AUGUST

On 16 August 2010, presenter Alex Jones made her debut on the BBC's flagship magazine programme *The One Show*.

A fluent Welsh speaker from Ammanford, Alex's television career began at S4C where she presented the travel series *Tocyn* (*Ticket*), an extreme sports show *Chwa* and a style and fashion programme *Salon*.

In 2009 Alex took part in *The Magnificent Seven*, a BAFTA-winning series which saw seven celebrities travel to a ranch in Arizona and learn to become cowboys.

Alex's popularity grew when she was a semi-finalist in *Strictly Come Dancing* in 2011 which she says was 'one of the best times of my life'. She has fronted several programmes for the BBC, such as *Shop Well for Less* and *Let's Dance for Comic Relief* and she was the host for the coverage of the Invictus Games. She fronted the critically acclaimed documentary *Alex Jones: Fertility and Me* and has filmed two further series, *Reunion Hotel* for BBC2 and *Alex Jones: Making Babies* for the W Channel.

Alongside her television work, Alex authored the bestselling baby book *Winging It*, based on her personal experiences of raising her three children, and works actively with a number of charities.

17 AUGUST

On 17 August 1832, the future Queen Victoria was engaged in her first official visit to Wales. She was accompanying her mother, Victoria Duchess of Kent, on a visit celebrating the duchess's birthday. Bonfires were lit on Penmaenmawr, Twthill, Elidir Fawr and other mountains, and three thousand rock canons (gunpowder inserted into bores in rocks to cause explosions) were fired in honour of the visit.

The then Princess Victoria was delighted with a doll dressed in Cambrian costume presented to her at The Hand Hotel in Llangollen. When they passed through Bangor later in the tour, the duchess and princess wore Welsh hats 'in compliment to the fair maids of Cambria'.

On one of Victoria's later visits to Wales with her husband Prince Albert in 1859, a special one-ton slate bed was commissioned by the wealthy Pennant family of Penrhyn Castle in honour of the Royal visit. Victoria refused to sleep in it because it reminded her of a tomb. The bed can be seen there to this day.

18 AUGUST

On 18 August 2016, Jade Jones (born 21 March 1993) made history by becoming a double Olympic gold taekwondo champion in the Rio Olympic Games. Four years earlier at the London Olympics, she became the first ever British athlete to win a taekwondo gold medal.

Born in Bodelwyddan, Jade credits her grandfather Martin for all her success. She was a troublesome youngster and he tried introducing her to a variety of sports to channel her energy before finding taekwondo. Jade fell in love with the sport immediately and, at sixteen, she left school to take it up full time. Martin would drive her an hour to Manchester four times a week to train and four hours to Cardiff on Sundays so that she could work with the Welsh squad.

Jade is nicknamed 'The Headhunter' because she prefers to score points from her opponent's head. She was the winner of the gold medal at the inaugural Youth Olympic Games in

2010 and she is also three-time European champion (2016, 2018 and 2021) and the 2019 world champion.

19 AUGUST

On 19 August 1991, a memorial service was held for Gwenfron Moss (1898–1991) at Minny Street Chapel in Cardiff. Gwenfron was a pharmacist who became a Christian missionary carrying out work in India, Zambia and, most notably, in pre-revolutionary China.

Born in Coedpoeth, Gwenfron was educated in Wrexham before training as a pharmacist in London. There, she regularly attended the Welsh Congregational Church in King's Cross. In 1925, convinced of her calling to become an interdenominational evangelical, she applied to the London Missionary Society, who arranged for her to be trained and then sent to China. She set sail in August 1928.

After learning the Chinese language, Gwenfron was appointed as a pharmacist at the Mackenzie Memorial Hospital in Tianjin. She was forced to return to Wales during the Second World War but went back to China to work at the Roberts Memorial Hospital in Tsangchow in 1946.

This was at a time of seismic cultural change in China and the area was governed by the Communist Party, which was hostile to religion. Christians, especially missionaries, were subject to persecution. Gwenfron was eventually compelled to leave China in 1949 as part of the 'reluctant exodus' following the declaration of the People's Republic of China.

In 1953, Gwenfron was sent to India, where she also arranged for the sale of local crochet, lace and embroidered goods to European markets including some in Wales. She returned home in 1964 after a four-month stay at the Kawimbe Centre in Zambia.

Gwenfron's papers including her letters home from China and India are now held in the Llyfrgell Genedlaethol Cymru (National Library of Wales).

20 AUGUST

On 20 August 1655, Margaret ferch Richard was convicted of witchcraft and sentenced to death by hanging in Beaumaris, Anglesey. She was the last person in Wales to be executed for being suspected of being a witch. Margaret was a widow and local healer in her forties. She was accused of casting a spell that caused the death of another woman.

Witchcraft in medieval Wales was a common fear. Women who looked after the preparation of poultices and medicines to assist with healing were often accused of being witches. The Acts of Union from 1536 to 1543 brought Wales under English rule and resulted in the practices of magic and witchcraft being made illegal. There were only thirty-seven prosecutions in Wales during the sixteenth and seventeenth centuries and only eight people were found guilty, with five of those sentenced to execution. In England, during the same period, it is estimated that five hundred witches were executed and, in the rest of Western Europe, the total is nearer 200,000.

The earliest record of trial and execution on charges of witchcraft in Wales is that of Gwen ferch Ellis in Denbigh in 1594. Gwen, from Llandyrnog, was a weaver and herbal healer of people and animals who had married and settled in Betws-yn-Rhos. She was accused of leaving a charm at the home of Thomas Mostyn in Llandudno, intended to cause him and his family harm. It was claimed that Gwen was acting on behalf of Jane Conway, of nearby Marle Hall, who had quarrelled with Mostyn. However, it is also suspected that Mostyn fabricated the charge, as he was having an illicit affair with Jane, of which Gwen had knowledge. Despite her protestations of innocence, local magistrates ordered investigators to search her home, where items were found linking her to the old (banned) Catholic religion. Seven witnesses testified against her, and the combined forces of the Church, the court and the gentry outweighed her spirited denials and secured her conviction.

21 AUGUST

On 21 August 1917, an inquest was held in Llanelli following an explosion at the Pembrey Munitions Factory in July that year which had killed six people including two women. The two women, Mildred Owen and Dorothy Wilson, received the almost unprecedented honour of being buried in Danygraig Cemetery with full military honours. The inquest, however, could not offer an explanation for the explosion. A further explosion the following year killed Mary Fitzmaurice, Jane Jenkins and Edith Copham.

During the First World War, when millions of men signed up to join the armed forces, women were recruited to work in industries that had previously been dominated by men. The critical munitions factories became the largest employer of women during the war years and by 1917 the factories were producing over fifty million shells a year.

Existing buildings were requisitioned to become National Shell Factories including large production units in Grangetown, Porthmadog, and Landore in Swansea. It was dangerous work, particularly for those who worked with the explosive substance TNT which was also highly poisonous. It contained picric acid, which caused toxic jaundice and turned the skin and hair of the women who worked with it yellow, giving rise to the nickname 'Canary Girls'. Prolonged exposure could lead to liver failure, anaemia and irreparable damage to the immune system. Many suffered burns and skin rashes which led, in some cases, to amputation. Many babies born to women workers at this time were born with a yellow discolouration of their skin.

At the peak of wartime production, 55 per cent of Welsh workers involved in the war effort were women, the highest percentage in Britain. They often clocked on seven days a week, risking life and limb to supply weapons and ammunition to the front line.

22 AUGUST

Folklore Day is celebrated on 22 August every year in countries around the world.

Wales abounds in folklore, and many of the most prominent figures in Welsh legends are women. One of the most loved tales is that of 'The Lady of Llyn y Fan Fach', also known as 'The Lady of the Lake' but entirely separate to the Arthurian legend of the same name.

A widow with an only son lived in a smallholding by the River Sawdde in the foothills of Carmarthenshire's Black Mountain. She sent him to graze their small herd of cattle by Llyn y Fan Fach, where he saw a beautiful woman combing her hair using the lake as her mirror. The boy fell in love with her and offered her bread, but she plunged below the surface, saying that the bread was stale.

He told his mother who made several attempts at baking the perfect loaf of bread. Eventually, his mother succeeded and the lady of the lake agreed to marry him, summoning a herd of fine cattle which walked on the surface of the lake to the shore. They were married on condition that if he should strike her three times she would return to the lake. For some years they lived happily on a farm and had three sons. Eventually, the farmer broke the conditions of their marriage pact, and the lady returned to the lake, taking her cattle with her.

Years later she appeared to her eldest son Rhiwallon and gave him a bag of herbal medicinal recipes, saying that he and his brothers had a calling to heal the sick. All three brothers chose healing as their mission in life and became the first gifted healers in the long line of the famous medieval Physicians of Myddfai.

23 AUGUST

Today is the feast day of St Tudfil. The town of Merthyr Tydfil is named in her honour as the place where she was martyred in c. AD 480. *Merthyr* means 'martyr' in Welsh.

Tudfil was the daughter of Brychan, King of Brycheiniog and, by some reports, his twenty-third daughter by his fourth wife. Many children of royalty travelled to spread the word of Christianity. Tudfil established a Christian community in the Taff Valley where she became known for her strong faith, her compassionate nature and her ability to heal people and animals.

During a visit from her father, she was attacked by a group of Picts, who killed Tudfil as she knelt and prayed. She was buried within the community she founded and eventually a Norman stone church was built and dedicated to her. A church has existed on this site since then but it was rebuilt in 1808 and 1894. It still stands at the lower end of the High Street in Merthyr Tydfil.

24 AUGUST

Incorporated on 24 August 2009, Ruth Jones and her husband David Peet incorporated Tidy Productions, following the huge success of the BAFTA-award-winning sitcom *Gavin and Stacey*, which was co-written by and starred Ruth and fellow actor James Corden.

An actress from Porthcawl, Ruth has since gone on to play the much-loved comedy actress Hattie Jaques in the major hit BBC biopic *Hattie* in 2011. In 2012, Tidy Productions created fifty-eight episodes of the comedy *Stella*. Written by Ruth, it saw her star as a single mother with a large and complex array of friends and family. Ruth was awarded an MBE in 2014, and has since published three successful novels: *Never Greener, Us Three* and *Love Untold*.

25 AUGUST

Rosie Swale Pope is probably the most famous female adventurer to come from Wales. On 25 August 2008, she completed her most challenging adventure: running around the world to raise money for the Prostate Cancer Charity, the disease that claimed her husband's life in 2002. Starting from her home town of Tenby on her fifty-seventh birthday, Rosie ran through Europe, Russia, Canada, the USA (taking the time to run the Chicago marathon), Greenland, Iceland, Ireland and Scotland, before making her way back to her home in Tenby. Her total distance travelled was 19,900 miles.

Rosie always had a natural thirst for adventure. She moved to London to work in journalism but soon quit her job hitch-hike through India, Nepal and Russia. In 1971, accompanied by her husband, Colin, and their children, Eve and James, she sailed a catamaran from Gibraltar to Australia, arriving in 1973. She met her second husband, Clive, during her preparations for her solo sailing across the Atlantic in 1983. She aimed to become the fourth woman to complete the crossing and raise money for a CAT scanner for the Royal Marsden Hospital. She arrived at Staten Island within seventy days. The following year, she rode across Chile on horseback.

Rosie has run multiple marathons all over the world. In 2016, she completed a 3,371-mile run across America, from New York to San Francisco and, in 2020, she became the oldest woman to walk from Land's End to John O'Groats.

During her adventures, Rosie has been caught in a desert sandstorm; broken two ribs in a fall from a horse; was lost in a rainforest without food; was nearly shipwrecked and has been held up at gunpoint. When she arrived in Tenby after her run around the world in August 2008, she was on crutches due to stress fractures but still finished her mission.

26 AUGUST

On 26 August 1938, actress and singer Glynis Johns (1923–2024) made her screen debut at the age of fifteen in the film *South Riding*.

Glynis was born in Pretoria, South Africa, in 1923 but only because her parents were on tour. Her father was an actor and her mother was a concert pianist, both from Wales. Glynis was always proud of her Welsh roots and took delight in playing the female lead opposite Richard Burton in the classic 1972 film *Under Milk Wood*. She is best known for her light comedy roles, such as the suffragette mother in *Mary Poppins* (1964), although she showed early in her career that she could take on serious roles as well with her role in *Frieda* (1947) where she played a war widow. She is probably best loved for her roles in *Miranda* (1948) and *Mad About Men* (1954). And Glynis showed her longevity, with her role in *Superstar* (1999).

Although predominantly an actress, Glynis's husky singing voice was also exceptional. Her soulful and heartfelt rendition of 'Send In the Clowns' was a highlight in the Broadway production of *A Little Night Music* (1973).

In 2020, Glynis became the oldest living Academy Award nominee and, in 2021, the oldest living Disney Legend.

27 AUGUST

On 27 August 1955, the *Guinness Book of Records* (now published as *Guinness World Records*) was first published. Many Welsh women have featured in the pages of the annual publication since then, including:

- **Helen Ryvar** is the current women's record holder for running the most consecutive half marathons. She runs in aid of the mental health charity Mind following the tragic and sudden death of her ex-husband in 2020. A single mother of three, Helen gets up at four o'clock each morning to complete her daily run before work. In 2024, she set about breaking her own record and aims to have run 1,000 half marathons by 2025.

- **Heidi Gannon and Jo Baines** from Welshpool are the first set of twins to be born in different countries. This unusual occurrence arose as their mother Carol Munro was unaware she was carrying twins. On 23 September 1976, she gave birth to Heidi in Welshpool in Wales but then went into labour again. For the second birth, she was taken to Shrewsbury in England.

- **Sylvia Pope** from Swansea – otherwise known as Nanna Baubles – broke the world record for the largest collection of Christmas baubles in December 2021. Sylvia passed away in 2023 and left her amazing collection to her family.

- **Catherine Pendleton** from Merthyr Tydfil, has the nickname 'The Merthyr Mermaid' because she achieved a Guinness world record for the most southerly ice swim when she became the first woman to swim a mile inside the Antarctic Polar Circle. The swim took thirty-two minutes and fifty-four seconds in a water temperature of 0.03°C (32°F).

28 AUGUST

The Qualification of Women (County and Borough Councils) Act gained royal assent to become a law on 28 August 1907. This meant that, for the first time, women were eligible to stand for positions in local government.

Gwenllian Morgan from Defynnog near Sennybridge (9 April 1852–7 November 1939) became the first woman in Wales to serve on a borough council. In 1910 she was elected as Mayor of Brecon, and was also the first woman in Wales to hold mayoral office.

Gwenllian was devoted to benefiting others and helping those in need. She understood the hardships people faced, treating them with kindness and understanding. She was also a passionate advocate of providing children with a good education. She volunteered her services to every branch of social work, dealt with public affairs and was a member of a long list of committees.

Gwenllian was described as a 'woman of wide culture and pronounced literary gifts' when awarded an Honorary MA degree by the University of Wales in 1925 for her valuable research into the life of the seventeenth-century Welsh poet Henry Vaughan. The award also acknowledged her work in Brecon, referring to her as a 'pioneer in the emancipation of women' and highlighting the impact her work would have on the future of women in Wales.

29 AUGUST

On 29 August 1536, the priory of Benedictine nuns in Usk was destroyed under Henry VIII's dissolution of the monasteries.

Usk was one of only three nunneries in medieval Wales, the other two being at Llanllyr in Deheubarth and at Llanllugan in Powys. These communities were small, with probably no more than a dozen women in each religious house.

There were few nunneries in medieval Wales compared to other countries and one possible explanation is that most of the abbeys in Wales were run by the Cistercian order, which was particularly hostile to women as they brought a 'risk of corruption' they were thought to bring with them. By 1228, there was a prohibition on new Cistercian nunneries being established.

Native Welsh law may also have presented a challenge to women wishing to take holy orders as, under the law of Hywel Dda, families with daughters entering holy orders would have to pay *ambor* (recompense) to the local lord, just as they would pay a dowry if a woman from their family was getting married. Few women in Wales held land in their own right so that made independent endowments difficult and reduced the likelihood of women being able to act as independent patrons. More common in Wales were independent enclaves of saintly or spiritual women. These were mainly made up of members of the nobility, such as the communities founded by St Melangell in the Berwyn mountains, by St Erfyl in Llanerfyl, and by St Gwenffrewi (Winifred) at Treffynnon.

30 AUGUST

Mary Hopkin, born in Pontardawe in the Swansea Valley, released her debut single 'Those Were the Days' on 30 August 1968. It was produced by Paul McCartney and Mary was the first artist to record on the Beatles' Abbey Road record label.

Mary began her career as a Welsh-language folk singer, rocketing to fame after winning *Opportunity Knocks,* a television talent programme hosted by Hughie Green. She went on to represent the UK in the 1970 Eurovision Song Contest singing 'Knock Knock Who's There' which came second in the contest, narrowly beaten by 'All Kinds of Everything', performed by Irish singer Dana.

Mary married Tony Visconti in 1971 and she partially withdrew from the pop music world to focus on raising a family. However, she continued to write songs, to record and contribute vocals to an eclectic range of pop legends such as Marc Bolan, Thin Lizzy and David Bowie.

She continues to write and perform, releasing an album of duets co-written and performed with her daughter Jessica Lee Morgan, called *Two Hearts,* in 2023.

31 AUGUST

Born on this day 1910 in Croydon, Esmé Kirby was a conservationist who, together with her husband Peter Kirby, formed the Snowdonia National Park Society (Cymdeithas Eryri) in 1967.

The Snowdonia Society works to protect and enhance the beauty and special qualities of Eryri (Snowdonia). Volunteers undertake practical conservation such as clearing litter, maintaining footpaths, tackling invasive species and improving habitats for wildlife. The society campaigns to protect Eryri from inappropriate development or any erosion of its natural and cultural heritage.

In 1997, Esmé's initiated the eradication of grey squirrels from Anglesey which resulted in the island now containing the largest red squirrel population in Wales.

Esmé first husband was Thomas Firbank, whose bestselling book, *I Bought a Mountain*, describes their married life during the 1930s on the farm Dyffryn Mymbyr, near Capel Curig. When Thomas and she separated she continued to live there until her death in 1999. Esmé left the farm to the National Trust.

1 SEPTEMBER

Katheryn of Berain (Catrin o Ferain; born 1535) was buried on 1 September 1591. She was posthumously referred to as *Mam Cymru* (Mother of Wales) as her four marriages meant that she had many descendants among the Welsh nobility. Notable among Katheryn's descendants were the powerful and influential Salusbury and Wynn families of north Wales.

Katheryn's grandfather was the illegitimate son of Welsh-born King Henry VII of England. As the heiress to the Berain and Penmynydd estates in Denbighshire and Anglesey, she was seen as a desirable bride and her four marriages each added to her substantial wealth and power.

Her first husband, John Salusbury of Lleweni, died at the age of twenty-two after they had had two sons together. Her second was Sir Richard Clough, one of the richest merchants of his time, and they had two daughters. Her third husband was Maurice Wynn, Sheriff of

Caernarfonshire, with whom she had a son and a daughter. Her fourth and last husband was Edward Thelwall of Plas-y-Ward, who outlived her.

As three of her husbands predeceased her, there were inevitable rumours at the time – the most outrageous of which suggested that she had murdered them by pouring molten lead in their ears as they slept. She was also said to have arranged her second and third marriages at the funeral of her first. Both Richard and Maurice had proposed to her on the day of John's funeral but Richard had proposed on the way into the service and Maurice on the way out. Katheryn allegedly accepted the first offer but told Maurice that she would marry him when 'there was a vacancy'. Other sources, however, show Katheryn to have been a dedicated wife and mother who was the victim of cruel gossip caused by jealousy of her immense wealth.

2 SEPTEMBER

On 2 September 1783, Frances (Fanny) Williams from Whitford Parish in Flintshire was sentenced to death for stealing from the artist Moses Griffith. Fanny was held in the old gaol in Flint until August of the following year when her sentence was reduced to transportation to Australia for seven years. On 13 May 1787, she left Portsmouth with a group of around 1,400 others on board eleven ships – a voyage known as 'The First Fleet'. During the journey, Fanny began a romance with Robert Ryan, a Royal Marine from Ireland. The ships arrived at Port Jackson (now Sydney) on 26 January 1788.

Initially, life was hard for the settlers. Crop failures, drought and bush-fires were common and the cattle they had brought with them became lost in the bush. To alleviate the food shortage, some of the party, including Fanny, were sent to settle on Norfolk Island. Fanny and Robert had a daughter in 1790 and Fanny died sometime in 1801.

Another Welsh woman who travelled to Australia with the First Fleet was Mary Watkins, from Cowbridge. Mary had been sentenced to seven years' transportation for stealing sixpence worth of clothing. Mary was also sent to Norfolk Island, where she and her partner, Isaac Tarr, converted some bush-land into farmland. The last record of Mary was in 1794 when she had returned to the mainland of Australia with her husband.

These women were some of the first Welsh settlers in Australia but it was the discovery of copper and gold in the early 1850s which caused the country's Welsh population to increase sharply. In Victoria, a *cymanfa ganu* (a festival of Welsh hymns) and the first Welsh-Australian Eisteddfod were held in 1863.

3 SEPTEMBER

On 3 September 1939 Britain declared war on Germany and the first child evacuees arrived in Wales as part of Operation Pied Piper. Throughout the Second World War, some 110,000 children were evacuated from urban areas of Britain to the safer rural areas of Wales.

Here are some notable women who came to Wales as evacuees:

- **Roberta Leigh** (born Rita Lewin) was evacuated from London to Prestatyn. There, she attended St Mary's Convent

School in Rhyl. It was during her time in Wales that she began writing by torchlight under the bedclothes. Roberta wrote romance novels but is perhaps best known for the puppet shows she created for television which included *The Adventures of Twizzle*, *Torchy the Battery Boy* and *Space Patrol*.

- **Nina Bawden** was a Golden PEN Award-winning novelist, and was evacuated from Ilford to Aberdare. Her novel *Carrie's War* (1973) describes the story of a brother and sister's experiences when they are evacuated to Wales.

- **Diana Wynne Jones** was a multi-award-winning novelist and was evacuated from London to Pontarddulais. She has been described as the best writer for children of her generation and is often cited as an inspiration for fantasy and science-fiction authors.

4 SEPTEMBER

Eldra Mary Jarman (née Eldra Mary Roberts), was born in Aberystwyth on 4 September 1917. She was a harpist, an author and a direct descendant of Abram Wood, thought to be the father of the Kale (*Sipsiwn Cymreig*), a group of Romani people in Wales.

Historically, the Romani lived a nomadic lifestyle moving from town to town, relying on agricultural seasonal work, handcrafts and fortune-telling to make a living. The Kale claim descendance from Abram Wood who was the first Romani to reside permanently in Wales in the early eighteenth century. They have a long tradition of music and speak a Roma dialect called Welsh Romani.

Eldra's great-grandfather was John Roberts, a well-known harpist who earned the sobriquet *Telynor Cymru* (The Welsh Harpist). Eldra learned the instrument as a child. She was the first generation to be born into a settled lifestyle. Her brother, who was ten years older than her, taught her about fishing, netting rabbits and hunting with ferrets and dogs, and her mother passed on to her the oral traditions and folklore of the Kale.

In 1943, Eldra married Alfred Owen Hughes Jarman, a lecturer in the culture and language of Wales at Cardiff University. He was also a Welsh speaker and he taught her to speak the language. Eldra became a keen Welsh nationalist. She also spent much of her time researching in detail the history and culture of the Kale. She published two intensely personal accounts of the history of the Roma in Wales: *Y Sipsiwn Cymreig* in 1979 (an English translation was published as *The Welsh Gypsies: Children of Abram Wood* in 1991).

Before she died in 2000, Eldra collaborated on a television script loosely based on her life as a child. *Eldra* aired on S4C in 2001.

5 SEPTEMBER ⚠

On International Day of Charity, we acknowledge and pay respect to some of the remarkable Welsh women who have been motivated to set up charities.

In 2012, Rhian Burke from Miskin lost her one-year-old son George, who collapsed suddenly with a seizure. As if this wasn't tragedy enough, Rhian's husband Paul died by suicide just five days later. Rhian's experience led her to set up the bereavement charity 2 Wish Upon a Star which provides bereavement suites, counselling and support groups, and to raise over £700,000 for the cause.

Shahien Taj is of Pakistani heritage and was born and raised in Wales. She founded the All Wales Saheli Association, now known as the Henna Foundation, which is a charity committed to supporting marginalised sections of Muslim communities. Shahien is a passionate advocate of equality and justice for women and a specialist in tackling the issues of 'honour' related abuses, forced marriages and radicalisation in Wales.

When Linda James discovered that one of her children was the victim of bullying she found a serious lack of support for children and families in her situation. As a result, in 2006, she established BulliesOut, a Cardiff-based anti-bullying charity founded to 'empower and inspire children, young people and adults to recognise their self-worth and achieve their full potential.'

In 2011, after eighteen years in an abusive relationship, Rachel Williams from Newport was shot by her violent partner. Rachel survived but spent several weeks in hospital and now lives with life-altering injuries. Her partner then died by suicide, as did her sixteen-year-old son Jack shortly after the attack. Rachel is the founder of SUTDA (Stand Up To Domestic Abuse) and works tirelessly to promote awareness of – and eventually end – domestic abuse.

6 SEPTEMBER

Imogen Stonehouse was born at Swansea's Singleton Hospital on 6 September 2022. She is Wales's most premature surviving baby. Her mother Rachel, from Bridgend, was only twenty-two weeks and five days pregnant at the time she went into labour and Imogen weighed just 515 grams (1lb 1oz) – the equivalent of a block of butter – when she was born.

Doctors told Rachel that Imogen had less than a 10 per cent chance of survival and she was immediately placed in a special incubator in the neonatal intensive care unit. Fighting for every breath, tiny Imogen overcame a heart murmur, a pulmonary haemorrhage, sepsis and numerous blood transfusions. Amazingly, after ninety-eight days, Imogen was able to be moved out of intensive care and into a special care baby unit at the Princess of Wales Hospital in Bridgend. There she spent a further thirty-four days before being allowed home.

DID YOU KNOW?

Wales's smallest surviving baby is Robyn Chambers who was born at the Grange University Hospital in Cwmbran on 8 March 2023, weighing just 328 grams.

7 SEPTEMBER

On 7 September 1816, Catherine Davies, born in Beaumaris, returned to Britain from Naples where she was governess for the children of the King and Queen of Naples: Joachim Murat and Caroline Bonaparte, the sister of the Emperor Napoleon of France. It was the final tumultuous months of the Napoleonic wars and the Murats were forced to flee and Catherine, unable to accompany them due to bad health, returned home.

Catherine Davies (1773–c.1841) had thirty-two siblings and step-siblings and she left her home in Wales to find work when she was fifteen. She worked as a nanny for a family in London who moved to Paris. Catherine followed but the position ended when hostilities broke out between Britain and France in 1802.

Caroline married Joachim Murat, an ardent republican and supporter of Napoleon. They had a young family and Caroline had great admiration for British governesses, so she employed Catherine to look after her children.

Napoleon, whom Catherine met on several occasions, was initially suspicious of her because of her nationality. When he asked her if she liked the French as well as the English, Caroline's sharp and honest reply was that she would be a hypocrite if she said that she did, but that she liked all people who were kind to her. This impressed him and she gained his respect. In 1808, when Caroline and Joachim were appointed as Queen and King of Naples, Catherine went with them to Italy.

She finally returned to Wales in 1818 and later related her experiences in a book *Eleven Years' Residence in the Family of Murat, King of Naples* which was published in 1841.

8 SEPTEMBER

Mavis Nicholson (née Mainwaring) born 19 October 1930 in Briton Ferry died on this day in 2022. She was a writer, a highly respected television and radio presenter, and the first solo female interviewer with a regular show on British television.

Mavis's father worked at the nearby steelworks. Her grandmother, Martha Jane, was an avid storyteller and instilled in Mavis the ability to communicate confidently. Mavis met her husband, the journalist Geoffrey Nicholson, at the University of Wales in Swansea. After graduating, the couple moved to London, where she worked as an advertising copywriter.

Her potential as a presenter was noticed when she was interviewed about a local dispute over school buses on *Thames Television News*. The famous television and radio presenter Eamonn Andrews noted that she was a natural. A year later, at the age of forty, she became host of a programme on the newly launched daytime television programme on Thames Television. Mavis was an instant success with her probing and engaging conversational style. She became a favourite of both the critics and stars she interviewed, including the likes of Elizabeth Taylor, David Bowie and Dudley Moore.

Mavis presented programmes such as *Afternoon Plus* and *Mavis On Four* on television as well as several radio shows, including *Woman's Hour*. She was also the resident agony aunt for *The Oldie* magazine until 2014. A lifelong socialist, Mavis could not abide injustice and was also an outspoken opponent of nuclear weapons.

9 SEPTEMBER

On 9 September 1843, the tollkeeper of the Hendy tollgate, seventy-five-year-old Sarah Williams, was shot dead when a group of men attacked her post during a series of civil protests known as the Rebecca Riots.

The Rebecca riots took place between 1839 and 1843 in rural west Wales. By the early nineteenth century, the population of the rural areas of Wales had doubled. This, combined with a series of wet harvests, placed extreme pressure on the mainly agriculture-based economy. There was widespread poverty and unemployment and a tipping point was reached with the introduction of a tollgate system to cover the costs of maintaining roads and the levying of taxes to pay for the building of workhouses. In protest, gangs of men dressed as women, calling themselves *merched Beca* (Rebecca's daughters) arrived under the cover of darkness to destroy the hated tollgates and workhouses.

Nobody was convicted of Sarah's murder, which caused outrage among locals. Following Sarah's death, the protesters recognised that the clandestine attacks were getting out of control and they began more open protests. Initially, the authorities clamped down and brought in troops to bolster the police forces. However, when this failed to quell the discontentment, the government was forced to call a commission of inquiry which ultimately resulted in the removal of the hated tollgates.

10 SEPTEMBER

Justina Jeffreys was born on this day in 1787 in Jamaica. Justina was the daughter of a freed Black woman and a white Scottish man. From her precarious beginnings, nobody could have foreseen that Justina – whose grandmother was an enslaved woman – would end up not only making her home in Wales but that she would rise to become a member of the Welsh gentry.

Justina's mother, Susan Leslie had been born into slavery but had gained her freedom. Justine's father was Captain Charles McMurdo, the senior British Army official on the island. She was sent to Wales when she was six to be raised as the adopted daughter of her father's junior officer, Edward Scott and his wife Louisa Maria Anwyl. Louisa was the heiress of the Bodtalog estate near Tywyn in Merioneth.

Justina grew up at Bodtalog, where, as a member of the local gentry, she received a good education and immersed herself in the language and culture of Wales. In 1814, Justina married wealthy lawyer George Jeffreys, from Shrewsbury, who had inherited land at Glandyfi, a picturesque hillside southwest of Machynlleth overlooking the Dyfi estuary. On this site in 1818, Justina and George built Regency Gothic style Glandyfi Castle as their home.

George and Justina had nine children and entertained lavishly in their grand new home. Among their friends was the author Thomas Love Peacock who used Justina as the inspiration for the heroine, Anthelia, in his novel *Melincourt*.

Justina inherited Bodtalog following the death of her father and also inherited Glandyfi when George died in 1868. She died the following year.

DID YOU KNOW?

Glandyfi Castle became the home of the notorious Sir Bernard Dockers, chairman of Daimler cars, and his wife, the socialite Lady Norah Docker. The couple made national headlines in the 1950s when it emerged that they were using the Daimler company to fund their extravagant lifestyle.

11 SEPTEMBER

Professor Julie Williams, one of the world's leading authorities in Alzheimer's research, was born in Merthyr Tydfil on 11 September 1957.

Julie is a professor of neuropsychological genetics at Cardiff University and was Chief Scientific Adviser for Wales from 2013 to 2017. Her research aims to identify and characterise genes which indicate a risk of developing psychological and neurodegenerative disorders such as Alzheimer's disease, developmental dyslexia, and schizophrenia. The former Minister for the Economy, Science and Transport in the Welsh Senedd, Edwina Hart said of Julie: 'She is a great role model for women in science … Her networks of national and international scientists will be crucial in opening the doors for Wales.' Julie was appointed a CBE for her contribution to Alzheimer's research in 2012 and is also a Fellow of the Learned Society of Wales.

12 SEPTEMBER

Born on this day 1861 in Blaina, Florence Eleanor Booth (née Soper) was an early officer of the Salvation Army and the wife of its second General, Bramwell Booth.

While visiting her aunts in London, a young Florence attended a meeting held by the co-founder of the Salvation Army, Catherine Booth, and was inspired to join. She was quickly promoted to lieutenant and married Catherine's son Bramwell in 1882. Florence then travelled with Catherine Booth to establish the Salvation Army in Switzerland and France.

In 1884, Florence pioneered the Salvation Army's Women's Social Work after she and Bramwell became concerned over the living conditions of many women and young girls. Unemployment and poverty meant that many women, including young girls, were finding themselves forced into sex work in order to survive. Her work involved the establishment of rescue homes which were safe havens for women in difficult circumstances. The success of her homes encouraged social reform and led to rescue homes being set up in many other countries by the Salvation Army.

13 SEPTEMBER

On 13 September 1957, *The Mousetrap* became Britain's longest-running play in the West End, when it staged its 1,998th performance. The success of the play and its author, Agatha Christie, have had a major influence on Welsh cultural life.

In 1951, Mathew Prichard was taken on his first theatre visit by his grandmother, Agatha Christie, to the Prince of Wales Theatre, Cardiff to see *Black Coffee,* a play which she had written twenty-five years earlier. The following year she signed the world rights of *The Mousetrap* to Mathew as a ninth birthday present. Agatha's only child, Rosalind, had married a Welsh man and lived near Colwinston. As a result, Agatha frequently visited and became very fond of Wales.

Prichard is now chairman of Agatha Christie Ltd which manages the literary and media rights to Agatha Christie's works around the world. He set up the Colwinston Charitable Trust, named after the village where he was brought up in the Vale of Glamorgan. The trust uses royalties from *The Mousetrap* (which continues to be performed in London today) to promote the arts in Wales. The Welsh National Opera, Wales Millennium Centre and Chapter Arts have all benefited from the Trust's financial support.

14 SEPTEMBER

On 14 September 1885, Elizabeth Phillips Hughes became the first principal of the University of Cambridge's Teacher Training College for Women. She was instrumental in the college being a great success and it was later named Hughes Hall in her honour.

Elizabeth Phillips Hughes (12 July 1851–19 December 1925) was born in Carmarthen and became a pioneer in women's education. She left a teaching post at Cheltenham Ladies' College to become the first woman student to take first-class honours at the University of Cambridge.

In 1899, she retired to Barry in Wales, where she carried on campaigning for improvements in secondary education and undertook lecture tours to America, Europe and even travelled to Tokyo to speak on the importance of physical education for women. She was an active member of the

Association for Promoting the Education of Girls in Wales and wrote numerous articles and pamphlets. In 1920, Elizabeth was the only woman on the committee which founded Swansea University.

15 SEPTEMBER

Greenpeace Day is observed on 15 September. It is a day dedicated to bringing about a change in the way we treat our environment in order to preserve our planet and its wildlife.

Sara Howell, from Dinas Cross in Pembrokeshire, is a Greenpeace activist who made headlines worldwide in 2017 when she swam into the path of the world's largest oil survey vessel, the 21,000 tonne *Amazon Warrior*, off the coast of New Zealand. She was protesting against offshore drilling and her actions stopped the ship from carrying out its work. She said later that her actions could be seen as 'troublemaking' but that she was motivated by 'standing up for what you think is morally right'.

Fellow Greenpeace activist Janet Barker, who lives with her husband in Llangammarch Wells on a farm that runs on renewable energy and produces ethical angora from rabbits, also made headlines in 2019 for her part in a protest. Janet was part of a group protesting at a black-tie event at Mansion House, London, where the then Chancellor of the Exchequer Philip Hammond was speaking about climate change. The protest was entirely peaceful and they intended to deliver a handwritten document to Hammond but fellow Tory MP Mark Field grabbed Janet by the back of the neck before pushing her against a column and forcibly walking her out of the event. Video of the event was widely circulated online and caused outrage.

Mr Field said he reacted 'instinctively' and 'deeply regretted' the incident. He was initially suspended as a Foreign Office minister while an investigation into the incident was carried out. Janet, however, who insisted the protesters' intentions were peaceful, said that she did not intend to press charges despite not receiving an apology from Mr Field. She thought the incident would be 'something best dealt with in the court of public opinion'.

16 SEPTEMBER

On 16 September 2001 – Owain Glyndŵr Day – actress Siân Phillips unveiled a memorial statue to his daughter Catrin in St Swithin's Church Garden, London.

Catrin ferch Owain Glyndŵr was probably the eldest daughter of Margaret Hanmer and Owain Glyndŵr. In November 1402, she married Edmund Mortimer. Mortimer had fought for Henry IV as a commander, but had been defeated and taken prisoner by Glyndŵr at the Battle of Bryn Glas. As Henry IV made no effort to pay a ransom for him, he switched his allegiance to Glyndŵr and married Catrin.

Mortimer died during the siege of Harlech Castle in 1409 and Catrin was captured along with her three daughters, her mother and one of her sisters. They were taken to the Tower of London. Their deaths, but not the cause of the deaths, are recorded as being in 1413. Catrin and her daughters were buried at St Swithin's Church.

Catrin's sister, Alys, also married a former enemy turned ally of her father, Sir John Scudamore of Herefordshire, who had held the castle at Carreg Cennen from Owain Glyndŵr and an army of 800 men in 1403.

It is thought possible that Alys and John sheltered Glyndŵr during the last years of his life at their home in the region between the Wye Valley and Monnow Valley in Herefordshire, at a time when King Henry V was offering rewards for information on Glyndŵr's whereabouts.

17 SEPTEMBER ⚠

Paula Yates (born 24 April 1959) died on this day in 2000. She was best known as the television presenter of the programmes *The Tube* and *The Big Breakfast,* for the levels of invasive media scrutiny she endured during her relationships with musicians Bob Geldof and Michael Hutchence and the tragic circumstances of her death.

Paula was born in Colwyn Bay, and brought up in the village of Rowen, near Llandudno. Her mother was Elaine Smith, a former showgirl, actress and writer of erotic novels. Until 1997, Paula believed her father was Jess Yates, host of the television programme *Stars on Sunday*. However, a DNA test that year revealed that her biological father was Hughie Green, the host of the television talent show *Opportunity Knocks*.

Paula began her media career as a music journalist but first came to public prominence in 1982 as co-presenter with Jools Holland of the Channel 4 pop music programme *The Tube*. She married Bob Geldof in 1976 and had the first of their three daughters in 1983. In 1992, she began presenting Channel 4's *Big Breakfast* show where she became known for her intimate 'on the bed' interviews. When Paula met Michael Hutchence, the lead singer of Australian rock band INXS, the two began an intense affair.

Paula and Bob divorced in May 1996 and a fierce battle

over custody of their daughters began. In July that year, Paula and Michael welcomed their daughter, Tiger Lily. In November 1997, Michael was found dead in a hotel room in Sydney, Australia. This tragedy, combined with the shock of her true parentage, shook Paula and she sought psychiatric treatment. In 1998 Bob Geldof won custody of their daughters and Paula attempted to take her own life.

Paula died at her home in London at the age of forty-one of a heroin overdose.

18 SEPTEMBER

On 18 September 1929, Iris de Freitas Brazão, became the first woman to practise law in the Caribbean, after graduating from Aberystwyth University.

Born in 1896, Iris was the daughter of a merchant in Guyana (then known as British Guiana). She registered as a student at Aberystwyth University in 1919 and studied botany, Latin and modern languages, law and jurisprudence. She lived in Alexandra Hall, the first purpose-built university hall of residence for female students in the UK, and became vice president of the university's Students' Representative Council and the president of the Women's Sectional Council. She graduated with a BA in 1922 and received her bachelor of laws in 1927. In 1929 she was admitted to the bar as the first woman to practise law in the Caribbean and was also the first female prosecutor of a murder trial there.

In 2016, a room in the Aberystwyth University's Hugh Owen Library was named in her honour and in 2018, she was included in a list of a hundred 'Brilliant, Black and Welsh' people.

19 SEPTEMBER

Today is International 'Talk like a Pirate' Day.

Wales's rugged coastline and remote, isolated bays and coves offered the ideal conditions for piracy and smuggling during the eighteenth century. Acts of piracy were mostly carried out by men but some women used this assumption to their advantage, and conducted their own pirating careers under the radar of suspicion.

Two such eighteenth-century women who feature in the legendary tales of piracy were Margaret Williams from Anglesey and Catherine Lloyd of Briton Ferry.

Anglesey was a popular centre of piracy due to its location on several sea routes in the Irish Sea. Margaret Williams was an intelligent and demure squire's wife who supposedly led a double life as the leader of a cut-throat band of pirates and smugglers who operated from their base at a cave near the village of Llanfair-yn-Neubwll on the west coast of Anglesey. Her story was used inspiration for the novel *Madam Wen* by W. D. Owen.

The coal ships returning to Neath from Ireland and the Channel Islands also offered opportunities for smugglers to bring in tea, cotton and brandy. Catherine Lloyd was the landlady of the Ferry Inn in Briton Ferry and the leader of a women-led smuggling gang. Her inn was where they stored the contraband collected by her all-women band of smugglers. Catherine's collective were hard uncompromising women. On one occasion in 1726 they had no problem in confronting a customs man sent to recover some seized brandy and wine. Catherine's activities, however, came to notice when she made the mistake of offering contraband Indian cotton to an off-duty customs officer from Llanelli.

20 SEPTEMBER ⚠

Actress Rachel Roberts was born on 20 September 1927 in Llanelli.

Initially a stage actress, Roberts made her film debut in 1954 in *Young and Willing*. She is perhaps best remembered for her role as the love interest of Richard Harris in *This Sporting Life* which saw her nominated for an Oscar. She also performed memorably in films including *Murder on the Orient Express, When a Stranger Calls* and *Charlie Chan and the Curse of the Dragon Queen*. Rachel also suffered throughout her life from depression and struggles with alcohol addiction.

She was married and divorced twice, the second time to Rex Harrison. She never recovered from the end of her relationship with Harrison. She was found to have died by suicide on 26 November 1980. Her journals were edited and published posthumously as *No Bells on Sunday: The Journals of Rachel Roberts* in 1984. The book is said to capture her 'hunger for love in all its miraculous and unrealistic aspects' and features memories of her from her close friends.

21 SEPTEMBER

World Alzheimer's Day takes place annually on 21 September. It is part of a global campaign to raise awareness and challenge the stigma around Alzheimer's disease and other forms of dementia.

The television and radio broadcaster Beti George is an outspoken campaigner on the Alzheimer's after her partner, writer and broadcaster David Parry-Jones, died from the disease in 2017.

In the final months of David's life, Beti let BBC cameras into her home to document his battle with the condition. The resulting documentary, *David and Beti: Lost for Words*, followed the couple and looked at the challenges and frustrations faced by carers in Wales. The programme was broadcast on BBC Cymru and BBC One and won a gold award at the New York Film Festival.

Beti was born in Coed-y-bryn near Llandysul in 1939. She is best known for presenting the nightly Welsh-language news programme *Newyddion*. She is a fervent supporter of Welsh independence and rejected an MBE in 2020 saying that, as a republican, accepting the award would be hypocritical. She was awarded an honorary degree by Swansea University in 2022.

22 SEPTEMBER

Emmeline Lewis-Lloyd (born 18 November 1827) died on this day in 1913. She was a pioneering female alpine mountaineer, and a member of the party that made the first recorded ascent of Aiguille du Moine in the French Alps in 1871. The summit of the peak is at an altitude of 3,412 m and it requires climbers to abseil on the descent.

Emmeline was born in a manor house in Nantgwyllt in the now-flooded Elan Valley. The Lewis-Lloyd Family were substantial property owners and her father was a Justice of the Peace but young Emmeline was far from the stereotypical Victorian gentlewoman. Her interests as a young girl were farming, hillwalking, fishing and otter-hunting. Her enthusiasm for Alpine climbing was inspired by Jean Charlet, a French mountain guide from Chamonix, who worked as a groom for a year on their family estate.

Emmeline subsequently climbed regularly in the Alps and the Pyrenees, being one of only half a dozen female mountain climbers active in Europe during the 1860s and 1870s. Few details survive about her ascents but she is known to have been the eighth woman to climb Mont Blanc. She introduced her friend Isabella Straton to climbing, with one of their first climbs being an attempt to ascend to the top of Matterhorn in 1869. The next year the two women completed a successful climb of Monte Viso, the highest mountain of the Cottian Alps in Italy in 1870 and became some of the first women to make the summit. Isabella later went on to climb with Jean Charlet before the two were married.

Emmeline was described as quite a character with a lively personality. In later life she was a noted raconteuse, entertaining people by talking passionately about her travels and exploits.

DID YOU KNOW?

There was no Lycra or Gore-tex for early women climbers like Emmeline Lewis-Lloyd. Instead, they wore long wool skirts and cotton or linen blouses with bow ties as well as wide-brimmed straw hats.

23 SEPTEMBER

On International Organic Farming Day, we celebrate the life and work of Dinah Williams, who farmed Wales's first organic dairy farm.

Dinah was born in 1911 in Crugiau House near Aberystwyth. Her father was Professor of Agriculture at Aberystwyth University, and her mother was the university's first instructor in dairy farming. The family owned Nantllan, a dairy farm in the Clarach valley near Cardigan. When Dinah's father died when she was twelve, she already had an active role on the farm with her mother. The 1920s brought harsh economic times and they found that they needed to be innovative in their farming methods. The team at Nantllan were pioneers in the use of seaweed as a fertiliser.

Dinah took a short course in agriculture at Aberystwyth University before returning to work at the farm. Her mother organised for Dinah to join a research trip to Ukraine to explore different farming practices. Towards the end of the 1930s, Dinah met her husband Stanley Williams.

After the Second World War, Dinah and Stanley moved to Brynllys, a farm in the Borth area, where she was able to develop her own ideas. She avoided using chemicals and, to the bemusement of the local farming community, experimented with newly developed strains of grasses, rotational grazing and composting techniques to produce organic fertilisers. She also began breeding a prize-winning herd of pedigree Guernsey cows and became a pioneering member of the Soil Association.

Dinah retired from farming in 1966 and left Brynllys to be run by her daughter and son-in-law. In her later years she became an active member of the Grassland Society, an activist within the National Farmers' Union and a Fellow of the Royal Agricultural Society, one of the very few women to have received the honour.

Dinah died in 2009 at the age of ninety-eight. In 2021 a Purple Plaque was installed on a cow byre at Brynllys Farm in recognition of her pioneering work in modern farming.

24 SEPTEMBER

World Rivers Day was first celebrated on 24 September 2005. It now occurs on the fourth Sunday of every September.

Two of Wales's major rivers have historical connections with mythical Celtic goddesses.

The River Severn (Afon Hafren in Welsh) is named after the goddess Hafren (Sabrina in Latin). The story of how the river came to get its name is recorded by Geoffrey of Monmouth in his twelfth-century chronicle *Historia Regum Britanniae* (*History of the Kings of Britain*). Legendary king of the Britons, Locrin, defeated an invading Germanic army and captured their leader's beautiful daughter, Estrildis. Locrin fell in love with Estrildis, but he already had a wife: Gwendolen. So he secretly met Estrildis in an underground cave and soon they had a daughter, Hafren. Gwendolen's father was the king of Cornwall and when he died, Locrin divorced Gwendolen and made Estrildis his queen. Consumed by rage, Gwendolen raised an army from Cornwall, killed Locrin in battle and declared herself ruler of Britain. She then ordered Estrildis and Hafren to be thrown into the mighty local river where they drowned. She named the river after Hafren as a reminder of Locrin's infidelity.

The River Dee is dedicated to Aerfen and is where sacrifices were made in her name to ensure victory in battle. In the ancient Brythonic language, from which Welsh is derived, the Brythonic word *dēvā* means 'river of the goddess'. The Romans later named their legionary fortress on the site of modern-day Chester Deva Victrix meaning 'the fortress on the Dee'.

25 SEPTEMBER

On this day in 1915, the Women's Institute secured government funding.

One of its original members was Charlotte Price White from Dumfries, one of the earliest female science graduates at the University College of North Wales, Bangor. She became the secretary and driving force of the Bangor branch of the National Union of Women's Suffrage Societies and was one of only two women who walked from north Wales to London as part of the suffragists' 'Great Pilgrimage' of 1913.

During the Second World War, Charlotte was secretary of a north Wales committee that raised funds to establish a Welsh hospital unit in Serbia and personally organised for a young Serbian refugee to receive a university education in Bangor. After the war, she played a prominent part in the Women's International League for Peace and Freedom and made another peaceful protest by walking to London as part of the National Peacemakers' Pilgrimage of 1926. That year she also became the first woman elected to Caernarfonshire County Council.

The WI movement began in Canada in 1897 and was set up in the UK to revitalise rural communities and to encourage women to become more involved in producing food during the First World War. It has since grown to become the UK's largest women's voluntary organisation with over 200,000 members in over 6,500 branches, offering women the chance to take part in a range of activities and to campaign on important local issues.

26 SEPTEMBER

Emily Charlotte Talbot (born 1840) was buried on this day in 1918. She was an industrialist and one of the wealthiest women in Britain but she also used her money for good.

Emily was the daughter and heiress of Christopher Rice Mansel Talbot, the Liberal politician and industrialist who owned the estates at Margam and Penrice. Emily did not marry, and used much of her wealth for the benefit of the local community.

Emily made land available for creating a port and railway system which, in 1901, helped to attract the new steelworks to Port Talbot and secure the town's future as an industrial centre. She reputedly ran Bryndu Colliery at a loss for ten years to keep its 500 workers in employment and funded a new waterworks at Margam. During the First World War, Emily gave £4 million to the war effort and converted Penrice Castle on Gower into an officers' hospital. She also funded the role of chair of preventive medicine at a local medical school as well as providing two large YMCA buildings and regularly donating large amounts of money to the Church.

When Emily died in 1918, she was buried in the family vault in Margam church. A newspaper obituary said of her: 'Her great gifts to benevolent, educational, and religious purposes were often anonymous and few knew what a large portion of her riches she devoted to the needs of others, particularly in south Wales, of which she was the true Lady Bountiful.'

27 SEPTEMBER

On 27 September 2008, Nicole Cooke won the cycling World Road Race Championships. In the Beijing Olympic Games earlier that same year she had won gold. She became the first British woman to achieve Olympic gold and win the World Championship road race in the same year.

Nicole was born in Swansea in 1983 and grew up in Wick, Vale of Glamorgan. She was cycling as a young child on tandems with her parents on family holidays and started racing competitively at age eleven with Cardiff Ajax Cycling Club. At sixteen she became the youngest rider to take the senior women's title at the British National Road Race Championships and at seventeen she became the youngest rider to win the senior women's title at the British National Cyclocross Championships. At eighteen, Nicole won a gold medal for Wales in the Commonwealth Games Road Race and subsequently became one of the world's greatest women cyclists for more than a decade. She became the youngest winner, and the first British cyclist, of any gender, to win a Grand Tour when she triumphed in the Giro d'Italia Femminile in 2004. She also won the Tour de France twice in her career. Her gold medal at the Beijing Olympics also made her the first British cyclist to win gold in any road discipline.

Nicole retired from competitive racing in 2012. Her autobiography, *The Breakaway*, published in 2014, highlighted her support for equality for women in cycling events, and condemned the abuse of performance-enhancing drugs in the sport.

28 SEPTEMBER

Born on this day 1895, Agnes Twiston Hughes was the first Welsh woman to qualify as a solicitor.

Agnes was educated at the Welsh Girls' School in Ashford, Surrey and Bangor County School for Girls before gaining a degree in economics from the University of London in 1918. She then achieved first-class honours from the Law Society in 1923 and became the first woman in Wales to qualify to practise law. Once qualified, Agnes worked at her father's firm of solicitors in Conwy, which she took over when he died. In retirement, she became a local councillor before becoming the mayor of Conwy in 1954.

29 SEPTEMBER

Julia Gillard, born in Barry on 29 September 1961, became the first female prime minister of Australia from 2010 to 2013.

As a child, Gillard suffered from a case of broncho-pneumonia and, for the benefit of her recovery, her parents decided to move to the warmer climate of Australia in 1966, settling in Adelaide.

Julia attended the University of Adelaide and then the University of Melbourne to study law. Here, she worked with the Australian Union of Students. In 1983 she became the second woman to be elected president of that union. She then worked in industrial law specialising in employee rights and workplace disputes but was still involved in politics. She resigned her position at the law firm in 1996 when she became the Labor Party's chief-of-staff in Victoria.

In 2006, she became the party's deputy leader and had responsibility for employment and workplace relations and social inclusion. In 2007, Julia was appointed the first ever Deputy Prime Minister and Minister of Education. In 2010, Julia mounted a successful leadership challenge, thereby making her Australia's first female prime minister. Her first year in office was productive, with her government promoting the education agenda and introducing legislation to reform the health system, citing Welsh Labour politician Aneurin Bevan as one of her political heroes. However, her popularity declined following her failure to produce major policy successes and she resigned in 2013.

Since her retirement from politics, Julia has published her autobiography and been the recipient of many international awards. She has also been closely involved with many leading charitable organisations, such as the Global Partnership for Education, Beyond Blue and the Wellcome Trust.

30 SEPTEMBER

On 30 September 1910, a meeting was held to establish what form the memorial to King Edward VII should take in Wales. It was decided that it would be a campaign to eradicate tuberculosis in Wales, and the King Edward VII Welsh National Memorial Association was founded. In 1921, the association purchased Craig Y Nos Castle, five miles northeast of Ystradgynlais, which they converted into a tuberculosis sanatorium known as the Adelina Patti Hospital. It remained in use until 1986, after which it was sold and converted into a hotel.

The pioneering hospital got its name because Craig Y Nos had been the home of the world-famous soprano Adelina Patti. She bought it when she retired in 1854 and settled in the Swansea Valley. Adelina was extremely popular locally, played a number of charity concerts in Swansea and Brecon and was fondly referred to as the 'Lady of the Castle' and the 'Queen of Hearts'.

In 1886, she had a railway station built on the Neath and Brecon Railway line and in 1891 opened a private theatre at Craig Y Nos. She was awarded the freedom of both Swansea and Brecon. In 1918, she gifted the Winter Garden building to the city of Swansea. This was rebuilt near the Guildhall and renamed the Patti Pavilion.

1 OCTOBER

Today is the International Day of Older Persons, a day dedicated to honouring and recognising the invaluable role that older people play in our communities.

With modern medical advances, people are now living longer and healthier lives. In the sixteenth century, life expectancy was only thirty-five years. By 1911, improved living standards and the introduction of public sewers increased life expectancy to fifty-four years for women and fifty for men in the UK. Today, life expectancy for women in Wales is now eighty-two years and seventy-eight years for men.

At the time of her death in 1982, Jeanetta Thomas, (born 2 December 1869) of Llantrisant, was, at the age of 112 years and thirty-four days, the UK's oldest person and the oldest Welsh-born woman at that time. Jeanetta spent her youth in London working as a seamstress and returned to Wales to open a drapery shop, which she ran until the age of ninety-eight.

Her record was broken in April 2024 by Wales's current oldest living woman: Mary Keir from St Davids. Mary was born on 3 March 1912 and worked as a nurse at Llandough Hospital in the Vale of Glamorgan. Mary keeps her mind sharp by doing daily crosswords and sudoku.

2 OCTOBER

On 2 October 1902 the first published edition of *The Tale of Peter Rabbit,* written by Beatrix Potter, went on sale in UK bookshops. Wales was a frequent destination for Beatrix and a huge inspiration in her work.

Beatrix's inspiration for the tales of Peter, her most well-known character, is said to have come during a stay at Croft House in Tenby in 1900. In letters to cheer up the children of her former governess, Annie Moore, who was recovering from scarlet fever, Beatrix wrote stories about the rabbits living in the cliffs around Tenby. She also sketched the property's lily pond which features in the book.

In 1909, Beatrix was inspired to write *The Tale of the Flopsy Bunnies* during her visits to her aunt at Gwaenynog Hall near Denbigh. The walled gardens there feature as the backdrop for her illustrations of Mr McGregor and the rabbits. McGregor's potting shed still stands and is a popular tourist attraction.

In 1888, on another visit to Wales, Beatrix wrote in her diary of her frustration that a train journey from Shrewsbury to Machynlleth had taken four hours. She was more complimentary of the countryside, which she described as beautiful, and of the Welsh people who seemed to her to be 'pleasant' and 'intelligent' even if she also thought they would be 'awkward to live with'.

3 OCTOBER

Today marks the day, in 1990, when the former German Democratic Republic officially joined the Federal Republic of Germany and Germany became unified. It is also recognised as Germany's national day. Wales has many connections with Germany and one is that they share a saint.

St Ursula was one of medieval Europe's most popular saints and Welsh legend claims she was from Ceredigion where there is a church dedicated to her.

Ursula's story goes back to the fourth century. She was the daughter of a British king and reluctantly agreed to marry a pagan prince in order to save her father's kingdom. She insisted on one final pilgrimage to Rome before the marriage and was accompanied by 11,000 virgins. Ursula and the virgins never returned. Legend has it that they were besieged by Huns in Cologne. All the virgins were beheaded and Ursula was fatally shot with an arrow.

The church at Llangwyryfon (the Church of the Virgins) near Aberystwyth in Ceredigion is the only one dedicated to Ursula in the United Kingdom. The Virgin Islands are also named after St Ursula and the 11,000 virgins. The name was given to them by Christopher Columbus who sighted the islands in 1493 on his second voyage to the Americas.

4 OCTOBER

Alice Matilda Langland Williams – known as Alys Mallt or Y Fonesig Mallt Williams – was a political writer and prominent supporter of Welsh home rule. She was born on this day in 1867.

Alys was born in Brecknockshire to an English-speaking family but was inspired to learn Welsh after being welcomed into the circle of the influential promotor of Welsh culture, Augusta Hall, Baroness Llanover. In 1896, Alys was the second person to join Urdd y Delyn, a movement for young people in Wales to promote Welsh arts and culture.

In 1889, Alys published the novel *One of the Royal Celts* under the pseudonym Y Ddau Wynne with her sister Gwenfrieda. The novel's main character can trace his ancestry back to the last true Welsh prince. Alys published her second novel *A Maid of Cymru* in 1901. It was a romance, again with strong patriotic themes that explored the failure of the campaign for Welsh home rule at the time.

Between 1911 and 1916, Alys helped found the radical nationalist group Byddin Ymreolwyr Cymru (Army of Welsh Home Rulers) and was also an active member of Welsh nationalist movements, such as Cymru Fydd and Plaid Cymru.

Alys's commitment to Welsh independence was uncompromising. She was also an outspoken supporter of other nationalist causes. She was an animated opponent of the establishment of an RAF training camp at Penyberth on the Llŷn Peninsula and dubbed them *ysgolion fomio* (bombing schools).

Alys died in 1950 and her ashes were scattered in the churchyard at Llansanffraid, Brecknockshire.

5 OCTOBER

Today is World Teachers' Day and we celebrate two notable women who have made a significant contribution to education in Wales.

Norah Isaac, from Caerau near Maesteg, was the headteacher of Wales's first Welsh-medium school, Ysgol

Gymraeg yr Urdd in 1939. When it first opened, Norah had just seven pupils but, by 1945, there were seventy-one. Norah was also an author and a playwright who went on to become a lecturer in Welsh and drama at Trinity College, Carmarthen, where she established the first Welsh drama department in Wales. She has been described as 'the most influential individual in the history of Welsh-medium education'.

Bev Lennon was Wales's first Black female teacher of the Welsh language. When she moved from Brixton to Barry in 1987, she was fascinated by the bilingual signs and decided to learn Welsh. She began by listening to Radio Cymru, watching Welsh-language television and reading translations of Noddy cartoons. Beverley took a beginner's course in the language in the early 1990s and went on achieve an A* grade at GCSE and then an A grade at A level. Bev went on to study for a degree and train to be a teacher. In 1997 she was offered a job teaching Welsh at Cantonian High School in Cardiff. Bev admits that she was met with surprise and occasional prejudice in her new role but it was 'never from pupils'. Bev was admitted as a member of the Gorsedd at the National Eisteddfod in 2019.

6 OCTOBER

On 6 October 1884, Martha Hughes Cannon secretly married Latter-day Saints leader and Mormon pioneer, Angus M. Cannon. He was twenty-three years her senior and she became his fourth plural wife – joining his three other wives in their home together.

Martha Maria 'Mattie' Hughes Cannon (1 July 1857–10 July 1932) was born in Llandudno and when she was four, she emigrated to Salt Lake City, Utah. Her family were converts of the Church of Jesus Christ of Latter-day Saints. It is speculated that it was the deaths of her younger sister, who died during the wagon journey across the plains, and her father, who died within days of arriving in the Salt Lake Valley, that instilled in Martha the desire to become a doctor. By the age of twenty-five, Martha had obtained four degrees including an MD and in 1882, she became one of Utah's first female doctors as the resident physician at Deseret Hospital in Salt Lake City.

Martha's marriage had to be a secret as, in 1882, polygamy had become a felony in the United States punishable by a fine and prison time. In 1885, Martha left Utah for Britain, France and Switzerland where she worked and learned in hospitals and nursing schools.

In 1888, Martha returned to Utah where she established a nursing school and became involved in politics as a leader in Utah's women's suffrage movement. In 1896 Martha became the first woman elected as a state senator for Utah where she helped introduce a law regulating working conditions for women and girls, spearheaded funding for the education of speech- and hearing-impaired students, and helped establish the Utah State Board of Health.

7 OCTOBER

On 7 October 1980, singer and jazz legend Iris Williams was given her first television show by the BBC.

Iris was born on 20 April 1944 in Rhydyfelin. Raised initially in a children's home in Tonyrefail, she was later adopted by her family. She won a scholarship to the Welsh College of Music and Drama after being made redundant from a glove factory in Llantrisant.

The first success of Iris's subsequent music career was in 1971 with '*Pererin Wyf*' (a Welsh version of 'Amazing Grace') and her biggest UK hit was 'He Was Beautiful' which followed in 1979. Her music success meant that her BBC show ran for two series.

Iris relocated to New York in the early 1990s, where she performed with Bob Hope, made an appearance with Rosemary Clooney and performed for former president Gerald Ford. She has returned to perform at the Royal Variety Performance several times and was one of the stars at the concert to celebrate the opening of the Senedd (National Assembly of Wales) in 1999. She was admitted to the Gorsedd of Bards in 2006.

8 OCTOBER

On 8 October 2019, the eXXpedition all-women Round the World voyage, led by Welsh woman Emily Penn, set sail from Plymouth.

Emily, born in Swansea and raised in Penarth, founded eXXpedition in 2014. It is a non-profit organisation aimed at helping people understand the true impact of plastic on our oceans and harnessing their skills to solve the problem.

Emily earned a place in the Welsh sailing squad aged fourteen. She left the University of Cambridge with a degree in architecture and soon after joined the team on *Earthrace*, a record-breaking bio-fuelled speedboat, on a voyage to Australia where she intended to pursue a career as an architect. It was on this journey that she had a moment which changed both her focus in life and her career path. *Earthrace* sailed through the Pacific garbage patch, a flotilla of mostly plastic waste. What she saw made her decide to dedicate her career to solving the issue of plastic pollution in the planet's oceans. She began with community clean-ups and subsequently organised the largest ever clean-up from the beaches of a tiny Tongan island.

The Round the World voyage was brought to an abrupt end by the beginning of the Covid-19 pandemic but Emily's work has continued. She was awarded The Fitzroy Award at the 2016 Ocean Awards as well as the Hotung Medal of the Scientific Exploration Society in 2018. She was also the youngest and only female recipient of both the Yachtmaster of the Year and the Seamaster of the Year award. In 2021 she was awarded a British Empire Medal in the Queen's New Year's Honours List.

9 OCTOBER

Dilys Price, born in 1932 and known as 'Daredevil Dilys', died on this day in 2020.

On 13 April 2013 Dilys, aged eighty, carried out a charity parachute jump. At the time it made her the world's oldest solo woman parachutist.

A retired Cardiff-based lecturer, Dilys made her first parachute jump at the age of fifty-four. She completed well over a thousand jumps for charity, raising tens of thousands of pounds for charitable causes. During her time as a teacher, she worked with specialist schools to help children using wheelchairs take part in sports and dance. In 1996, she also founded The Touch Trust (now known as Two Rhythms). The organisation is now a centre for promoting movement education (called 'touch therapy') for people with autism, dementia and profound disabilities.

10 OCTOBER

The first and only time the title 'Princess of Wales' was recorded in an independent Wales was when Eleanor de Montfort married Llywelyn ap Gruffydd in October 1278. However, since Llywelyn's death at the hands of King Edward I in 1282 and the English king's subsequent subjugation of Wales, the English Crown has awarded the title to the wife of the heir apparent to the English and later British throne.

The first time it was awarded in this manner was on 10 October 1361 when Joan, Countess of Kent married Edward the Black Prince, son and heir apparent of King Edward III.

Including Joan, there have been ten English Princesses of Wales. The other nine are:

- **Anne Neville** married Edward of Westminster in 1470. Edward killed at the Battle of Tewkesbury in 1471 and Anne married Richard, Duke of Gloucester who went on to become Richard III in 1483 making Anne Queen of England until her death in 1485.

- **Catherine of Aragon**'s first husband, Arthur Tudor, died in 1502 making his younger brother Henry the heir to the throne. Henry married his brother's widow after his coronation. Henry declared their marriage invalid so he could marry Anne Boleyn in 1533. Catherine was thereafter acknowledged only as the dowager Princess of Wales.

- **Caroline of Ansbach** married George Augustus, who would become George II of England, on 22 August 1705. Caroline was the first women to receive the title of Princess of Wales at the same time as her husband received the title of Prince of Wales.

- **Augusta of Saxe-Gotha** gained the title when she married George II's son, Frederick Louis on 17 April 1736. She never became queen consort though, as Frederick died suddenly in 1751. However, their son became King George III in 1760.

- **Caroline of Brunswick** married George IV on 8 April 1795. They had one daughter, Charlotte, but lived separate lives thereafter. George tried to divorce Caroline. She refused and returned to take her position as queen but was barred from his coronation in 1821.

- **Alexandra of Denmark** married Edward, the son of Queen Victoria, on 10 March 1863. She was the Princess of Wales from that date until 1901 when Victoria died, which is the longest anyone has held the title.

- **Mary of Teck** married George, son of Edward VII on 6 July 1893. George would go on to become George V in 1910. Her son, Edward VIII, later abdicated to marry the American socialite Wallis Simpson.

- **Diana Spencer** married Charles, Prince of Wales on 29 July 1981. The couple had two sons, but their marriage ended in divorce in 1996. Diana was regarded as a fashion icon and was thought to be one of the most photographed women in the world. She died in a car accident on 31 August 1997.

- **Catherine Middleton**, known as Kate, married William on 29 April 2011. When Elizabeth II died on 8 September 2022, they became Prince and Princess of Wales. They have three children. Catherine underwent treatment for cancer in early 2024 and announced that she had completed chemotherapy in September 2024.

11 OCTOBER

On 11 October 1957, actress Anna Kashfi married Marlon Brando, at the time one of the world's most famous actors. Afterwards, Anna became the focus of intense media attention over the mystery of her true parentage. What was eventually revealed about Anna's real story led back to a butcher's shop in Cardiff.

The day after the wedding, a factory worker from Cardiff called William Patrick O'Callaghan claimed that he and his wife Phoebe were Anna's parents and that her real name was Joan O'Callaghan.

Joan – or Anna as she preferred to be known – was born in India in 1934. She was raised in Kolkata (Calcutta) until she was thirteen, when her Welsh mother decided it was time to move back to Cardiff in 1947. There she attended school and then worked as a waitress and as an assistant in a butcher's shop.

When she was in her twenties, she moved to London to become a model. An agency encouraged her to transform herself into 'ethnic Indian' model and actress Anna Kashfi. Anna's good looks soon brought her to the attention of Hollywood film directors and she enjoyed a brief acting career in the 1950s, starring in films with Spencer Tracey, Rock Hudson and Jack Lemmon. It is reported that Brando was instantly smitten on first seeing Anna, describing her as 'probably the most beautiful woman I've ever known'. After a brief romance which resulted in an unplanned pregnancy, they married.

When questions about her were raised after their wedding, Anna claimed that her father was a man called Devi Kashfi and her mother was a woman called Selma Ghose. The O'Callaghans back in Cardiff still insisted that Anna was their daughter. It was suspected and widely reported, although unsubstantiated, that Phoebe had engaged in an affair with an Indian man and that William had raised Anna as his stepdaughter. This was backed up by Anna's own account in her autobiography published in 1979, *Brando for Breakfast,* although Phoebe has always denied this.

12 OCTOBER

Ruth Manning-Sanders (born 21 August 1886) died on this day in 1988. She was a prolific poet and author who was best known for her *A Book of…* series of children's books in which she collected and retold fairy tales from all over the world. She published more than ninety books during her lifetime.

Ruth was born in Swansea and moved with her family to Sheffield and Manchester, where she won a scholarship to study English literature and Shakespeare studies at the University of Manchester. A serious illness forced her to leave university, however, and after returning from a trip to Italy to recover, she moved to Devon where she met and married the artist George Sanders. They spent much of their early married life touring Britain in a horse-drawn caravan and working in a circus before settling in Cornwall.

Ruth started by writing poetry but, inspired by a lifelong fascination with the subject, she then concentrated on collecting fairy tales. Her first book, *A Book of Giants*, was published in 1962. This was quickly followed by another volume every year until 1984. The series covered dragons; princes and princesses; dwarfs; witches; spooks and spectres; and ogres and trolls. Ruth introduced readers to fairy tales from across the globe including Baba Yaga and Anansi, publishing over ninety books in a variety of genres including prose fiction, poetry and non-fiction.

13 OCTOBER

On 13 October 2019, Lucasfilm executive vice president and general manager, Lynwen Brennan was honoured by BAFTA Cymru with a Special Award for Outstanding Contribution to Film and Television. Lynwen is best known for her work on the *Star Wars* and *Indiana Jones* franchises.

Lynwen grew up in Penally in Pembrokeshire. As a child she was in awe of the film industry and remembers seeing her first film at the cinema, the blockbuster hit *Jaws*.

Lynwen had just graduated when she fell from a bobsled-style rollercoaster. Her injuries were so severe that doctors considered amputating her foot. Her mother spent twelve hours massaging her leg to revive a pulse in her foot. Lynwen recalls this in an interview and noted that she came from a long line of determined Welsh women. She recovered but the process took a whole year. It was during this time that she started working in special effects with her brother, who was setting up his own software company.

One of their first clients was George Lucas's Industrial Light & Magic (ILM) which was working on *Jurassic Park*. Lynwen knew the moment she saw the dinosaurs brought back to life on the screen that she wasn't going to work anywhere but in the film industry.

In the late 1990s, she was offered a junior position at ILM working on *Star Wars: The Phantom Menace*. She worked her way up the ranks, eventually becoming president in 2008. In 2015, Lynwen began serving as general manager of Lucasfilm. She told *The New York Times* that she is on a 'crusade' to remedy the entrenched gender inequality in her industry. She has been recognised by BAFTA Cymru and made an honorary fellow of the Royal Welsh College of Music and Drama.

14 OCTOBER

The Senghenydd colliery disaster which took place on 14 October 1913 remains the worst mining disaster in British history. A tragic total of 439 men and boys died in the explosion at the Universal Colliery, leaving 217 women widowed and 522 children without a father. One woman had eight coffins in her house for the bodies of her husband, three brothers and four sons.

The subsequent inquiry into the disaster proved to be controversial. Although the inquiry was critical of the owners and management for the poor safety standards at the mine, Universal Colliery only had to pay the equivalent of £4,000 in fines (in today's money) and was back in operation by the end of the following month. The treatment of the widows of the victims was also chauvinistic. The compensation paid by the mine to the affected families was the equivalent (in today's money) of £26,000 per man. It was decided that widows would be paid in weekly instalments as it was doubted that they could be trusted with a lump sum. Conditions were also put in place by the male-only executive committee and board of trustees that the women would lose their payments if they took paid work. They also had to avoid 'all immoral habits', stay chaste and not remarry.

An iconic image of the disaster, published all around the world, showed thirteen-year-old Agnes May Webber waiting for news from the colliery with her baby sister. It is the inspiration for a sculpture carved from the trunk of a sycamore tree in the grounds of the National and Universal Mining Disaster Memorial Garden in Senghenydd.

15 OCTOBER

It is thought to have been 15 October 1204 when Joan (Siwan) (born c.1191), the illegitimate daughter of King John of England, was betrothed to Llywelyn ap Iorwerth otherwise known as Llywelyn Fawr (Llywelyn the Great), Prince of Wales.

Little is known of Joan's early life but she seems to have spent part of her childhood in France, as King John brought her to England from Normandy in 1203 in preparation for her wedding to Llywelyn. After their marriage Joan came to be known as 'The Lady of Wales'. Joan and Llywelyn had at least two legitimate children together: Elen ferch Llywelyn and Dafydd ap Llywelyn. Llywelyn reputedly built the Church of St Mary, Trefriw, Conwy, for her.

In 1211, King John invaded north Wales and Joan acted as a negotiator between her husband and her father. In 1216, when Henry III came to the throne, Joan continued to plead for Gwynedd's independence with the English court.

In 1230, William de Braose, who was being held captive by Llywelyn at the time, was discovered with his queen in the royal bedchamber. Llywelyn had de Braose hanged and placed Joan under house arrest for twelve months, although she was subsequently forgiven by Llywelyn, and restored to favour.

Joan died on 2 February 1237 at the royal home at Abergwyngregyn and Llywelyn founded a Franciscan friary nearby, on the coast at Llanfaes, in her honour. Her stone coffin can still be seen in Beaumaris parish church, Anglesey.

16 OCTOBER

Pobol y Cwm, the Welsh-language soap opera was first screened on television on 16 October 1974. It is the longest-running television soap opera produced by the BBC. In 1994, it was briefly shown across the whole of the United Kingdom on BBC2 with English subtitles. It is now screened by S4C and is regularly its most-watched programme.

The setting for the show is the fictional village of Cwmderi, located in the Gwendraeth Valley, the area lying between Carmarthen and Llanelli. Storylines are centred around the village pub, Y Deri; the comprehensive school, Ysgol y Mynach; and a local farm, Penrhewl.

The village's oldest character is Megan Harries played by the show's longest-serving cast member Lisabeth Miles. Lisabeth comes from Waunfawr near Caernarfon and was an original member of the cast in 1974.

17 OCTOBER

On 17 October 1838, Lady Charlotte Guest published the first volume of her translation of the *Mabinogion,* a collection of medieval Welsh prose which has become the most influential text of Welsh medieval legend.

Charlotte Elizabeth Guest (1812–1895) was born in Uffington, Lincolnshire, the daughter of wealthy aristocrat Albemarle Bertie, 9th Earl of Lindsey. She was an intelligent child. She showed a particular aptitude for languages and was fluent in several languages by the time she was an adult.

In 1833, Charlotte married John Josiah Guest, a part-owner of the Dowlais Iron Company, near Merthyr Tydfil, which was, at the time the world's largest iron producer. Guest was twenty-six years older than the twenty-two-year-old Charlotte, which caused something of a scandal, but it appears to have been a happy union and they had ten children during their nineteen years of marriage.

In her new home, Charlotte became fascinated with Welsh culture and mythology and learned Welsh. She was approached by historian Thomas Price and the Reverend John Jones, both associated with the Abergavenny Eisteddfod, to support the publication of Welsh manuscripts. Instead, she decided to do the translation herself. Working from the library of Dowlais House, she primarily used selected tales from the medieval Welsh manuscripts, the *Red Book of Hergest* and the *White Book of Rhydderch*. Charlotte wasn't the first to publish English translations of these particular tales, but when she brought them together as the *Mabinogion*, they attracted a much wider public audience than they had before.

Following her husband's death in 1852, Charlotte ran the Dowlais Ironworks for three years. She was proactive in improving the education and health of the workers as well as writing a history of the iron trade in the UK. In later life, she campaigned for Turkish refugees and for better treatment for hansom cab drivers. She was also an avid collector of china, ceramics, fans and playing cards from throughout Europe, which were donated to the Victoria and Albert Museum after her death.

18 OCTOBER

Eryri (Snowdonia) National Park was established on 18 October 1951. It was the first national park in Wales and the third in the United Kingdom. There have been a number of women who have played a vital part in protecting this precious part of Wales.

In 1895 Dinas Oleu, a gorse-covered hillside in the Mawddach Estuary near Barmouth, became the first property donated to the National Trust. The 4.5 acres of land, home to rare species of plants and birds, were given to the Trust by Fanny Talbot, a friend of Octavia Hill who was one of the Trust's founders.

Eryri's Dark Sky Officer is Dani Robertson. DarkSky International seeks to restore night-time environments from the harmful effects of light pollution. The park was awarded Dark Sky Reserve status in December 2015. There are only twenty Dark Sky Reserves in the world, and two of them are in Wales, the other being the Bannau Brycheiniog (Brecon Beacons) National Park.

In 2022, Annwen Hughes, councillor for Harlech and Llanbedr, was elected as chair of the Eryri (Snowdonia) National Park Authority. She was the first woman to take up the post and it was the first time ever that there was an equal number of men and women on the board.

19 OCTOBER

Today is National 'Evaluate Your Life' Day. It is the day when people are encouraged to look at their lives and life choices and commit to making the changes for the better. Steph Jeavons, from Old Colwyn, did just that.

Born in Canada, Steph has lived most of her life in Wales and considers herself Welsh. Steph's turning point came during her darkest hours. She found herself serving a two-year prison sentence as a result of heroin addiction. One night she looked out of her prison cell window and, instead of being in a cold cell, she imagined herself under a baobab tree with a sleeping lion in its branches, and decided to change her life.

In 2014, after she had served her sentence, she set off on her trip around the world on Rhonda the Honda (her motorbike). Despite not being a mechanic or speaking other languages, Steph completed her journey through the hottest, driest, wettest and coldest places on earth in just under four years, relying on good luck and the kindness of others. During her journey, Steph visited fifty-three countries and covered over 74,000 miles. She got caught in a Hindu pilgrimage in India, a Himalayan landslide on the highest road in the world, and politely turned down six marriage proposals.

On her return, Steph set up a business teaching beginners how to ride and, in 2019, led the first ever all-female motorcyclist trip to Everest base camp. She says that she hopes her story can inspire other women to chase their dreams.

20 OCTOBER

Born on this day in 1919, Frances Môn Jones MBE was an internationally acclaimed harpist.

Frances won the solo harp competition at the National Eisteddfod of Wales three years in a row from 1937 to 1939 and was admitted to the Gorsedd in 1953. She was instrumental in establishing the Llangollen International Eisteddfod in 1947. From 1954 to 1981, she sang *penillion*, traditional Welsh verses accompanied by the harp, during the Eisteddfod's opening ceremony. She became the honorary president of the Society for the Traditional Instruments of Wales in 1996.

The harp is the national instrument in Wales. In 2000, King Charles III, then Prince of Wales, revived a tradition of having Welsh harpists in the royal household to foster and encourage young musical talent in Wales.

The holders of the post of official harpist to the Prince of Wales since then have all been women from Wales:

- Catrin Finch (2000–2004)
- Jemima Phillips (2004–2007)
- Claire Jones (2007–2011)
- Hannah Stone (2011–2015)
- Anne Denholm (2015–2019)
- Alis Huws (2019–2024)
- In July 2024, Mared Pugh-Evans was appointed to the newly created post of King's Harpist.

21 OCTOBER ⚠

On 21 October 1966, a colliery tip above the village of Aberfan collapsed and engulfed Pantglas Junior School and twenty houses in the village, killing 144 people, including 116 schoolchildren. One of the many heroes that day was Nansi Williams, a dinner lady at the school, who sacrificed her own life to save five children.

The children had just sung 'All Things Bright and Beautiful' at their morning assembly. Nansi was collecting school dinner money when they realised something terrible was happening. Nansi told the children in front of her to get on the ground and then flung herself on top of them. She was killed instantly as a wall collapsed on them. All five of the children she was shielding survived.

Karen Thomas was one of the children and she told a BBC Wales documentary what happened: 'At the other end of the hall glass started coming down the corridor from the headmistress's room and Nansi … jumped on top of us. The wall I think more or less pushed us all together and she took the full impact.'

Nansi is buried in Aberfan Cemetery.

22 OCTOBER

The documentary *Blodyn Haul: Stori Heulwen Hâf (Sunflower: Heulwen Hâf's Story)* was broadcast on S4C on 22 October 2009. It shows Heulwen speaking about her experience of breast cancer.

Heulwen, from Corwen, was a former model and a distinguished actress appearing on television shows such as *Pobol y Cwm, Casualty* and the S4C drama series *Lan a Lawr*. She became the voice of S4C as the channel's sequence announcer.

Blodyn Haul was followed by a second documentary and a book of the same name, *Bron yn Berffaith* (*Nearly Perfect*), which looked at Heulwen's life after receiving treatment. Both the documentaries and the book have proved to be an inspiration to thousands of women living with breast cancer. Heulwen also raised a lot of money for and awareness of breast cancer charities.

Following Heulwen's death on 5 December 2018, fans and friends paid tribute to her. Actor and close friend Stifyn Parri wrote: 'Sadly we said goodbye to Heulwen Hâf today. May summer sunshine shine brightly forever.'

23 OCTOBER

On 23 October 1952, Queen Elizabeth II carried out her first official engagement in Wales as the reigning monarch. The Queen arrived at Llandrindod railway station for the opening of the Claerwen Reservoir in Powys.

Some of Queen Elizabeth II's many connections to Wales include:

- She can claim Welsh descent through Henry VII's daughter Margaret Tudor, who was the great-grandmother of James I of England.
- In 1946, she was made an honorary bard in the Gorsedd of Bards at the National Eisteddfod of Wales.
- In 1948 she was given the Freedom of the City of Cardiff.
- At her coronation on 2 June 1953, Elizabeth's gown was embroidered with the emblems of the Commonwealth countries, including a leek representing Wales.
- Pembroke Welsh Corgis were her favourite breed of dog and she kept more than thirty as pets during her reign.
- Her son Charles was invested as Prince of Wales at Caernarfon Castle in 1969.

- On 1 March 2006, the Queen opened the permanent home for the Senedd in Cardiff.

- A gift of a kilo of Gwynfynydd Welsh gold was given to the Queen on her sixtieth birthday in 1986. Her wedding ring was also made of Welsh gold.

24 OCTOBER

Sylvia Sleigh (born 8 May 1916) died on this day in 2010. Born in Llandudno, Sylvia was a realist painter who, in later life, lived and worked in New York City. She is known for her role in the feminist art movement and for reversing traditional gender roles with her paintings of nude men and men in poses that were traditionally associated with women.

Over her career, Sylvia had more than forty-five solo exhibitions and was a founding member of two renowned all-women art galleries. In 2008, she was honoured with the Distinguished Artist Award for Lifetime Achievement by the College Art Association. She was also recognised by the Women's Caucus for Art, which posthumously awarded her the organisation's Lifetime Achievement Award in 2011.

25 OCTOBER

Today is the feast day of St Canna.

Canna (born c.520) was a daughter of the Breton King Tewdwr Mawr. She came to Wales with her husband Sadwrn. The couple had a child who became St Crallo. There are many depictions of her in art and she is often holding a flowering staff. The legend was that, upon feeling the pangs of childbirth, she grasped at a dry rowan stick which immediately burst into leaf.

Canna became a nun and the church at Llangan is named after her. Her name is also associated with two suburbs of Cardiff, Canton and Pontcanna.

26 OCTOBER

Hillary Clinton (née Rodham) was born on this day in 1947. She is known throughout the world as the former Democratic nominee for US President and was America's First Lady during the presidency of her husband but she can also trace her roots back to Wales.

Hillary's great-grandmother was Mary Griffiths who was born in Merthyr Tydfil around 1850. She was fatherless by the age of one and worked as a servant from the age of twelve. Mary emigrated to Scranton in Pennsylvania, following her brother in seeking a life in the new world. Life was still hard for Mary in America. She had fourteen children but only four survived and one of them was Hannah – Hillary's grandmother. Hannah Jones was born sometime between 1882 and 1883 and her son Hugh Rodham (Hillary's father) was born in Scranton in 1911. Hannah lived long enough to meet her granddaughter, Hillary.

Hillary has confirmed that she is extremely proud of her Welsh roots and said, 'as an American of Welsh descent, I have always had a special place in my heart for Wales – both the beauty of its land and the determination of its people.' She was awarded an honorary doctorate by Swansea University in 2017 in recognition of her commitment to promoting the rights of families and children around the world.

DID YOU KNOW?

Martha Washington, the wife of George Washington and First Lady of the United States between 1789 and 1797, was of Welsh descent.

27 OCTOBER ⚠

On 27 October 1916, a statue of Boudica – known in Welsh as Buddug – was chosen by a public vote of the Welsh public as one of the 'Heroes of Wales' and was unveiled by David Lloyd George in the Marble Hall at Cardiff City Hall.

The choice of Boudica is both surprising and interesting. Although she is not usually considered to be what has come to be understood as Welsh, she lived at a time when Britain was divided into areas controlled by Celtic tribes. As queen of the Iceni tribe, Boudica would have been culturally Celtic and would have spoken an ancient language known as Common Brittonic (*Brythoneg*) from which modern Welsh is derived.

Boudica famously led an uprising against the might of the invading Roman Empire in AD 60. The uprising failed but she has endured as a symbol of the struggle for independence.

The statue depicts a defiant Boudica standing with her arms around her two daughters who were raped by the Romans as their mother was flogged.

28 OCTOBER

Llyn Celyn Reservoir in the Tryweryn Valley was officially opened on 28 October 1965, despite ten years of passionate protest by local residents. The official ceremony lasted less than three minutes because protesters cut the microphone wires and the chants of the dissenting crowd made the speeches inaudible. Elizabeth Watkin Jones, a local teacher, was a leading figure among the protesters.

The construction of the new reservoir in the Tryweryn Valley was to provide a new water supply for Liverpool but it involved drowning the Welsh-speaking village of Capel Celyn near Bala. Protest from the residents of the village was encouraged and lead by Elizabeth. She was secretary of the Capel Celyn Defence Committee and appeared in many television and newspaper interviews, often with her harp. She organised numerous public meetings and was proactive in protest marches in London and Liverpool bringing the protest to the rest of the country's attention.

The reservoir was built despite the opposition of thirty-five out of thirty-six Welsh members of parliament. Although Elizabeth's campaign failed, it led to an increase in support for the Welsh nationalist party, Plaid Cymru, and also gave fresh impetus to the idea of Welsh devolution.

29 OCTOBER

Val Feld, former Labour Welsh Assembly Member and an inspirational cancer campaigner, was born on this day in 1947.

Val was the founder and first director of Shelter Cymru. In 1989 she was appointed head of the Equal Opportunities Commission for Wales. She was also a leading campaigner for Welsh devolution. In July 2001 after suffering from cancer, she became the first member of the National Assembly for Wales to die in office.

The first Purple Plaque to be placed on the Senedd building was one commemorating Val Feld.

30 OCTOBER

Elizabeth Andrews was born on this day in 1882 and gained national recognition when, on 26 February 1919, she gave evidence to the Sankey Commission regarding the hardship of the lives of women in mining communities. She emphasised how important it was for the miners to have pithead baths as, otherwise, women had to carry out the heavy and dangerous work of boiling water for baths and cleaning clothes in the home. Her evidence was instrumental in the introduction of bathing facilities at coal-mine locations.

Elizabeth grew up as one of eleven children in a poor mining family in the Cynon Valley. She went on to become one of the most influential female political activists of the twentieth century and a key figure in the establishment of the Labour Party in Wales. Elizabeth was particularly interested in improving health and education and was responsible for the first nursery school in the Rhondda. She was elected a member of the Glamorgan Executive Health Committee in 1948 and received an OBE in 1948 for her services to the public. Elizabeth published a book telling her life story in 1956, *A Woman's Work is Never Done.*

31 OCTOBER

Nos Galan Gaeaf (Winter's Eve) is celebrated on 31 October. It marks the end of the harvest and the beginning of winter. It is also a time when Christian and pagan traditions have become intertwined. *Nos Galan Gaeaf* is an *ysbrydnos* (a 'spirit night') and is associated with Halloween. And what better time is there for the tale of the famous Welsh female ghost, Y Ladi Wen.

Y Ladi Wen (The White Lady or The Woman in White) is a terrifying ghost and she is most often seen at this time of year. Her story has been passed down through Welsh oral tradition. She is often evoked to warn children about bad behaviour. She is particularly associated with the villages of Ogmore, Ewenny and St Athan.

Legend has it that she wandered Ogmore until a man approached her. She led him to a haul of treasure hidden beneath a stone in Ogmore Castle and allowed him to take half of the gold. But the man became greedy and returned for the rest. The spirit reappeared, her fingers now claws, and attacked the man. Confessing his greed, the man died. Y Ladi Wen is still said to haunt Ogmore and both White Lady's Meadow and White Lady's Lane are named after her.

1 NOVEMBER

When S4C was launched on 1 November 1982, the first programme aired was the Welsh-language animated series *SuperTed*.

SuperTed was produced by Siriol Animation, a company set up by Liz Young. Liz was raised at Old Wallace Farm in Dyffryn in the Vale of Glamorgan. She and her husband Mike, from Cwm, Ebbw Vale, established the company and were determined to keep their productions both local and Welsh speaking. *SuperTed* was later dubbed into English and broadcast on the BBC throughout the UK.

Following the series' phenomenal success, Liz and Mike moved to Los Angeles in 1989, where they founded Splash Entertainment, an animation studio producing children's television series. Their relocation was a significant risk as they were setting themselves up to compete with established studios but they have succeeded in growing the company to be a multi-award-winning studio that is one of the largest and most prolific independent animation studios in the US. They are also involved in the production of the animated series of *Bratz*, linked to the high-fashion dolls.

2 NOVEMBER

On 2 November 1982, Carol Vorderman made her first appearance on the television game show *Countdown*. Carol remained with the show for twenty-six years. During that time, and she has become a well-known celebrity, appearing in numerous shows as a presenter or participant.

Carol was born in 1960 but her parents separated just weeks after her birth and so she moved with her mother and two elder siblings to Prestatyn, her mother's home town, where she was raised and educated.

After graduating with a degree in engineering from Cambridge, Carol moved to Leeds to become a management trainee. An advert by Channel 4 was placed in *The Yorkshire Post*. They were looking for a woman with good mathematical skills for an upcoming television show based in Leeds. Carol's mother submitted her and her journey into television began.

Carol is the presenter of the *Pride of Britain Awards* and was a competitor in the second series of *Strictly Come Dancing*. She is also an established author of books on education and health and runs an online mathematics coaching system.

Carol has been awarded an MBE as well as an honorary degree (MA) from the University of Bath and an honorary fellowship from Bangor University.

3 NOVEMBER

Today is the feast of St Winifred, or Gwenffrewi in Welsh.

St Winifred was a seventh-century Welsh Christian. Her parents, legend claims, were Tyfid ap Eiludd, a noble chieftain of Tegeingl, and Wenlo, who was St Beuno's sister or niece. When Winifred decided to take holy orders, an enraged suitor, Caradog, decapitated her. A healing spring miraculously appeared where her severed head came to rest. Winifred was restored to life but Caradog fell dead on the spot and was swallowed by the earth. St Beuno decreed 'that whosoever on that spot should thrice ask for a benefit from God in the name of St Winefride would obtain the grace he asked if it was for the good of his soul.'

Winifred is the focus of many tales and legends. A spring called St Winefride's Well in Holywell is claimed to have healing powers, and has been a place of pilgrimage for nearly 1,400 years, making it among the oldest of any British saint. It is known as 'the Lourdes of Wales'.

4 NOVEMBER

Bonnie Tyler made her television debut on *Top of the Pops* on 4 November 1976, singing her breakthrough hit 'Lost in France'. Her distinctively husky singing voice is the result of a 1977 throat operation to correct nodules on her vocal cords.

Bonnie, whose real name is Gaynor Sullivan (née Hopkins) was born in Skewen in 1951. She was inspired to pursue a singing career after competing in a local talent contest and changed her name to Sherene Davis to avoid confusion with folk singer Mary Hopkin. In 1975, RCA Records recommended that she change her name. After the success of 'Lost in France' (1976) she released 'It's a

Heartache'(1977). In 1983, Bonnie became the first Welsh singer to have a transatlantic number-one hit with 'Total Eclipse of the Heart'. It has sold over six million copies, making it one of the bestselling singles of all time.

DID YOU KNOW?

The video for Bonnie's 'Total Eclipse of the Heart' has over a billion views on YouTube.

5 NOVEMBER

The Gunpowder Plot failed on this day in 1605. It was an attempt by a group of Catholics to blow up the House of Lords during the State Opening of Parliament and a protest against King James I's policy of repression against Catholicism. In the aftermath, a woman called Anne Vaux found herself under suspicion.

Many women were involved in the clandestine operations to keep Catholicism alive in Britain, including the concealment of Jesuit priests from the authorities. Anne Vaux was one of them. Northeast Wales at this time was a centre for Catholic resistance and, in late August 1605, Anne organised a Catholic pilgrimage to the holy shrine at St Winefride's Well in Holywell. This trip was later suspected as being a ruse for the conspirators to organise and gather support. Anne was arrested shortly after the discovery of the plot and although she admitted to receiving conspirators at her house, was found innocent of treason. Although Anne had no direct role in the plot, she was certainly aware of it and was suspected of being the author of an anonymous letter warning an MP to avoid parliament on that day.

6 NOVEMBER

Born on this day 1934 in Butetown, Cardiff, Betty Campbell was Wales's first Black headteacher. She was also a community activist and a champion of Black history in education in Wales.

Betty's father was killed during the Second World War and she was raised by her Barbadian mother. Her dream was always to become a teacher and, despite negative social stereotyping and the lack of encouragement she received from her teachers, she was determined to do that. Betty excelled at school and earned a place at Cardiff Teacher Training College. She got her first job in Llanrumney before returning to Butetown to work at Mount Stuart Primary School, where she later became headteacher.

Betty admits that she experienced hostility from some parents. 'They hadn't seen a Black teacher before. It was as if you could do a good job, but if you're Black you weren't quite as good.' Betty began teaching children about Black history including slavery and the system of apartheid that operated in South Africa at the time. She was invited to meet Nelson Mandela during his visit to Wales in 1998.

Over her career, Betty served on the Home Office's race advisory committee and was appointed to the Commission for Racial Equality. She was elected to represent her community as a councillor from 1999 to 2004 and was awarded an MBE in 2003 for services to education and community life.

In 2015 Betty was awarded with a lifetime achievement award by Unison Cymru's Black Members' group for her contribution to Welsh education and Black history. In 2019, Betty was selected by a public vote to be one of the Welsh women who deserved to have a statue erected in their honour. The statue is in Cardiff.

7 NOVEMBER

World-famous soprano Dame Gwyneth Jones was born in Pontnewynydd, Monmouthshire, on this day in 1936.

In her teens, Gwyneth gained success in *eisteddfodau* in Wales and worked as a secretary before receiving a grant from the local council to study at the Royal College of Music. She then went to Europe, and studied in Siena and later in Zurich, where she eventually settled down.

At the Royal Opera House in 1963 she achieved instant fame when she was called as a stand-in for Verdi's *Il Trovatore*. She expanded her repertoire, winning acclaim in operas by German composers like Strauss, Beethoven and Wagner. She is now regarded as one of the greatest Wagnerian sopranos of all time. As well as performing across the United States and Europe, she has returned to give many concert performances in Wales.

Gwyneth was made a Dame of the British Empire (DBE) in 1986 and has branched out as a director and costume designer in recent years. She has also been the president of the British Wagner Society since 1990.

8 NOVEMBER

Dorothea Bate was born in Carmarthen on this day in 1878. She was a palaeontologist, a pioneer of archaeozoology (scientific evaluation of animal materials retrieved from archaeological sites) and a world expert on the fossils of Mediterranean mammals.

Dorothea had very little education and was disinherited by her parents so her brother could be provided with a dowry in order to marry a wealthy woman. At the age of nineteen, she was given a job at the Natural History

Museum sorting through specimens. It is likely that she was the first woman employed by the museum as a scientist. She worked there for fifty years. Through her work, she explored the Mediterranean islands of Cyprus, Crete and the Balearics and would often walk for hours over mountainous terrain, scrambling down cliffs and through caves to find fossils. Dorothea survived scarlet fever, nearly drowned on several occasions and suffered seasickness and appalling mosquito bites in her dedication to her work. She is credited with collecting the fossils of many extinct Mediterranean island species, including dwarf elephants, dwarf mammoths and the Majorcan mouse-goat.

Dorothea died on 13 January 1951, but her pioneering work continues to inform and inspire new generations of scientists.

9 NOVEMBER ⚠

On 9 November 1961, Rosemarie Frankland, from Rhosllaner-chrugog near Wrexham, became the first British woman to win the Miss World title.

Rosemarie had previously won Miss Wales and later Miss United Kingdom. She was crowned by the pageant's compere Bob Hope who declared that she was the most beautiful girl he had ever seen. She later reportedly had an affair with Hope for some years.

Rosemarie went on to have a brief acting career. Her last role was in *I'll Take Sweden* in 1965 alongside Bob Hope. She married guitarist Warren Entner in 1976 and together they had a daughter but divorced in 1981. Rosemarie battled depression throughout her life and she died from a drug overdose in 2000 in California. Her ashes were returned to Wales for burial.

10 NOVEMBER

Maria Jane Williams (born 4 October 1795) died on this day in 1873. She was a pioneer in the field of Welsh folk music and credited with playing a significant role in the promotion and preservation of Welsh culture and tradition in the nineteenth century.

Maria was born into a wealthy family at Aberpergwm House in Glynneath. She showed a great interest in and talent for music which was encouraged by her family. Her singing voice was especially admired and she acquired the name '*Llinos*' ('Linnet').

In 1844, she published a collection of Welsh music *The Ancient National Airs of Gwent and Morgannwg*, acknowledged as a significant contribution to the knowledge of traditional Welsh music. Maria's passion for Welsh traditional music ultimately led to the formation of the Welsh Folk-Song Society (Cymdeithas Alawon Gwerin Cymru) in 1906.

The Society continues to flourish today in large part due to the enthusiastic efforts of other notable women.

- **Ruth Lewis** (1871–1946) was born and raised in Liverpool but she fully embraced Welsh culture and language after she married Herbert Lewis, a prominent north Wales politician and committed nationalist. Ruth became central to the Society's activities, serving as secretary, chair and president. The chief competition for individual folk singers at the annual National Eisteddfod of Wales is The Lady Herbert Lewis Memorial Competition.

- **Dora Herbert Jones** (1890–1974), from Llangollen, was a singer who performed folk songs on radio and television. She represented Wales at the International Arts Festival held in Prague in October 1928, which inspired the composer Gustav Holst to become interested in Welsh folk songs for his works. She served as president for the Society.

- **Lady Amy Parry-Williams** (1910–88) from Pontyberem was a singer and writer with a special interest in Welsh folk traditions. She was an early director of the Welsh television company HTV and another serving president of the Welsh Folk-Song Society.

11 NOVEMBER

On 11 November 1918, Germany signed an agreement for peace (an armistice) and the horrors of the First World War, which had commenced on 28 July 1914, finally came to an end.

Over the course of the war, 272,924 Welshmen took arms (21.5 per cent of the male population) and approximately 35,000 lost their lives. As a symbol of the commitment of the Welsh people to the League of Nations and its efforts for international peace, the Welsh National Temple of Peace and Health in Cathays Park was opened on 23 November 1938.

Minnie James, from Dowlais, had lost three sons during the conflict and was chosen to lead a group of twenty-four war-bereaved mothers from across the UK, its Empire and the United States in the opening ceremony. Minnie, who was wearing three sets of medals that had belonged to her sons, was presented with a golden key to open the building and then led the mothers in a procession down the central aisle in front of hundreds of guests from all over the world who stood in tribute and respect.

12 NOVEMBER

On 12 November 1766, Charlotte Jane Windsor (1746–1800) married John Stuart, 1st Marquess of the Isle of Bute. She was heiress to the Herbert estates in Glamorgan and he was the Scottish son of British Prime Minister John Stuart. Charlotte became the first Marchioness of Bute and mother of the wealthy and influential Bute family dynasty that dominated Cardiff and Glamorganshire for the next two centuries.

The union also marked the start of the Bute family's philanthropy in the Cardiff area. The Bute Estate included the castles of Cardiff, Caerphilly and Castell Coch as well as a vast amount of land in the south Wales coalfields. By leasing the mineral rights and developing the docks at Cardiff along with its connecting railway infrastructure, the Butes became one of Britain's wealthiest families and Cardiff developed into one of the greatest coal-exporting ports in the world. Charlotte's grandson, the 3rd Marquess of Bute, John Crichton-Stuart (1847–1900) became one of the wealthiest men in the world.

DID YOU KNOW?
Charlotte is often credited with being the person who introduced the dahlia to Britain. She procured them from the Madrid Botanical Gardens and brought them back to Kew Gardens.

13 NOVEMBER

On 13 November 1970, Bernice Rubens from Splott in Cardiff was named as the Booker Prize winner for her novel *The Elected Member*. Her writing was almost unknown at the time and she was the first woman and, to date, the only Welsh author, to win the award.

Bernice's father, Eli Rubens, was a Lithuanian Jew who, at the age of sixteen, fled Europe hoping for a new life in America. However, he had been deceived by the ticket seller and, instead of New York, he found himself in Cardiff. Settling in his unexpected new home, he married Dorothy Cohen, a Polish immigrant, teacher, chemist and suffragist.

The Rubenses were a musical family and Bernice's two brothers and her sister were all professional musicians. Bernice's instrument of choice was the cello, which her parents could not afford and so she described herself as the 'listener'. She studied at the University of Wales, Cardiff, and then became an English teacher and documentary film-maker.

Bernice began writing at the age of thirty and frequently used Jewish themes in her work. She said of herself, 'I don't love writing. But I love having written.' She wrote over twenty books.

14 NOVEMBER

Nell Gwyn (born 2 February 1650) died on this day in 1687. She became one of the most famous figures of her time. She was a working-class girl who became an actress and was elevated to the status of a celebrity in her time when she became the long-term mistress of King Charles II.

Nell was not born in Wales but a number of historians believe she had Welsh ancestry, most likely on her father's side. Gwyn is certainly a name of Welsh origin. Nell's father was an army captain who fought during the English Civil War on the side of King Charles I, and subsequently moved to Hereford where he became a brewer.

Nell and her sister were raised by their mother in Covent Garden, London. When she was old enough, she worked selling fruit and vegetables from a barrow to customers of the Theatre Royal, Drury Lane. It was not long before Nell's good looks and effervescent personality came to the attention of the theatre's management and she was given her first acting role in 1665 at the age of fifteen. Charles II, who often attended performances, soon became an admirer of Nell and they started a love affair that lasted until Charles's death in 1685.

15 NOVEMBER

Petula Clark (Sally Olwen Clark) was born in Epsom, Surrey, on 15 November 1932. Her mother was Welsh and, as a child, she frequently visited her grandparents in Abercanaid near Merthyr Tydfil where she learned to speak Welsh and sang in their chapel.

She first began recording in her teens, and during the 1940s and 1950s recorded for EMI, Decca and Pye. During the Second World War, she performed on numerous occasions to entertain the troops. At this time she also featured in the film *Medal for the General,* and went on to have thirty other film credits. Since then she has been a regular guest on radio shows and hosted her own television series in the 1960s.

The single 'Downtown' launched Petula's American career and earned her a Grammy Award in 1964. Throughout that decade, she released numerous chart hits, starred in musicals and appeared frequently on television. Even now, she remains a popular performing artist.

16 NOVEMBER

On 16 November 1902, a reported hunting trip attended by American President Theodore Roosevelt was satirised in a cartoon in *The Washington Post*. It was said that the president had been on a bear-hunting trip in Mississippi in 1902 where he had failed to locate a single bear. To save his embarrassment, some of his fellow hunters cornered a black bear and tied it to a willow tree, offering the president a free shot. Roosevelt, however, deemed this to be extremely unsportsmanlike and refused to shoot the bear. A couple of shop owners from Brooklyn who had a hobby making and selling stuffed toy animals were inspired by the story and decided to create a stuffed toy bear for the president. They called it 'Teddy's Bear' and the teddy bear was born. Not many know that it was a small business run by a woman in Wales that played a key role in its continued worldwide popularity.

Wendy Boston was working as a designer for Cadbury in Birmingham. When the Second World War began in 1939, she began making toys to cheer up friends and family. After Wendy's home was bombed, she and her husband decided to relocate to Crickhowell. In Wales, Wendy was able to concentrate on her bears. She set up a company to sell her toys in 1941. Wendy was behind many innovations in toys. She invented screw-locked plastic eyes in 1948 and the world's first fully washable non-jointed teddy bear in 1954. In 1955, the BBC showed the washable bear being washed and then squeezed through a mangle. By 1964, Wendy Boston Playsafe Toys Ltd was producing over a quarter of the UK's soft-toy exports.

17 NOVEMBER ⚠

On 17 November 1888, the death certificate for Mary Jane Kelly was issued. On 9 November, Mary had become the final victim of the 'canonical' five victims of the serial killer, Jack the Ripper, who was active in the Whitechapel district of London in 1888. Much is known about Mary's death; little is known about her life. But historians have recently retraced her journey to Whitechapel and it started in Wales.

Mary said that she was born in Limerick in Ireland and had moved to Carmarthen as a young child with her family. If she grew up in Wales then it is likely that she would have been able to speak Welsh. One account reports that she married a local coal miner at sixteen and was forced to relocate to Cardiff to live with a cousin when her husband was killed in an explosion.

In 1884, Mary moved to London, where she worked for a tobacconist and as a domestic servant before meeting a French woman who introduced her to a high-class brothel where Mary became one of the most popular girls. Mary made the journey to France after an invitation from a client but she returned within weeks. Some historians have theorised that she escaped a sex-trafficking ring and was therefore unable to return to the relative safety of the brothel.

In November 1888 Mary was renting a small room in Miller's Court. It was here that she spent her last hours. Mary was last seen alive on the night of 8 November with a smartly dressed customer, heading back to her lodgings. She was heard by neighbours singing until about one o'clock in the morning. Her body was discovered the following morning by the rent collector. She was twenty-five years old.

18 NOVEMBER

On 18 November 2000, Catherine Zeta-Jones married fellow Academy Award-winning actor Michael Douglas at the Plaza Hotel in New York City.

Catherine was born in Swansea in 1969 to parents, Dai and Pat Jones, owners of a sweet-shop. She showed an early interest in entertainment, starring in Swansea Grand Theatre stage versions of *Bugsy Malone*, *The Pajama Game* and *Annie*. She played the lead role in the West End production of *42nd Street* at seventeen.

She had some early film roles but her breakthrough came on television when she was cast as Mariette in *The Darling Buds of May* in 1991. She then went on to appear in many more films, making her Hollywood breakthrough in *The Mask of Zorro* in 1998.

Over her career, Catherine has won many awards, including a British Academy Film Award, a Tony Award and the Academy Award for Best Supporting Actress in the musical *Chicago* (2002).

Catherine is a patron of Swansea's Longfields Day Centre for people with disabiities and an ambassador of the National Society for the Prevention of Cruelty to Children. She also launched the Full Stop appeal in Wales to raise awareness of child abuse and is one of the members of the Cinema for Peace Foundation. In 2010, Catherine was awarded a CBE for her film and charity work and, in 2019, was honoured with the Freedom of the City of Swansea.

19 NOVEMBER

On 19 November 1999, the Stirling Prize was awarded to Future Systems for designing the Lord's Media Centre. Amanda Levete was one of the directors of the company alongside Jan Kaplický. The design was widely acclaimed as the most elegant and state-of-the-art media centre in the world and was the world's first all-aluminium semi-monocoque building – one in which the outer skin bears a considerable amount of the structural load.

Other high-profile examples of Amanda's work include the Belgrade Philharmonic Concert Hall, the Paisley Museum in Scotland, the Selfridges department store in Birmingham, the Victoria and Albert Museum, the

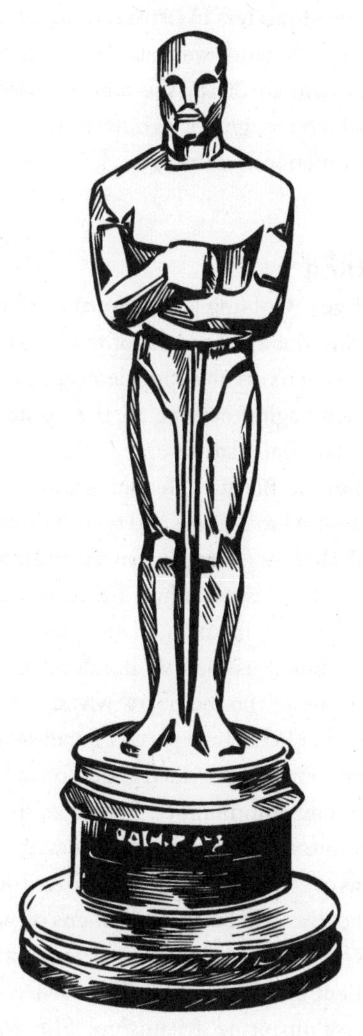

Museum of Art, Architecture and Technology in Lisbon, the D'Ieteren headquarters in Brussels and three hospitals in Cyprus. In 2017 Amanda was awarded a CBE for services to architecture and in 2018, she was awarded the Jane Drew Prize, which recognises significant contributions to the status of women in architecture.

20 NOVEMBER

Margarette 'Peggy' Golding (née Owen) was born on this day in 1881. She was the founder of the Inner Wheel, an international women's organisation dedicated to promoting friendship, encouraging service to the community and fostering international relations.

Peggy was born in Blaenau Ffestiniog and raised in Hay-on-Wye. She trained as a nurse and served throughout the First World War before setting up a successful business with her husband in Manchester, supplying nurses' uniforms.

Her husband was a member of the Rotary Club. The organisation excluded women so she decided to organise a meeting of some of the members' wives. This led to her setting up the Inner Wheel as a partner organisation in 1924. The Inner Wheel initially provided goods, often homemade, to the poor of their communities. The ethos spread rapidly through the country and then abroad. Today, it is open to all women and has over 100,000 members in over 100 countries, making it one of the world's largest women's organisations.

Peggy was described as an intelligent woman who was 'an excellent speaker, with a lively sense of humour and the gift of inspiring friendship'. She was also an active philanthropist, supporting the Manchester Girls' Orphanage and Ancoats Hospital.

DID YOU KNOW?

The Inner Wheel has consultative status at the United Nations, meaning that elected members assist UN Commissions on issues such as human rights, the condition of women, elderly people and family issues.

21 NOVEMBER

Twelve-year-old Adeline Coquelin drowned when the ship *La Jeune Emma* ran aground on Cefn Sidan on 21 November 1828. Adeline, the niece of Napoleon Bonaparte's ex-wife Joséphine de Beauharnais, was on her way from France to the West Indies. Instead of reaching her destination the poor little girl ended up in a grave in Wales.

The disaster, in which thirteen of the nineteen passengers drowned, came about as a result of the ship's captain mistaking the Bristol Channel for the English Channel. Cefn Sidan is Welsh for 'satin sands' and is a long sandy beach filled with dunes that stretches nearly eight miles. The shore had proved treacherous to ships before and the sinking of *La Jeune Emma* was not the only time a vessel had become lost in those waters.

Some sympathetic villagers made valiant attempts to rescue the survivors. However, some locals made the best of the regular wrecks on their shores. Known as *gŵyr-y-bwelli bach* (people with little hatchets), they would even entice ships into danger using fires so they could loot their cargo. By the time the militia from Carmarthen arrived, the cargo of sugar, sherry, spices, coffee, cotton, rum and ginger were all gone, and all that was left of the cargo was three hundred gallons of rum. *Gŵyr-y-bwelli bach* were most active in the early nineteenth century. However, by 1886, the establishment of the militia barracks at Pwll meant that their lucrative period had ended.

Adeline is buried at St Illtyd's Church, Pembrey, alongside her father.

22 NOVEMBER

Mary Ann Evans, known better by her pen name George Eliot, was born on one of the farms of the Arbury Hall estate in Nuneaton, Warwickshire, on 22 November 1819. Her father was Welshman Robert Evans, the estate's land agent, and she attended a Welsh Baptist school in Coventry.

Mary became one of the leading writers of the Victorian era, publishing seven novels mainly set in provincial England. As female authors at the time were considered incapable of writing anything other than lightweight romances, she used a male pen name to ensure her works would be taken seriously. Formidably intelligent and knowledgeable across a range of subjects, she was unconventional in her religious and political outlook. She spoke several languages including Hebrew, German and Greek. Her first collection of stories, published in 1858, brought acclaim from prestigious critics such as Charles Dickens and William Makepeace Thackeray. Her first novel Adam Bede was an instant success and she was said to have been the favourite novelist of Queen Victoria.

DID YOU KNOW?

Mary's soulmate was the philosopher and literature critic George Henry Lewes. The couple never married but lived together for many years. It was he who suggested that she should consider writing fiction while the couple were on holiday in Tenby.

23 NOVEMBER

On 23 November 1963, the very first episode of *Doctor Who* was broadcast. Today it is the longest-running and arguably most successful science-fiction television series in the world. This is despite the fact that the show was off the air for sixteen years from 1989 until its enormously successful revival in 2005, made from that point on in Wales.

Notable women who have been involved in that success and the spin-off series include:

- **Julie Gardner** was born in 1969 in Neath and raised in Glynneath. She was an executive producer for the 2005 revival of the show, *Torchwood* and *The Sarah Jane Adventures*. She is a co-founder of the Cardiff-based production company Bad Wolf. In 2024, BAFTA Cymru awarded her the Outstanding Contribution to Television award.

- **Eve Myles** was born in Ystradgynlais in 1978. Eve made her acting breakthrough with a role in *Doctor Who*. She went on to be cast in *Torchwood* and won a BAFTA Cymru award for Best Actress for her portrayal of Gwen Cooper. She has since starred in the BBC Wales drama *Belonging* and the fantasy series *Merlin*. She has also had leading roles in the television drama series *Frankie*, *Broadchurch* and *A Very English Scandal*. In 2017, Eve learned to speak Welsh for the drama *Un Bore Mercher* (*Keeping Faith*).

- **Helen Raynor and Elwen Rowlands** were the first female script editors in the history of *Doctor Who*. Helen hails from Swansea and Elwen from Cardiff.

DID YOU KNOW?

Lily Connors from Swansea is the Guinness world record holder for the biggest collection of *Doctor Who* memorabilia. Among her collection of over 10,000 items are two full-size Daleks and a full-size Cyberman.

24 NOVEMBER

Ellen Edwards (born 1810; née Francis) was a pioneering teacher of navigation and died on this day in 1889.

Ellen was born and raised in Amlwch, Anglesey. Her father was an experienced seafarer who retired in 1814 and opened a school of navigation in Amlwch. It was here where Ellen also learned about navigation and mathematics. The school soon became so successful and Ellen so proficient that they opened another in the rapidly growing port town of Caernarfon. Ellen, who at the time was only twenty years old, would run it.

Ellen was breaking societal norms not only by working but by teaching a subject usually thought of as being in the male domain. She was a good teacher though, and when she was unfairly criticised in a report from non-Welsh-speaking Anglican commissioners, there was an outcry by the ship's captains she had taught. The mariners of Gwynedd came to call her the 'Misses'.

Ellen retired in 1880, having taught more than 1,000 mariners how to navigate the seas. She died on 24 November 1889 and her funeral at Llanbeblig Church was attended by a large contingent of ship's captains and mariners of all grades.

25 NOVEMBER

Born on this day 1910 in Abertillery, Thora Silverthorne was a nurse during the Spanish Civil War and a pioneer for the establishment of nursing unions.

Thora's father was a miner and founder member of the local Communist Party. She joined the Young Communist League at sixteen and remained loyal to the party for the rest of her life. Thora's mother died when she was young and she followed her sister to Oxford to pursue a career in nursing. There, she volunteered to act as a nurse for the strikers marching to London as part of the National Hunger March in 1932. In 1936, she volunteered as a nurse during the Spanish Civil War, caring for anti-fascist soldiers of the International Brigade. Such was her efficiency and popularity that she was elected by her contemporaries as matron at Granen Hospital.

On her return to the UK, Silverthorne was instrumental in the establishment of the nurses' union the National Nurses Association. She was also part of a delegation that met Clement Attlee to discuss the founding of a British National Health Service in 1948.

26 NOVEMBER

Today is celebrated as Egyptology Day. It marks the day in 1922 that archaeologist Howard Carter opened King Tutankhamun's tomb in Egypt's Valley of the Kings for the first time in more than 3,000 years.

Käthe Bosse-Griffiths was a brilliant young Egyptologist, who would make a unique contribution to Welsh literature.

Käthe was born in Wittenberg, Germany in 1910. In 1935, after studying for her doctorate in classics and Egyptology she began working at the Berlin State Museums. However, the Nazis were gaining power in Germany and she was dismissed from her post when it emerged that her mother was Jewish. Her mother later died at Ravensbrück concentration camp, but Käthe fled to Britain and found research work at University College London and the Ashmolean Museum in Oxford. In Oxford, she met and later married fellow Egyptologist John Gwynedd Griffiths. He was from Porth, Rhondda, and was also a Welsh nationalist and political activist.

The couple returned to the Rhondda. During the Second World War, they founded *Cylch Cadwgan* (the Cadwgan Circle), a Welsh-language intellectual group dedicated to pacifism. Käthe developed a passion for the Welsh language and began writing fiction in Welsh about the lives of Welsh women including taboo subjects such as abortion, adultery and religion.

The couple later moved to Swansea where Käthe became Keeper of Archaeology at Swansea Museum. As part of her work, she researched Sir Henry Wellcome's Egyptian collection of over 5,000 items, which is now held at the Egypt Centre at Swansea University.

27 NOVEMBER

Storm Arwen reached its peak on 27 November 2021. The storm saw sustained winds and gusts in excess of 90 mph which caused mass destruction, particularly in north Wales. Hundreds of trees were downed and 13,000 homes lost power. Hundreds of thousands of pounds' worth of damage was done to Bodnant Garden in Conwy and live broadcasts and filming of *I'm a Celebrity… Get Me Out of Here!* at Gwrych Castle were massively disrupted.

In 2015, the UK's Met Office started naming storms that had the potential to cause disruption or damage in an effort to prepare the public better for them. A new list is issued every September for the year.

Despite sounding Welsh, the name 'Arwen' was actually invented by J. R. R. Tolkien, based on Welsh linguistic patterns, when he named the elven character in *The Lord of the Rings*. It has become popular as a Welsh girl's name despite not being authentically Welsh. Arwen was the first and, to date, the only Welsh girl's name to be used for a storm.

Other Welsh names listed as possible names for future storms are:

- **Olwen** meaning 'white footprint'. In Welsh mythology, Olwen is the beautiful daughter of the giant Ysbaddaden. She is the heroine of the story 'Culhwch and Olwen' in the *Mabinogion*.
- **Gladys** which derives from Gwladus or Gwladys, meaning 'princess' or 'ruler'.
- **Heulwen** which, amusingly, caused surprise among Welsh speakers as it translates as 'sunshine', or 'blessed by the sun' – hardly an appropriate moniker for a period of stormy weather.

28 NOVEMBER

Born on this day 1964 in London to Welsh parents, Sian Williams, journalist and current affairs presenter, is best known as a co-presenter on *BBC Breakfast* and the *BBC News at Six*.

Williams spent over a decade reporting and editing news programmes for BBC Radio, before moving into television news. During the BBC Cymru television series *Coming Home*, Williams discovered that she was the first member of her family to have been born outside Wales in 350 years. She said, 'I think it's not about where you're born, it's about where generations of your family come from. I can now proudly say I'm Welsh, it doesn't matter that I was born in Paddington, I'm Welsh, yes I am, and very proud of it too.'

29 NOVEMBER

On 29 November 1947, the United Nations General Assembly passed a resolution calling for Palestine to be partitioned between Arabs and Jews. It allowed for the formation of the Jewish state of Israel. However, almost immediately after the plan was approved, violence broke out between Palestinian Arabs and Jewish Zionists.

Yehudit Anastasia Grossman was an author who wrote under her pen name Judith Maro. She actively campaigned to establish the state of Israel, but despaired of the racial conflict and bloodshed. She left the Middle East for Britain with her husband, the sculptor Jonah Jones. They settled on the Llŷn Peninsula, where she became passionate about her new home. She immersed herself in the debate about the future of the Welsh language, drawing interesting parallels between the political and linguistic situation in both Wales and Israel. She insisted that her three children learned Welsh and would only allow her books to be published in English after they had been translated into Welsh. Her books include *Hen Wlad Newydd* (*New Old Land*) which is a reflection on the similarities between Wales and Israel. She is recognised as one of the authors who has done the most to understand the relationship between Wales and the Jewish people.

30 NOVEMBER

The University of Wales was founded on 30 November 1893 as a federal university with three colleges: University College South Wales and Monmouthshire (now Cardiff University) founded in 1883; University College North Wales (now Bangor University) founded in 1884; and University College Wales (now Aberystwyth University), founded in 1872.

Sixteen-year-old Louise Davies was the first woman to formally enrol full-time at the University College of Wales in Aberystwyth in 1884. There had been two part-time women students there since 1875: Kate Rees and Lizzie Edwards (both from Aberystwyth)studied music under Joseph Parry, famous for composing the love song 'Myfanwy' (see 21 May).

The first degree ceremony of the newly established University of Wales took place in 1897. The first degree to be awarded at Cardiff was a Bachelor of Science to Miss Maria Dawson. Maria went on to carry out pioneering research at the Cambridge Botanical Laboratories exploring how the addition of nitrogen and nitrates to soil improves crop yields.

In 1898, Mary (Eppynt) Phillips, from Merthyr Cynog, became the first female doctor to qualify from Cardiff University. She was regarded as an innovator in the field of care during and after pregnancy. During the First World War, Mary worked at typhoid hospitals in Calais and Serbia. In Malta she treated ANZAC casualties from Gallipoli. In recognition of her service, she was awarded the Medal of the Order of Saint Sava by the King of Serbia, as well as a medal from the French Red Cross, the British War Medal, the Allied Victory Medal and the Scottish Women's Hospital Medal.

By 1911, 35 per cent of students at the University of Wales were women. Currently, the figure is closer to 55 per cent.

1 DECEMBER

On 1 December 2015, Wales became the first country in the UK to introduce a soft opt-out system of organ donation. All adults in Wales are considered to have agreed to be an organ donor when they die unless they have recorded a decision not to consent.

Helena Jones from Glynneath (1933–2018) was a tireless campaigner for the introduction of the opt-out system after four of her five children required kidney transplants. Helena, who was on dialysis herself, dedicated most of her adult life to fighting kidney disease. In conjunction with Kidney Research UK, she set up a campaign called Helena's Hope. To raise funds, she abseiled down Brunel House in Cardiff aged sixty-nine and skydived out of an aeroplane when she was seventy. Helena was named UK Charity Award Volunteer of the Year in 2003 and is thought to have inspired more than thirty thousand people to become organ donors before the opt-out system was established.

Baroness Ilora Finlay of Llandaff first introduced the private members bill to seek a change in the system in 2007 and was another campaigner on the issue. Ilora is a doctor and professor of palliative medicine at the Cardiff University School of Medicine. She is vice president of Hospice UK and Marie Curie, and a former president of the Royal College of Medicine. She was also the first person to propose a bill to ban smoking in public buildings in Wales.

2 DECEMBER

On the International Day for the Abolition of Slavery, we celebrate Jessie Donaldson (1799–1889), from Swansea, who fearlessly fought to end slavery during the American Civil War.

Jessie was the daughter of prominent abolitionist Samuel Heineken. She opened a school in Swansea with her sister in 1829 and joined the Swansea Anti-Slavery Society, the largest of many abolitionist groups in Wales. She moved to Cincinnati with her husband Francis Donaldson in 1854. Their home stood on the opposite side of the Ohio river from Kentucky, a state where slavery was still widespread.

The couple became part of the famous 'Underground Railroad', a network of safe houses and routes set up by abolitionists to help runaway slaves achieve their freedom in the north. Risking fines and prison sentences, they ran their home as a safe house and helped people from the other side of the river to escape slavery.

The USA abolished slavery in 1865 and the couple returned to Swansea the following year. In 1874, the Fisk Jubilee Singers from Nashville, the first choir of freed slaves to sing in concert halls, honoured Jessie by performing in Swansea. Jessie died in 1889, aged ninety-one, at her home in Sketty.

In 2021, Swansea City Council honoured Jessie with a Blue Plaque, unveiled on 19 June – or Juneteenth – the oldest-known celebration of the ending of slavery in the United States.

3 DECEMBER

Politician and teacher Glenys Kinnock, (née Parry) died on this day in 2023. She was born on 7 July 1944 in Roade, Northamptonshire. Her family were Welsh-speaking churchgoers who returned to their native Anglesey when Glenys was two.

Her father, Cyril, was a railway signalman and active trade unionist. Her mother, Elizabeth, took in washing and ran a café. Glenys's interest in politics came from her parents. By her mid-teens, she had joined the Labour Party, the Campaign for Nuclear Disarmament and the Anti-Apartheid movement.

She met her husband, future Labour Party leader Neil Kinnock, at University College, Cardiff, where he was chairman and she was secretary of the Socialist Society. Glenys studied education and history and then embarked on a career in teaching in 1965. In 1989, she founded the charity, One World Action, which aims for a world free from poverty and oppression where strong democracies safeguard people's rights.

In 1994, Glenys was elected to represent Wales in the European Parliament. She became the Labour spokeswoman on international development and remained an MEP until 2009 when she became Labour's Minister of State for Europe and later for Africa. She was also awarded a life peerage, becoming Baroness Kinnock of Holyhead.

Throughout her career, Glenys was immensely proud of her Welsh identity and it was during her tenure as Minister for Europe that the status of the Welsh language was elevated to make it equal with several other European minority languages.

4 DECEMBER

On 4 December 2011, sisters Gemma and Sarah Griffiths along with Louise Francis carried out Wales's first all-female lifeboat rescue when they assisted a swimmer who had got into difficulties in the estuary of the River Teifi, Cardigan.

Since its foundation in 1824, the Royal National Lifeboat Institution (RNLI) has saved countless lives at sea through the courage, dependability and trustworthiness of its volunteers. Lifeboat crews have been predominantly male, but many women have selflessly put themselves forward to assist those in peril on the seas.

In 2005, Aileen Jones, Porthcawl lifeboat's first female crew member, was awarded the Institution's Bronze Medal of Gallantry for her part in the rescue of two fishermen. She was the first lifeboat woman in 116 years to be given such an award. In 2016, she was awarded an MBE.

The first Welsh women lifeguards to receive an award for bravery were Martha and Margaret Llewellyn from Fishguard in 1847. The two women had waded into the rough sea during a storm with ropes lashed around their bodies to rescue three men from a stranded vessel on Fishguard beach in 1846.

5 DECEMBER

Gwladus Ddu (Gwladus of the dark eyes) was thought to have been born on 5 December 1194. She was the daughter of Llywelyn ap Iorwerth, otherwise known as Llywelyn Fawr (the Great) of Gwynedd. There is some debate as to who her mother was. Some claim that she was Llywelyn's illegitimate daughter by Tangwystl Goch, but she is more widely accepted as the legitimate daughter of Llywelyn's wife Joan, whose father was King John of England.

A valuable political pawn, Gwladus was married twice. First, when she was very young, to the elderly Marcher lord Reginald de Braose (a union that was probably unconsummated). Upon Reginald's death, she married the equally powerful Ralph de Mortimer, Marcher lord of Wigmore, with whom she had five children. Marrying Gwladus brought Ralph closer to Gwladus's uncle, the young King Henry III.

When Ralph died in 1246, his lands were inherited by his and Gwladus's son, Roger de Mortimer. As Roger was only fifteen, he shared the administration and management of the estate with his mother.

6 DECEMBER

Rosie Moriarty-Simmonds, from Cardiff, was born on 6 December 1960, without arms or legs after her mother had been prescribed the drug thalidomide during her pregnancy. Rosie attended Ysgol Erw'r Delyn, a school for children with physical disabilities in Penarth, and then Treloar School near Alton in Hampshire, which at the time was the only school in the UK to offer an academic education for students with disabilities. Rosie became adept at writing with her mouth and was Cardiff University's first disabled student, graduating in 1985 with a degree in psychology.

Rosie initially worked in the civil service before establishing RMS Disability Issues Consultancy in 1995. She regularly appears on radio and television to talk about disability issues and was a leading campaigner for the creation of the Thalidomide Memorial in Cathays Park, Cardiff, which opened in 2016. In 2007 Rosie published her autobiography *Four Fingers and Thirteen Toes* and is also a member of the Association of Mouth and Foot Painting Artists of the World (AMFPA). She was awarded an OBE in 2015 for services to the equality and rights of disabled people. In 2017 Cardiff University awarded her an Honorary Fellowship.

7 DECEMBER ⚠

On the morning of 7 December 1989, workmen at a house in Cardiff discovered skeletal remains of a young girl wrapped in a carpet and buried in a shallow grave. The subsequent police investigation proved to be one of the UK's most baffling cases and changed the course of murder investigations across the world.

The unidentified victim became known as Little Miss Nobody as she didn't match anybody who had been reported missing. Forensic experts were able to determine that the girl had been dead for approximately ten years, and had been fifteen years old when she was killed. The investigation team used two pioneering and untested techniques to try to identify her. They used the victim's skull to create a facial reconstruction of the girl, which was shared with the public. They then tested the DNA from a couple who thought the victim might be their daughter. They were finally able to identify the victim as Karen Price, a teenager who had run away from a children's home in Pontypridd in 1981.Facial reconstruction had been used in archaeology but never in a crime investigation and it was also one of the first cases to use DNA technology to identify a victim.

Alone and vulnerable, Karen had met Alan Charlton, a nightclub bouncer and a man described as having a 'fearsome' reputation. Charlton has appealed his conviction but is still serving a life sentence for her murder.

8 DECEMBER

Fanny Parkes (née Frances Susanna Archer) was born in Conwy on this day in 1794. She was a travel writer who became famous for her extensive journals about colonial northern India, where she lived for twenty-four years.

In 1822, Fanny married Charles Crawford Parks, who worked for the East India Company. Charles was first appointed to a post in Kolkata (Calcutta), India. They then subsequently moved to Kanpur (Cawnpore) in 1830 and finally settled at Prayagraj (Allahabad) in 1832. Charles was extremely well paid and they lived in relative luxury, with Fanny running a household employing fifty-seven servants (with an additional fourteen in the hot months). The couple were childless and Fanny spent her time horse-riding and travelling.

Fanny was fascinated by and deeply admired the richness of Indian culture. She befriended Baiza Bai, a queen from the semi-autonomous state of Gwalior and a prominent opponent of the East India Company. Fanny learned Persian, Hindustani and Urdu. During her travels she endured frequent storms, treacherous rocks in rivers and the risk of being attacked by robbers, to quench her thirst for adventure.

Fanny and Charles returned to Britain in 1846 and Fanny began publishing her memoirs and travel journals. They give an important pre-colonial perspective of northern India and its people and customs and also record the economic impact and domestic problems associated with Britain's colonial rule in India. Fanny died in 1875.

9 DECEMBER

Actress Ruth Madoc (born Margaret Ruth Llewellyn Baker) died on 9 December 2022. Her portrayal of Gladys Pugh, one of the lead characters in the television sitcom, *Hi-de-Hi!* (1980–88) made her a household name and one of the most recognisable Welsh voices in the UK.

Ruth was born in Norwich but that was by accident. Ruth said, 'My mum couldn't get home quick enough to have me, so I was born in Norfolk … I'm Welsh to my core and I thank the Lord that I am Welsh. I don't care if I was born in England, I'm a Welsh woman through and through.'

After studying at RADA, Ruth secured roles in the film versions of *Fiddler on the Roof* (1971) and *Under Milk Wood* (1972). The role of Gladys Pugh, one of the Yellowcoats at the fictional holiday camp Maplins, defined her career but she also appeared, alongside her first husband, Philip Madoc, in the highly acclaimed television drama serial *The Life and Times of David Lloyd George* in 1981. Ruth returned to comedy as Daffyd Thomas's mother in the comedy series *Little Britain*. Ruth was awarded an honorary degree by Swansea University in 2006.

10 DECEMBER

On 10 December 1964, former Wales international footballer, Laura McAllister, was born in Bridgend. Laura won twenty-four caps for Wales and served as team captain. She now serves as a political adviser to the Welsh government and a senior sports administrator for UEFA.

Jayne Ludlow (born 7 January 1979 in Llwynypia and raised in Treherbert) is another notable Welsh football international. Her former coach, ex-player Jarmo Matikainen described her as 'the most successful player that Wales has ever had'. She won nine league titles and six FA cups with Arsenal and captained the team that won the UEFA Women's Champions League title in 2007. She is the club's all-time top goal scorer and was voted Players' Player of the Year in 2001, 2003 and 2004. She was appointed as the manager of the Welsh women's team in 2014, and in 2021 she became the technical director of Manchester City Girls' Academy.

Jess Fishlock (born 14 January 1987 in Cardiff) was the first Welsh player, of any gender, to earn a hundred caps for the national team. She was named Welsh Footballer of the Year in 2011, 2012, 2013, 2014 and 2019 and was a member of the FFC Frankfurt team that won the UEFA Women's Champions League title in 2015. Jess has used her platform as a high-profile gay athlete to campaign on a number of issues. In 2018, was awarded an MBE for services to women's football and the LGBTQ+ community. In 2020, she was named a member of the Stonewall Sports Champion Team, a group that believes that every person should have the ability to feel comfortable being themself in organised sports.

DID YOU KNOW?

In 2018, Cheryl Foster from Llandudno became the first Welsh woman to referee a Welsh Premier League game. She also refereed the 2023 UEFA Women's Champions League final and in the same year became Wales's first woman to referee a Women's World Cup match.

11 DECEMBER

Bridget Bevan (born 1698) died on 11 December 1779. She was a benefactor and manager of the Circulating Welsh Charity School system, which it is estimated taught over 200,000 Welsh people to read and helped Wales achieve one of the highest literacy rates in Europe.

Bridget was born at Derllys Court in Llannewydd, Carmarthenshire. She was the daughter of John Vaughan, a financial supporter of the Society for Promoting Christian Knowledge (SPCK). In 1721, she married Arthur Bevan, a local lawyer and MP for Carmarthen. In 1731 she helped Griffith Jones, a local preacher, to establish an experimental school in Llanddowror. It was this school which developed into the Circulating Welsh Charity School system, which moved from village to village throughout Wales, educating both children and adults. After Jones's death in 1761, Bevan took on the management of the project. It is estimated that, between 1736 and 1776, half the population of Wales attended a circulating school and Bridget came to be known as Madam Bevan.

12 DECEMBER

On 12 December 2010, Martha Musonza-Holman began her twenty-two-mile barefoot walk along the canal from Brecon to Llanfoist to raise money for local community projects and to highlight the plight of people in her native Zimbabwe.

Martha was forced to flee her homeland in 2001 when she was accused of teaching politics to students. She found a new home in Abergavenny where she became a Fair Trade entrepreneur and worked to create links between Wales and the country of her birth. Her astonishing walk was to raise awareness about poverty levels in her home country where people often have to walk many miles barefoot, simply because they cannot afford shoes.

Martha founded the Love Zimbabwe Community Interest Company and regularly visits Zimbabwe where she ensures that Fair Trade producers receive financial remuneration. In 2016 and 2017 she made trips with anthropology students from University of Wales Trinity Saint David to participate in extensive community projects. In 2017, she won an award in the social and humanitarian category of the Ethnic Minority Welsh Women Achievement Association (EMWWAA) awards for women who have made a significant contribution to Welsh life.

13 DECEMBER ⚠

On 13 December 1956, artist Nina Hamnett fell forty feet out of her apartment window and died three days later. It has always been debated as to whether her death was caused by a drunken accident or whether she had intended to take her own life.

Nina was an artist and a writer who came to be known as the Queen of Bohemia. She was born in Tenby in 1890. After studying at the London School of Art, she went to the artist Marie Vassilieff's Academy in Paris. During her lifetime, Nina was associated with many leading figures in the artistic community, including Dylan Thomas, Augustus John, Gertrude Stein, Nancy Cunard and Pablo Picasso. She was flamboyant, unconventional and sexually liberated. She once danced nude on a Montparnasse café table 'just for the hell of it'. Her work was held in high esteem by fellow artist Walter Sickert who also painted her as a subject. She later published a memoir, *Laughing Torso,* which became a bestseller.

Nina struggled with alcoholism during her life and there is still a mystery around her tragic death. Her last words were reported to be: 'Why don't they let me die?'

14 DECEMBER

The opening of the railway to their village on 14 December 1867 facilitated the expansion of the business and reputations of the cockle women of Pen-clawdd. The branch line from Gowerton, nicknamed the 'Cockle Line', meant that fresh cockles from the area could be transported and sold all over south Wales and parts of England. Before this, the cockle women, who were famed for their durability and determination, would walk the eight miles to Swansea Market with their wares loaded on donkeys or they would sell door-to-door in local villages.

The women would typically collect between 100–150 kg of cockles per day using a jumbo – a long plank of wood with a handle at either end – to soften the sand and suck the cockles to the surface. The cockles were then loosened from the sand using a curved scraper called a scrap, before being put into piles using a three-pronged iron fork called a cram. The cockles were sorted into size using a large mesh sieve called a riddle, before being placed into large wicker baskets known as tiernals, and taken ashore in donkey carts.

In 2023, the film *She Sells Shellfish* focused on the work of the cockle women of Pen-clawdd and highlighted the contribution of two Welsh women to the shellfish and seaweed industries of south Wales. Carol Watts's great-grandmother was a cockle-picker and she has been selling Pen-clawdd cockles and laverbread at Swansea Market all her working life. Megan Haines works on a regenerative ocean farm off the coast of St Davids that grows oysters, mussels and seaweed sustainably. The film looks at the unique relationship between the women, their work and the environment.

15 DECEMBER

No one really knows when rugby was first played by women in Wales but the women's game certainly came to prominence during the First World War. One of the most notable matches from that period took place at Cardiff Arms Park on 15 December 1917 when Cardiff Ladies, a team made up entirely of workers from the Hancock brewery, played Newport Ladies, with the visitors winning 6–0. A photograph of the Cardiff team taken prior to the match is believed to be the world's oldest image of a women's rugby team.

Other landmarks in women's rugby in Wales include:

- Wales women's national rugby union team played their first official match on 5 April 1987 when they took on the England Women's side at Pontypool Park.
- Wales hosted the first Women's Rugby World Cup in Cardiff in 1991.
- The Welsh Women's Rugby Union was created in 1994.
- In 2015, Aileen Richards, from Cardiff, became the first woman to be appointed to the board of the Welsh Rugby Union.
- In 2016, Sian Williams, from Wrexham, was granted elite athlete status by the RAF, enabling her to continue to be employed by the forces while also being able to train full-time for rugby. It was the first time any Welsh woman had signed a professional rugby contract.
- In 2022, the Welsh Rugby Union offered professional contracts to women rugby players for the first time.
- In 2023, Abi Tierney became the Welsh Rugby Union's first female chief executive officer.

16 DECEMBER

Mary Jones, from Llanfihangel-y-Pennant, was born on this day in 1784. In 1800, when she was fifteen, she famously walked for twenty-five miles, barefoot, over rugged land and mountains to purchase a Bible in Bala.

Mary came from a very religious family and, from a young age, had been educated in a circulating school, where the Bible was used as a central part of learning. She was therefore very keen to obtain her own copy and reportedly saved for nearly six years in order to buy one.

One of the few people in north Wales who sold copies of the Bible at that time was the Calvinistic Methodist clergyman Thomas Charles from Bala, so Mary set out on the long walk to get one. However, when she arrived, she discovered that Charles had sold out. Impressed with her determination, he found somewhere for her to stay for two days to wait for new supplies to arrive and then sold her three copies for the price of one.

DID YOU KNOW?

The Mary Jones Pilgrim Centre, a visitor and education centre that tells Mary's story, was opened in Llanycil in 2014.

17 DECEMBER ⚠

The pioneering work of forensic ecologist Patricia Wiltshire was instrumental in the conviction on 17 December 2003 of Ian Huntley for the murders of two ten-year-old girls, Holly Wells and Jessica Chapman, in Soham, Cambridgeshire.

Patricia was born in Cefn Fforest, near Blackwood, in 1942. Her schooling was interrupted from the age of seven when she sustained serious burns in a domestic accident which caused repeated chest infections and permanent damage to her lungs. As she recovered, she spent her time reading books and going on nature walks with her grandmother, which inspired her interest in the botanical world.

After working as a medical laboratory technician, Patricia studied and later lectured at King's College London, before taking up a post at the Institute of Archaeology at University College London as a palynologist (studying pollen). When she was in her fifties, she pioneered the use of pollen as evidence in criminal cases. She has since worked as a forensic scientist with every police force in the UK. Her ability to analyse traces of soil and plants to link perpetrators to the scenes of their crimes has been invaluable. Patricia has been involved in solving several other high-profile crimes, including the murders of Sarah Payne, Milly Dowler and the cold case of Christopher Laverack as well as the serial murders of Steve Wright in Ipswich.

18 DECEMBER

Mandy Rice-Davies (born 21 October 1944) died on this day in 2014. She was one of the main protagonists of the Profumo Affair, a scandal that forced Cabinet Minister John Profumo to resign in 1963 and which discredited the Conservative government led by Harold Macmillan.

Mandy was born in Pontyates and moved to Solihull with her family before getting a job at the Earls Court Motor Show when aged sixteen. She subsequently became a model and showgirl which was when she met Christine

Keeler. Christine introduced her to the osteopath Stephen Ward with whom Mandy began a relationship. In December 1962, Christine Keeler was visiting Mandy when one of Keeler's former boyfriends attempted to enter the property and ended up firing a gun several times at the door. His subsequent trial brought attention to the girls' involvement with many influential people, including the War Minister John Profumo and Soviet spy, Yevgeny Ivanov, who were both having affairs with Keeler.

Mandy's boyfriend, Stephen, was later brought to trial, charged with living off the immoral earnings of Keeler and Rice-Davies. Mandy was giving evidence on the stand when the prosecuting counsel pointed out that Lord Astor, who has been accused of having had an affair with Mandy, had denied ever meeting her. Mandy replied, 'He would, wouldn't he?' It was a phrase later immortalised by the Oxford Dictionary of Quotations.

Later in life, Mandy traded on the notoriety and attention the trial brought her. She converted to Judaism and married an Israeli businessman, with whom she opened nightclubs and restaurants in Tel Aviv. She also made a series of unsuccessful attempts to become a pop singer in the mid-1960s.

19 DECEMBER

On 19 December 1911, Sarah Jane Howell, aged twenty-one and a teacher at Brynmenyn Council School, lost her life in the Llynfi River near Bridgend while rescuing one of her pupils from drowning.

The school had no playground but a local farmer allowed the children to play in one of his fields near the bank of the

River Llynfi, which that year was in flood and fast flowing. Sarah noticed some of the boys playing football in the field and, as she called them in for their lesson, their ball rolled into the river. When Sarah went over to help them retrieve the ball, one boy, Bertie Gubbins, slipped and fell into the water.

Selflessly, Sarah jumped in to rescue Bertie. She managed to grab hold of him and get him to the safety of the riverbank before being swept away and dragged down into the river herself. Sarah's body was recovered further downstream.

Sarah's heroic actions were posthumously recognised by the Royal Humane Society and the Carnegie Hero Fund Trust. A plaque commemorating her bravery was placed at Brynmenyn Primary School and an annual award in her name is presented to a pupil who has excelled in their schoolwork.

20 DECEMBER

On 20 December 1971, all-girl group the Jonson Sisters won the special 'All Winners Show' of talent-spotting television series *Opportunity Knocks*, witnessed by an audience of 20 million viewers. The band is perhaps better known as The Fabs and they were Wales's first girl pop group.

In 1963, band leader and impresario Wally Waldini had the idea of forming an all-girl version of the Beatles. The band he put together comprised of Sarah Wrigley (née Johnston) from Cardiff, Linda Mazey from Barry, Margaret Lewis from Bedwas and Newport's Maria Kitsom. Wally supplied the instruments and they began performing covers of popular songs in clubs around south Wales.

In 1964, The Fabs performed at US Army bases in Germany and proved to be very popular. Sarah said that, 'after four months of playing six nights a week, four hours a night, we did rapidly improve.'

The girls were met with cynicism from other male-dominated bands. Roger Daltrey of The Who reputedly told Sarah, 'You're quite good, love, but you won't get anywhere.' Nevertheless, The Fabs were given a contract for a nightclub residency in Mexico City in 1967. There, they made an album and performed at the 1968 Olympics. They were also taken to dinner by Steve McQueen who was intrigued by the presence of four Welsh girls in Mexico.

After the band changed their name and won the talent show they really hoped that their career in the UK would take off. They were offered a record contract but their producer told them that selling the idea of a girl band was too hard. The band's final appearance was at Cardiff's New Theatre in 1972. The book *Twenty Pairs of Pants and a Passport,* written by Sarah and published in 2022, documents the band's story as well as detailing the discrimination and misogyny of the music industry at the time.

21 DECEMBER ⚠

The inquest into the death of Sarah Jacob was held on 21 December 1869. The results confirmed that she had starved to death. Tragically, groove marks on her toes indicated that she had tried to open a water bottle in a desperate attempt to get water.

Sarah was born in 1857 on a farm near Llanfihangel-ar-arth in Carmarthenshire. When she was nine, she became seriously ill and was confined to bed for a considerable period. She passed the time by composing poems and reading the Bible, but then, according to her parents, Evan and Hannah, Sarah suddenly began to refuse food. However, she did not suffer any ill effects and seemed to be thriving. Sarah became 'The Welsh Fasting Girl' and her ability to do without nourishment was dubbed a miracle.

Sarah became famous and people travelled from all over Wales and England to see her lying in her bed, surrounded by flowers and reading the Bible. They were encouraged to give her gifts and money.

Some people, however, were sceptical and arranged for some nurses to carry out an observation of Sarah. Just a week after they began their work, Sarah slowly lapsed into semi-consciousness, before dying on 17 December 1869.

It was widely thought that Sarah's parents and her doctors were responsible for her death. They were prosecuted for unlawful killing. Carmarthen magistrates subsequently imprisoned Sarah's parents. The doctors, however, were only criticised for their 'foolish behaviour'.

22 DECEMBER

The winter solstice in the Northern Hemisphere usually occurs on 21 or 22 December. It is the shortest day and the longest night of the year when the sun's daily maximum elevation in the sky is at its lowest.

Dôn is the Welsh legend who is celebrated at this time of year. Celtic druids were said to have recognised the winter solstice as the rebirth of the sun. Dôn was associated with the powers of light and constantly in conflict with the powers of darkness. She is also regarded as the Celtic mother goddess who gave birth to up to fourteen other gods and goddesses in the Celtic pantheon by her husband, Beli. She is also credited with giving the gift of speech and metalworking to the Welsh and had the power to change her form.

Dôn appears in the *Mabinogion* as the mother of five significant children including Arianrhod, a sky goddess and symbol of fertility who was the mother of the hero Lleu Llaw Gyffes, and Gwydion who was a magician and trickster. Gwydion lends his name to a Welsh phrase for the Milky Way, *Caer Wydion*, meaning 'the castle of Gwydion'. Dôn's domain of *Llys Dôn* (the Court of Dôn) is the traditional Welsh name for the star constellation Cassiopeia.

23 DECEMBER

On 23 December 1688, King James II of England was forced into exile in France following the invasion of England by William of Orange, the husband of James's daughter Mary.

Elizabeth Herbert, Marchioness of Powis (c.1634–1691) and her husband William Herbert, of Powis Castle near Welshpool, were Catholics and staunch supporters of James.

Elizabeth had served as lady of the bedchamber to Catherine of Braganza, queen consort of King Charles II, but in 1678, her husband William was imprisoned. He had been accused by the renegade Anglican priest, Titus Oates, of being part of the Popish Plot, a fictitious Catholic conspiracy to assassinate the king. Elizabeth's frantic efforts to secure William's release led her into unwise dealings with the double-crossing Thomas Dangerfield and she narrowly escaped being convicted for treason herself.

In 1685, King James II came to the throne and, although

he had a policy of religious tolerance, he was met with increasing opposition as he was Catholic. The situation became more critical when his son, James Francis Edward Stuart was born, as it made the return of a Catholic line of succession more likely. At the invitation of influential Protestant leaders, William of Orange led a large invasion fleet that resulted in a change of regime that became known as the Glorious Revolution. When James fled to France, Elizabeth and William Herbert went with him. Elizabeth acted as first lady of the bedchamber to James's queen, Mary of Modena, and as governess to their children.

24 DECEMBER

At least eighty members of the *Y Gwylliaid Cochion Mawddwy* (The Red Bandits of Mawddwy) were captured and executed on 24 December 1554. The matriarch of this band of red-haired outlaws from the area of Dinas Mawddwy, in the mountains above Dolgellau, was Lowri, daughter of Welsh nobleman Gruffydd Llwyd.

In this remote, desolate territory, there were great difficulties in maintaining law and order and *Y Gwylliaid* terrorised the area for many years, stealing cattle, money and possessions at will. Householders were forced to take drastic action to protect themselves and their property. Some farmers reputedly kept sharpened scythes inside their wide chimneys to prevent the bandits from breaking in.

Tales of *Y Gwylliaid* eventually reached the court of Queen Mary I, and apparently on her direct orders, an army was gathered by Baron Lewis Owen of Dolgellau to round up the bandits. Eighty of the hundred bandits that were captured were hanged immediately by Owen. Lowri's two sons were executed in front of her eyes – one of whom was no more than a child. In her grief, Lowri ripped open her bodice, exposing her breasts and vowed vengeance on Owen: 'These yellow breasts have given suck to those who shall wash their hands in your blood!'

A year later, Owen was murdered while riding through the valley at Bwlch yr Oerddrws. His bodyguards were cut down by a hail of arrows and his throat was slit by John Goch (Red John), a relative of the dead boys. It was said that Lowri fulfilled her promise and washed her hands in his blood. She was tried at Bala in 1558 but avoided execution because she was pregnant at the time. No record exists to confirm her fate.

25 DECEMBER

There are many Welsh Christmas traditions historically carried out by women.

The night before Christmas, women would invite their family and friends to *noson gyflaith* (toffee evening) for an evening of toffee-making and storytelling.

When the mixture had cooled, the women would cover their hands with butter, and while the toffee – known as *taffi, dant, ffani* or *cyflaith* – was still warm, would pull and twist it until it became a golden yellow colour. The process passed the hours until it was time to join the torchlit procession to church, and provided the chance for women to talk and share stories together.

There was another Christmas tradition that was less celebratory for women. On *Gwyl San Steffan* (Boxing Day) young men and boys would beat the girls with holly branches on their arms and legs until they bled. Known as *curo celyn* (holly beating), it was sometimes inflicted on the last person to get out of bed. Thankfully this custom died out during the nineteenth century.

26 DECEMBER ⚠

Ann of Swansea died on this day in 1838. She was a popular novelist in Britain in the early nineteenth century.

Born 29 April 1764 as Ann Julia Hatton, she was the daughter of travelling actor, Roger Kemble. Her sister Sarah Siddons also became an actress. Ann had an eventful few years where she married a bigamist, worked in a London brothel and attempted to take her own life in Westminster Abbey. In 1793, she travelled to America with her legitimate husband, William Hatton. Her libretto, *Tammany: The Indian Chief*, was the first known libretto by a woman and achieved Broadway success. Ann and William returned to Britain and settled in Swansea, where Ann became a writer. She wrote poetry and fourteen gothic novels using the pseudonym 'Ann of Swansea'.

27 DECEMBER

On 27 December 1912, the famous Dan yr Ogof cave system in the Swansea Valley was discovered by the Morgan brothers. The farming brothers were searching for the source of the River Llynfell which flowed through their land. They managed to cross a lake in a coracle but their exploration was halted when they came across a narrow passage which deterred even the most experienced and daring potholers. They had discovered the Long Crawl – a 350-foot tight tunnel into the rock.

In 1963 Eileen Davies, a local domestic science teacher, was a young and relatively inexperienced caver. But she became the first person to pass through the Long Crawl and discover the cave systems beyond. Eileen, nicknamed 'the ferret', went through and her fellow members of the South Wales Caving Club followed. Beyond it they discovered a network of caverns, blood-red stalagmites several feet high, a crystal pool fringed with flower-like formations and a hundred-foot waterfall cascading from the roof.

The National Showcaves Centre for Wales at Dan yr Ogof is now one of the country's top tourist attractions.

28 DECEMBER

When the horse Dream Alliance won the Welsh Grand National at Chepstow on 28 December 2009, it was something of a fairy-tale moment for one Welsh woman.

Jan Vokes was working as a barmaid from Cefn Fforest near Blackwood when she overheard one of the punters talking about a racehorse. Inspired, she had the idea that she too could breed a champion. Jan and her husband bought a mare for £350 and, with the help of a local syndicate each paying £10 a week, reared and trained her chestnut foal on Jan's allotment. They named him Dream Alliance. The syndicate was soon able to have Dream professionally trained and, despite a disappointing start, he won his first race in 2006 and then the Perth Gold Cup the following year.

Disaster struck when Dream sliced a tendon while training for the 2008 Grand National and it was touch-and-go as to whether he would have to be put down. The syndicate decided a try a new but expensive stem-cell treatment that included surgery and fifteen months of rehabilitation to save him. The treatment proved successful and Dream Alliance went on to win the 2009 Welsh Grand National.

> **DID YOU KNOW?**
> The improbable story of Dream Alliance is told in the 2020 film *Dream Horse* starring Damian Lewis, Toni Collette and Owen Teale.

29 DECEMBER

Ada Vachell (born 27 December 1866) died on this day in 1923. She was a remarkable and determined supporter of the poor and disabled of Bristol.

Ada was born in Cardiff, the daughter of William Vachell, a wealthy iron merchant and mayor of Cardiff. An epidemic of scarlet fever took the lives of two of her older siblings and left her deaf. This traumatic series of events prompted her parents to relocate with Ada and her surviving younger brother to her mother's home town of Bristol.

Ada took little interest in education or forming relationships, instead devoting her time to horse-riding, travelling and amateur dramatics. She was also devoutly Christian and, after visiting Bristol's roughest slums, became committed to charitable work.

Ada founded The Guild of Poor Brave Things in Bristol in 1896, probably Britain's first building to have disabled access as part of its design. The Guild acted as a social club for poor and disabled people and it later bought a holiday farm in Somerset where disadvantaged adults and children could experience the countryside and farm life. The Guild continued until the introduction of the welfare state following the Second World War. It was disbanded in the 1980s and its headquarters are now used by the NSPCC.

30 DECEMBER

On 30 December 1887, a petition was handed to Queen Victoria signed by over a million English women, appealing for public houses in England to be closed on Sundays – as they had been in Wales for several years.

Temperance campaigners had been active in Wales for several decades. They wanted to reduce opportunities for the consumption of alcohol before and during work hours, and for the Sabbath to be a day of sobriety. The Sunday Closing Act (Wales) 1881 required the closure of all public houses in Wales on Sundays. It was the first legislation since the annexation of Wales to apply specifically and only to Wales.

Women often suffered from the effects of their menfolk drinking excessively: alcohol-fuelled domestic violence and the squandering of money needed for family food became significant drivers in the burgeoning temperance movement.

The North Wales Women's Temperance Union was established in Blaenau Ffestiniog in 1892, and branches began to spring up. Meetings were chaired and led by women, who would protest publicly and vociferously against the evils of drink. This was followed in 1901 by the Women's Temperance Union in south Wales, led by the bardic poet Cranogwen (see 9 January), who was particularly concerned with violence against women. Lady Llanover of Abergavenny, motivated by her Calvinistic Methodist faith, was so convinced of the importance of temperance that she closed all the pubs on her estate.

The campaign for the closure of pubs in England on Sundays ultimately failed, but pubs remained closed in Wales on a Sunday until the Licensing Act 1961 enabled counties to vote every seven years on whether to be 'wet' or 'dry' on Sunday. Dwyfor in Gwynedd was the last district to drop the ban in 1996.

31 DECEMBER

The Nos Galan Races take place on New Year's Eve each year in Mountain Ash in Rhondda Cynon Taf. They commemorate the legendary athletic prowess of a local man, Guto Nyth Brân.

Guto Nyth Brân, or Griffith Morgan, was born in Llwyncelyn in the Rhondda in 1700. He lived on his family's farm near Porth. Guto was an extraordinarily fast runner. It was said that he managed to chase and catch a live hare and a bird in flight and that he once ran seven miles from his home to Pontypridd in the time that it took his mother to boil the kettle. But it was his wife and local shop owner, Siân, who would give focus to Guto's amazing talents.

Siân o'r Siop (Siân from the shop) organised races for Guto and the first was against an unbeaten English captain stationed at Carmarthen. Guto won the four-mile race easily and he and Siân collected the £400 prize money. Siân continued to arrange races for Guto but word got out that no one could defeat him and challengers became harder to find.

They were about to retire when a new runner, known as 'Prince of Bedwas' emerged as a challenger. He was unbeaten and Siân persuaded Guto, then aged thirty-seven, to enter into a twelve-mile race from Newport to Bedwas. Prince took an early lead in the race but Guto surged past his opponent in an uphill sprint near the end to take victory. Unfortunately, the exertion proved too much for Guto, who collapsed and died in Siân's arms.

ABOUT THE AUTHORS

Huw Rees and Sian Kilcoyne run 'The History of Wales' Facebook page. They are a brother and sister team, dedicated to improving their knowledge of their country and sharing it with a wider audience. Their aim is to provide objective and (hopefully!) interesting information, to help them and their readers better understand who we are as a nation, highlighting major past events, items of interest and the famous Welsh people that have shaped us into what we are today.